David M. Faris is Assistant Professor of Political Science at Roosevelt University, where he teaches Egyptian and Middle Eastern Politics. He holds a PhD in Political Science from The University of Pennsylvania.

DISSENT AND **REVOLUTION** IN A **DIGITAL AGE**

SOCIAL MEDIA, BLOGGING AND ACTIVISM IN EGYPT

DAVID M. FARIS

I.B. TAURIS
LONDON · NEW YORK

New paperback edition published in 2015 by
I.B.Tauris & Co Ltd
London • New York
www.ibtauris.com

First published in hardback in 2013 by I.B.Tauris & Co Ltd

ISBN: 978 1 78453 207 9
eISBN: 978 0 85773 942 1

A full CIP record for this book is available from the British Library
A full CIP record is available from the Library of Congress

Library of Congress Catalog Card Number: available

Typeset by Newgen Publishers, Chennai

For Sheerine

CONTENTS

ACKNOWLEDGEMENTS

Writing a book is an enormous undertaking, and I would like to take this opportunity to extend my sincerest gratitude to the dozens of people who both helped make my work possible and improved it in myriad ways. This project began as a doctoral dissertation on the political effects of the Internet in Egypt. My dissertation advisor, Ian Lustick, worked extensively with me on this project from the very beginning, supporting it from when it was just the kernel of an idea to the finished product, reading countless chapter drafts and helping to secure funding opportunities for me in many places. Robert Vitalis was also enormously helpful in helping to refine ideas and push me toward my final goal. And I am deeply indebted to Deborah Wheeler, who believed in the importance of this work from the start, helped arrange speaking opportunities at many conferences, and led the way in showing how this kind of work is important for political science.

My fieldwork in Egypt was supported by two generous grants from the Foreign Language and Area Studies (FLAS) program administered by the United States Department of Education, one for the summer of 2007 and one for 2007–2008. Additionally, I am indebted to support from the Political Science Department at the University of Pennsylvania, the College of Arts and Sciences at Roosevelt University, and Roosevelt's Department of Political Science and Public Administration, which allowed me to return to Cairo twice for further research and interviews. I am most grateful to Lynn Weiner, Dean of the College of Arts and Sciences at Roosevelt University, for everything she has done to help bring this project to fruition, as well as to my colleagues in the Department of Political Science and Public Administration at Roosevelt University: Jeffrey Edwards, Naser Javaid, Bethany Barratt, Jeannine Love and Paul Green.

In addition, I am indebted to numerous scholars who commented on various aspects of this work at conferences and panels, including Zeynep Tufekci, Marc Lynch, Philip Seib, Murad Idris, Eric Trager, Shanthi Kalathil, Abby Jones, Kevin Wallsten, Chris Anderson, Elham Gheytanchi, Babak Rahimi, Amber Davisson, Antoinette Pole, Laura Hosman, Joshua Stacher, Nivien Saleh, and Laura Roselle. I am particularly indebted to David Karpf for his role in helping to craft the theoretical framework for this book, and for providing extensive comments on various chapters. I am also deeply indebted to Murad Idris for his assistance with transliteration, and to Sara Nimis for her generous work on the index.

I am also most grateful to countless scholars and individuals who were critical in helping me navigate fieldwork in Cairo. First I must thank Ahmed Abdel Fattah, who kindly scheduled countless interviews for me and arranged for me to spend April 6, 2008 with the activists behind the day's events. I also owe sincere gratitude to Mohamed El-Gohary, who put me in touch with so many activists, Rania Al-Malky, who was so helpful in gaining me access to Egyptian journalists, and Tarek Atia, who asked various bloggers to speak with me in 2007. I conducted several interviews jointly with Courtney Radsch, who was enormously kind and helpful to me during my stay in Egypt. I was also blessed with a supportive community of scholars, reporters and friends in Egypt who also deserve thanks, including Stephanie Boyle, Rebecca Johnson, Nadim Audi, Erin Snider, Anne Zimmerman, Jon Jensen and Jeffrey Culang. I am further thankful for the dozens of Egyptians who agreed to be interviewed by me and who frequently provided key insights and ideas to follow-up upon.

I would be remiss if I didn't also thank my amazing partner, Sheerine Alemzadeh, as well as my parents, Ralph and Jane Faris, and brother and sister-in-law, Jason and Katie Faris, who were tremendously supportive of my endeavors, and without whose support I would have been unable to see it through to the finish.

Finally, I would like to thank my editor at I.B.Tauris, Maria Marsh, whose belief in and support for this project has helped to make it a reality.

David M. Faris

LIST OF ILLUSTRATIONS

CHAPTER 1

SOCIAL MEDIA AND
AUTHORITARIAN POLITICS
IN EGYPT

Introduction: 'Waiting for Baradei'

In February 2010, discussion of the upcoming 2011 presidential elections in Egypt centered around the potential candidacy of Mohamed ElBaradei, the former head of the International Atomic Energy Agency. ElBaradei, a Nobel Laureate who commanded broad respect inside Egypt for his achievements, had been living abroad in Vienna for decades. When ElBaradei's flight arrived in Cairo on 19 February, hundreds of supporters met him at the airport and greeted him like a saviour. Those present included not just ordinary supporters, but leading luminaries of Egypt's harried opposition, including the journalist and publisher Ibrahim Eissa, novelist and social critic Alaa Al-Aswany, Kefaya co-founder George Ishaq, and others.[1] ElBaradei had caused a stir earlier in the month when he hinted that he might run for president if the election were to be genuinely democratic, rather than the farce that had taken place in 2005. Observers, however, anticipated that power would be handed off from the ailing and ageing dictator Hosni Mubarak to his son and heir apparent Gamal, in another rigged election. It was in this context that a group of young Egyptians started a 'fan' page on the social networking site Facebook dedicated to ElBaradei's potential candidacy, called ElBaradei For President.[2]

Before long this group had over 150,000 members (out of roughly 2 million Egyptians on Facebook at the time). The use of Facebook was noteworthy because most ordinary paths to political participation were closed in Egypt at the time. Hosni Mubarak, the elderly president, had ruled Egypt without interruption since 1981 under an emergency law enacted after the assassination of his predecessor. Registering as a political party in Egypt was an onerous process that could take years – if a licence was even granted. Only in the past five years had any kind of independent print press taken root in Egypt, and as a result, the previous decade had seen Egyptians increasingly turn to the tools and applications of the Internet to express their dissatisfaction and challenge authoritarian rule. Over the course of those years, digital activists – bloggers, and later users of other forms of 'social media' like Twitter, Facebook and YouTube – scored a number of important victories over the regime, over issues largely revolving around human rights. A major youth political movement, the April 6 Youth Movement, had been born out of one of these instances of digital activism. And yet at the time of ElBaradei's Facebook campaign, many observers were deeply sceptical of the power of social media to reshape Egyptian politics in any fundamental way. Even after years of blogging, Tweeting, protesting and dissent, the Egyptian regime remained firmly in place, seemingly committed to perpetuating its own sclerotic rule and passing power down the Mubarak line.

ElBaradei's decision whether or not to participate in the election, and the swift growth of his dedicated Facebook group, renewed debates inside and outside the country about the effect of social networking sites like Facebook – and other forms of 'social media' like blogs, Twitter, and text messaging – on politics in Egypt. Many were sceptical that a platform which could be monitored by the regime, like Facebook, could have any effect.[3] Others worried that the ElBaradei supporters were wealthy elites who were disconnected from the broader population of Egyptians. Still others wondered whether membership of a Facebook group had any relationship to a group's actual power.[4] In other words observers were asking, yet again, a question to which scholars have sought the answer for years: is the Internet inherently a tool of democratization? The debate over the ElBaradei group would soon be rendered academic by events unfolding within Egypt itself. Within a year of ElBaradei's Facebook campaign, the authoritarian regime of Hosni Mubarak had been swept aside by a popular mobilization driven, at least in part, by digital media tools. That ferment largely swept aside ElBaradei and his Facebook group as well, although the group did play a role in launching the protests.[5] Veteran political activists in the April 6 Youth Movement, together with the administrators of a Facebook group called We Are All Khaled Said,[6] dedicated to a murdered Alexandrian, plotted national protests on January 25, 2011 – Police Day in Egypt –shortly after popular protests had ousted the Tunisian regime of Zine el-Abadine Ben Ali. With tens of thousands publicly committed through their online social networks, and with calls to public protest circulating through email networks, Facebook social clusters, and street organizing, the activists had set in motion a staged confrontation with the Egyptian regime, of the sort that the ElBaradei supporters could have only dreamed of a year previously. During the protests themselves, Twitter users created the hashtag #jan25 to coordinate dispatches from the field, organize supplies, outsmart security forces, and reach global audiences with word from the streets. The street mobilization, together with a general strike, eventually convinced elites within the military establishment that Mubarak needed to be ousted, and some semblance of democratic transition initiated. And so, 18 days after the revolt began, President Hosni Mubarak suddenly resigned, unleashing massive celebrations across Egypt. Was this the world's first true social media revolution?

The question of the role played by social media in Egypt's revolution deserves an in-depth and fully theorized account. Unfortunately much of the research on the impact of the Internet in the Middle East has been somewhat anecdotal. Driven by popular press coverage of the latest application (like Twitter) or the perceived success or failure of online activism in places like Iran, our understanding of the impact of these technologies seems to change with every new protest or Facebook group. The goal of serious research about digital activism, therefore, should not be to ask what the impact of any particular digital technology will be, but rather to generate robust theories that can help us understand events as they happen and make probabilistic predictions about the future. The development of digital activism in Egypt that led to the formation of ElBaradei's Facebook group, and ultimately to the removal from power of Hosni Mubarak's regime, offers the perfect opportunity to study this phenomenon in detail, and to determine whether the claims made for and against the power of digital activism have any merit in a critical case. The term *digital activism* is preferable to 'cyberactivism' or 'Internet activism' since so much activity takes place through mobile telephony networks that are digital but not necessarily 'online' in any meaningful sense of the word. Joyce defines digital activism as 'all instances of social and political campaigning practice that use digital net-work infrastructure'.[7] This book will therefore explain the impact of digital activism in authoritarian countries through a single case study (Egypt between 2005 and August 2011), and answer the following research questions. Does the use of digital tools lead to more collective action in authoritarian societies? Do digital activists generate media coverage of sensitive events and issues in authoritarian societies? What are the effects of digital tools on socially- or politically-marginalized groups in Egyptian society? And finally, why do some states (like China) seem more successful than others at controlling the effects of digital activism? These questions intersect with several distinct literatures in the fields of political science and communication, which I will review below before proceeding to an outline of the case selection, methodology, and chapter organization.

The Political Context of Social Media Networks in Egypt

In addition to addressing questions in the field about the Internet and politics, this book also engages with debates about the durability of authoritarianism. The Egyptian state has responded to the threat of online activism with strategies similar to those with which it has approached the control of the political sphere. Prior to the events of January 2011, most observers seemed to be in general agreement that the Egyptian political system was quite stable.[8] Brownlee argued in 2007 that the single-party system in Egypt provided incentives for individual elites to pursue opportunities with the NDP rather than joining the opposition, thus providing for long-term systemic stability.[9] Lust-Okar saw Egyptian domestic stability as predicated on an ingenious divide-and-rule strategy which kept the opposition off guard and at loggerheads.[10] Like various other semi-authoritarian regimes, Egypt allowed a number of legal parties to operate and organize in the political system. These parties included the reconstituted Wafd, and among their many privileges were able to set up and run their own newspapers. But one of the more popular organizations, the Islamist Muslim Brotherhood, was allowed to participate only indirectly, and was not recognized as a political party until rules were relaxed after Mubarak stepped aside in February 2011. In fact, since the election of Hamas in Palestine in 2006 the Brotherhood had been targeted aggressively by the regime, which believed that international events granted them new licence in eliminating the group's political influence. The crackdown on the Brotherhood included the arrest and prosecution of dozens of senior members of the group's leadership in 2007–2008. Overall, by allowing certain parties access to power and privilege, the regime drove a wedge between the opposition camps. As a result, just when the regime seemed the weakest (in the mid-1990s), the legal opposition groups became less likely to push for reforms in alliance with the excluded opposition.[11]

Kassem argued in 2004 that Mubarak had successfully consolidated control over the regime, so much so that it was widely expected that he would soon pass power to his son Gamal.[12] Bellin also views Middle Eastern regimes, and Egypt in particular, as employing 'robust and tenacious' coercive apparatuses.[13] Heydemann contended that authoritarian regimes in the region, including Egypt, survived and thrived by what he calls 'upgrading authoritarianism' – selectively creating openings in the electoral arena and the economic sphere while pursuing closer relationships with foreign powers that shared their lack of interest in human rights and democracy.[14] While El-Ghobashy and Rutherford both found some potential for change in the increasing density of civil society and judicial oversight, respectively, neither saw democratization as particularly likely.[15] Hanna argued in 2009 that the architecture of electoral control erected by the Mubarak regime made any challenge to

Gamal's ascendancy, and any long-term change, difficult at best; while Cook held that 'the underlying patterns and processes of Egyptian politics' would prevent further liberalization.[16] Regardless of where each particular author located Egyptian authoritarian stability, views of the regime in political science circles enjoyed as close to a consensus as there is in the discipline – the façade of democracy worked for the Mubarak regime, the coercive apparatus was strong and resilient, and there were no clear-and-present dangers to its authority on the horizon. Most of all there seemed to be wide agreement that the various opposition groups' capacity for mobilization was very low, and thus a change of regime or democratization was highly unlikely.

There were a small number of dissenters to this general consensus. El-Ghobashy saw in Egypt's constitutional battles the possibility of investing Egypt's institutions with real legitimacy through struggle.[17] El-Mahdi saw the Egyptian regime as 'likely to face further cycles of popular opposition' in the run-up to the 2011 presidential elections.[18] Beinin argued that it was 'unlikely that the Mubarak regime will be able to continue indefinitely with business as usual'.[19] Finally, whereas some saw stability, others saw the Mubarak regime as lurching toward a crisis, suggesting that, far from ensuring the continued existence of authoritarianism, the regime's policies were generating a confrontation with opposition groups.[20]

Kefaya and Protest Politics in Egypt

However, just beneath what appeared to be the stable surface of authoritarianism in Egypt were rumblings of potential unrest. The group that offered the stiffest challenge to the regime prior to the events of January 2011 was Kefaya (The Egyptian Movement for Change), a broad-based coalition of leftists, Islamists, and other opposition figures. Kefaya has always been difficult to categorize, and very little has been published about the movement since its inception in 2004. As the anonymous blogger Baheyya writes,[21] Kefaya

fits none of the available models found in the (admittedly dessicated) Egyptian political landscape. It's not an 'opposition party', it's not an NGO, it's not a professional association, it's not a solidarity committee, it's not a party-in-waiting (like *Wasat* and *Karama*), and it's not a grassroots initiative.[22]

According to Shorbagy, this movement sprung out of the detritus of the legal but severely restricted political parties, on the one hand, and the illegal Muslim Brotherhood on the other. Lacking an accepted, institutional voice, opposition politics in Egypt had come to a standstill during the early years of the new century.[23] Kefaya, a word with unique meaning in the Egyptian context (it is colloquial for 'Enough!'), included figures from across the political spectrum, galvanized to prevent Mubarak from assuming a fifth term as President of Egypt. This appeared to be the only focal point of agreement in the group. As Baheyya wrote, 'The only consensus is that Mubarak must go; everything else is up for debate'.[24] However, eventually this unwavering opposition to the Mubarak regime began to appear in the popular mind as an absence of any alternative, positive vision for the future.[25] The emergence of Kefaya, as well as the nascent opening perceived in the political system following the US-led war against Iraq, appeared to combine for a combustible situation, one that was ripe for organizing a movement against the state. As leading blogger Issandr El-Amrani noted, in 2005 'there was so much happening and there was a lot of attention on Egypt because President Bush had decided to highlight Egypt as a place to democratize'.[26] And for a time it did appear as though Kefaya was galvanizing people in a way that had not happened in a long time – their street protests were bold, and undertaken without the regime's permission, which in any case remained quite hard to obtain.[27] However, these protests eventually become rote, and easy enough for the regime to disrupt by banning or interfering with them and arresting activists after the fact. El-Mahdi argues that while the Kefaya movement eventually fizzled out, it ignited dissent in other quarters of Egyptian public life, particularly in the labour movement.[28]

Through Kefaya, the presence of protestors on the streets of Cairo became routine, making it seem ordinary for Egyptians to go into the streets to call for the resignation of Hosni Mubarak or for other major reforms.[29] The fact that between 2004 and 2011 Egyptians became accustomed to seeing so many of their fellow citizens in the streets could only have encouraged others to participate in such risky collective actions. Therefore, even though the movement itself did not have the desired effect on the political system, it should certainly be credited with setting the stage for other, more successful movements. Furthermore, the April 6 Youth Movement – which was ultimately one of the parties responsible for the January 25 protests – was an indirect outgrowth of Kefaya, born out of the group's Youth For Change wing. These movements will be discussed in further detail in Chapter 4.

The Egyptian Media Context

But Kefaya was not only important in and of itself – it also provided the institutional foundation for a new means of expression in the country, the growth of blogging as a tool for dissent and opposition. The appearance of blogs on the Egyptian scene in 2004 coincided with increased openness and reduced oversight of the press, which meant that opportunities for expression and dissent multiplied almost overnight. For years Egyptians had been subject to a moribund local print press, with the government-run dailies and their fawning coverage of the president more or less the only game in town. While the state had legally licensed the opposition parties to run their own newspapers, these organs were not trusted news sources, since their affiliation with the state in the form of acquiescence to its rules made them suspect in the eyes of many. That left Egyptians dependent on international press organs like Al-Jazeera, but regardless of the undeniable impact of satellite TV, there was still a conspicuous missing link since no one was on the ground honestly covering local Egyptian political issues in a way that earned widespread public trust. This was all to change in 2004, when the independent (as opposed to 'opposition') privately-owned daily newspaper *Al-Masri Al-Youm* was launched by Hisham Kassem. As we will see in Chapter 3, the existence and growth of the independent press allowed a kind of nexus to form between activist bloggers and human rights agitators – they fed into one another, in the sense that bloggers linked to and talked about the stories printed in the independent press, while journalists working for the independent press often relied on bloggers as sources. *Al-Masri Al-Youm* was a daily newspaper unlike anything that had been seen in Egypt in decades[30] – a privately-financed institution that was free to criticize the regime, make money, and publish hard-hitting investigative journalism. It may be that the kind of criticism carried in the pages of the newspaper emboldened bloggers to do the same on their new websites. And crucially this new nexus of blogger-journalist-activist created new kinds of networks – networks that the regime had never seen before.

The growth of communication on the Internet is, not coincidentally, also a major concern of scholars. Each information revolution – be it print, film and television, satellite broadcasting, radio, and now the Internet – has been hailed with the great hopes of revolutionaries and opposition leaders, and met with the realities of state hostility to free expression. This has long been the case in Egypt, whose film censorship office once employed the renowned novelist Naguib Mahfouz.[31] For a long time, Egyptian film served as a political battleground for ideas that could not be expressed in the public sphere. But in fact the censorship of films – particularly Western films – actually stretches back to the period of de facto British rule. The pre-revolutionary regime seemed to fear films in particular that depicted revolutions.[32] The post-revolutionary regime's belief that uncensored films presented a political and social threat to their continued hold on power can be seen in the recent controversy over the film version of Alaa Al-Aswany's best-selling novel *The Yacoubian Building*, a book which unflinchingly depicts corruption, homosexuality, torture, and other troubling features of Egyptian political and social life. Censors clipped parts of the film. But that was not enough for more vociferous critics, who wanted the movie banned altogether.

But greater things were expected from the print media and radio in the Middle East and Egypt. Lerner chronicled the Nasser-era state's takeover of print and broadcast media almost immediately upon its assumption of power:

Nasser then has converted his earlier view that Egyptian society was not 'ready' for mass participation into a more daring hypothesis – that he can use the mass media to achive national consensus without unduly raising public demands for full participation. This feat hinges upon effective control of the media, along with all other channels of access to the Egyptian mass.[33]

Modernization theory's expectation that rising literacy and increased access to media would change entrenched 'traditional' social attitudes has been mirrored by the regime's fear of those attitude changes and its insistence on manipulating them. Part of this strategy was the regime's nationalization of newspapers in 1960, muzzling what had once been a relatively free-wheeling discursive arena.[34] Indeed, Lerner argues that Egyptian newspapers were brought under 'central directive' long before that.[35] While the subsequent decades have eroded the state's desire and capacity to thoroughly regulate the print media, the atmosphere was still fairly well-regulated in the seven years prior to the revolution. As for radio, Lerner argues that the Egyptian State Broadcasting's (E.S.B.) Pan-Arab propaganda program Voice of the Arabs (Sowt al-Arab) may have been instrumental in fomenting revolutionary Nasserist fervor across the region in the late 1950s.[36] But the regime's desire and capacity to carry out state censorship and official control over these relatively new (to Egypt) forms of mass communication are the important factors.

One of the central conceits of modernization theory was the idea that the spread of mass communication and the changes in attitude might presage a greater role for ordinary individuals in the political universe. Mass media and the rise of literacy had the chance to make public opinion 'a real factor instead of a fine phrase in the arena of world politics'.[37] These hopes presaged later enthusiasm about the Internet and its potential to change entrenched attitudes about gender and politics. Lerner and other advocates of democratization did not see, or did not want to see, that mass communication could also be used by the defenders and articulators of tradition to safeguard against more 'cosmopolitan attitudes' brought by foreign media and economic influence. This reality is especially stark today in Egypt, where for every secular, cosmopolitan liberal blogging about government abuses, there are probably a dozen Islamists using the Internet, newspapers, DVDs, cassette tapes and other media forms to propagate ideas that Lerner and other modernization theorists would find 'traditional'. This reality underscores the idea that new technologies are value-neutral and can be used by anyone to accomplish most any social goal.

The Internet and Activism in the Middle East

In the past decade, scholarly work converged on a consensus that the Internet and its associated tools and applications might reduce the various costs of collective action. Rheingold argued that the coordinating capacity of tools like text messaging might allow activists in authoritarian countries to mobilize and avoid the repressive arm of the state.[38] Shirky, meanwhile, argues that what he calls 'social tools' spur group-formation and collective action by reducing the costs of communication and removing 'two old obstacles – locality of information, and barriers to group reaction'.[39] Karpf holds that these mechanisms allow for new and unexpected forms of political organization and contestation.[40] Bimber, Flanagin and Stohl argue that new media tools allow for easier crossings of the boundary between public and private domains, thus mitigating the collective action problem (which after all involves movement from the private to the public sphere).[41] Castells believes that the Internet produces a phenomenon which he calls 'mass self-communication', which challenges hierarchical corporate and state power structures through the wielding of 'counter-power', while Diamond (2010) has labeled the tools of social media 'liberation technologies'.[42]

A competing tradition in the literature holds that states have largely been successful at shutting down online dissent.[43] Others such as Faris and Etling, while recognizing the reduction in organizing costs and communication, argue that digital technologies have little effect on the institutions of authoritarianism.[44] Still others, while recognizing the way that the Internet empowers non-state actors, feel that regimes allow certain kinds of expression and deliberation online but refuse to change underlying structures, or worse, use that information for repressive purposes.[45] More recent work has been intensely critical of the idea that the Internet can be a global tool of liberation, and casts doubt on organized government initiatives to promote Internet usage.[46]

Few studies, however, have investigated the effects of the Internet on collective action in the Middle East, a region which is often regarded in the discipline as somehow exceptional.

Many scholars dismiss the Internet and Internet activism as chimerical and unimportant in the Middle East, due to limited access for most of the region's citizens and restrictions on the availability of certain websites. Lynch argues that limited accessibility has hampered the ability of the Internet to affect public affairs in the Arab world. And contrary to expectations, dictators have managed to design sophisticated systems of control that serve to prevent the free flow of information.[47] Given these limitations, researchers must ask whether the Internet and the new political influence of blogs has any traction at all in these societies. But the fact that states – particularly China – have responded so forcefully to the information potential of the Internet indicates that at least one savvy regime perceives a genuine threat. And while a very low percentage of the region's inhabitants might own personal computers with Internet connections, the proliferation and cheapness of Internet cafés in major metropolitan centres means that even people of limited means can gain internet access – and that news might be cheaper to obtain in cyberspace than in print. Along with other forms of new media like satellite TV, it can be argued that the Internet helps eradicate states' 'hegemonic control over the flow of information'.[48]

But regimes fear (and attempt to control) these other methods of mass communication as well. What is unique about the Internet? Anderson argues,

> In these respects, the Web is comparable in a contemporary context to early printing presses in the world of the scriptorium: it escapes the world of editors and arbiters of thought and interpretation by displaying the materials of interpretation and providing alternative organizations for them.[49]

Anderson was writing about Islam on the Web, but his comments could apply to any political writing and organization on the Internet – overwhelmingly populated by blogs, political organizations, online magazines and 'social media' like Facebook and Twitter, which operate through an individual's online social networks. The Internet allows political commentary and organizing in real time and fosters the creation of online communities and pressure organizations. Just as satellite television and call-in shows have undermined state control over the media and democratized the regional discourse in the Middle East, blogs,[50] chat rooms, and message boards have done the same – and are available to anyone who can afford the comparatively low cost of Internet access. And with the sheer number of blogs and web pages – as many as a million new web pages a day[51] – state censors will be perpetually challenged to keep up. Even in states that can claim to have successfully filtered Internet content, it would be impossible for governments to fully censor all political blogging and content. That said, free expression risks a serious response from the state. As Bucar and Fazaeli note in the Iranian context, 'When blogging is at its most politically powerful, it risks its greatest punishment'.[52]

Some scholars of the region have come to optimistic conclusions, in the sense that they believe the Internet is altering the balance of power between states and oppositions, about the potential impact of the Internet. In a statistical analysis, Best and Wade argue that Internet penetration is associated with an identifiable increase in democracy across the world. The authors identify a number of what they call 'democratic regulators' that might allow the Internet to increase the level of democracy in a given country. Encryption technology allows regime opponents to organize and communicate in secret; the increasing cheapness of Internet access allows organizations and dissidents to better communicate, inform, and organize; and the Internet's architecture disallows 'governments such as the United States from implementing back doors in the Internet to allow wiretapping'.[53] While they caution that each of these possible benefits has an authoritarian analogue (filtration software, political increases in the price of Internet access, etc.), Best and Wade argue that overall the Internet has been beneficial – although they specifically note that there has been no such positive effect in the Middle East, perhaps because during the course of the study the region did not become more democratic at all. Meier argued in 2009 that in some contexts, the Internet does seem to lead to more collective action outcomes – strikes, demonstrations, and protests – but that this finding depends on the level of Internet penetration. In higher-connectivity societies, the Internet does indeed lead to more collective action. In lower-connectivity societies, on the other hand, this does not appear to be the case. [54]

Rahimi lists occasions where new media technologies have helped undermine authoritarian regimes, including the use of email bulletins as resistance in rural Zimbabwe. He also points to the most likely use of the Internet as a form of resistance to authoritarian regimes – the exposure of corruption and abuses. His case study of Iran indicates that while the state has struck back against Internet activists in the context of a formerly loose environment, it has been unable to shut down dissent entirely, making the Internet a new site of contestation over political issues that remain 'red-lined' – unofficially forbidden by state censors – offline.[55] Similarly, Teitelbaum argues that in Saudi Arabia the Internet 'creates a more level playing field for the opposition'.[56] He also notes that despite the Saudi regime's generally successful attempt to control Web content, the censoring of sites has only led to dissent being transferred to other electronic arenas like email and chatting. The rise of mobile technology since Teitelbaum wrote in 2003 makes it increasingly likely that dissent also takes place through SMS and other mobile technologies. He also noted the Internet's utility in crossing traditional social boundaries, like gender.[57] Meanwhile, Wheeler argues that the Internet could lead to incremental changes in authoritarian societies through changes in democratic habits attained through interaction with other people, and through the creation of a democratic public sphere. Because of these interactions and the concomitant reshaping of individuals' politics and beliefs, she ultimately believes the state is 'fighting a losing battle'.[58]

Lynch describes the contours of the public sphere created out of such interactions:

> The Arab public sphere can mobilize public outrage, pressure leaders to act through ridicule or exposure, shape the strategic incentives for rational politicians, and even incite street protests. But it cannot, in and of itself, act.[59]

Lynch is referring mainly to the international public sphere created by Al-Jazeera and other Arab satellite television networks. Television, as noted years ago by Neil Postman, is a passive medium.[60] With the exception of the few individuals whose calls are taken by talk show hosts, satellite TV and the 'new Arab public' generated by it do not interact with each other. If Postman is correct that television culture is an inherent attack on print culture, then democratic enthusiasts should be happy to see the satellite TV phenomenon accompanied by the present-day explosion in online writing and activism. And therein, perhaps, lies the crucial difference between the new Arab public and the new Arab cyberpublic – while the Internet may be available to far fewer citizens than satellite TV, it is also, by its very nature, a far more interactive medium. One of the central features of most political blogs is the 'comments' function, where readers respond to posts – often acrimoniously – and help shape the scope and direction of the debate on each site. And of course, in the past seven years, three primary new applications have shaken the world of digital activism and brought new and even more powerful tools into the hands of invididuals. First, video-sharing sites led by YouTube emerged in 2005 and gave individuals the capability to self-publish videos of nearly any kind and to share them free of charge with both local and global audiences. Second, the rise of 'Social Network Sites', which Boyd and Ellison describe as

> web-based services that allow individuals to (1) construct a public or semi-public profile within a bounded system, (2) articulate a list of other users with whom they share a connection, and (3) view and traverse their list of connections and those made by others within the system. The nature and nomenclature of these connections may vary from site to site.[61]

Finally, 'microblogging' sites like Twitter brought even more participants into conversations, and enabled better coordination of protest and planning through 'hashtags'. All such sites operate under the principle of 'many-to-many' communication, enabling the creation of new publics that are geared explicitly toward conversation, co-creation and sharing. Wheeler argues that such back-and-forth encounters, even in the context of continued authoritarianism, can have positive feedback effects in terms of democratic culture.[62] Howard, writing presciently just before the Arab Spring, argued that the Internet, especially as used by young, urban elites, has contributed to the creation of 'democratic discourses' in Muslim publics, and that the networked nature of the technologies increasingly threatens authoritarian regimes.[63]

The Internet is also said to facilitate organization on specific issues. This kind of organization has been termed 'issue ad-hocracy'.[64] Groups of disparate activists may form around narrow issues but develop into a larger coalition based on shared interests – interests that they may not have been previously aware of, and which were brought together by online activism. In other words, the Internet is a tool that makes these kinds of meetings and happenstances possible – in part because of its own unique technological characteristics, and in part because of the ways states have been unable to entirely clamp down upon it.

On the other hand regimes have also been quite successful in responding to the threat of Internet activism – one need look no further than the Islamic Republic of Iran, where the Green Revolution of 2009 has turned into a bloody stalemate that still favours the repressive apparatus of the state.[65] So while the Internet is conceptualized in the popular imagination as a central hub that anyone can plug into, the reality is far different. In fact, contrary to expectations, ruling regimes have been able to design sophisticated schemes to filter Internet content before it reaches end users, including bloggers, activists, and their readers. While the Internet was designed to be a medium that eluded centralized control – based on the military origins of the technology – it has since evolved in ways that make such control possible. Boas details what he refers to as the 'architectural constraints' on Internet access constructed by China and Saudi Arabia, as opposed to institutional constraints like law, social norms, and the market. In contrast to institutional constraints, architectural constraints seek to actually interpose the power of the state between Internet providers and their users.[66] Zittrain has detailed the ways that software companies and states have designed hardware and applications that make it easier for governments to censor and monitor their citizens.[67]

While the Internet itself does not censor – as Boas writes, 'the core of the network performs simple data transfer functions that do not require knowledge of how the ends are operating' – it is possible in some ways to intercept information. The Internet is 'much less a single network of individual users as it is a network connecting separate computer networks'.[68] Since most individuals access the Internet through service providers (ISPs), states have managed to route all ISPs through a central state server which can, with varying levels of effectiveness, intercept content deemed to be objectionable by political or cultural authorities. For instance, Saudi Arabia's 1.46 million Internet users can sign up with different providers, but all providers access the Internet through the same centralized state portal. Control of the vastly larger number of users in China is more complicated, but operates on the same general principle. These techniques have allowed China and Saudi Arabia to establish what Boas calls 'effective' control – not perfect by any means and capable of being thwarted by savvy and determined users, but enough to satisfy the 'social, economic, and political goals' of the regime.[69]

The Open Net Initiative, which monitors the extent of government filtering of the Internet globally, argues that there are still no formal attempts to filter or block Web sites in Egypt.[70] Boas and Kalathil note that Egypt, in contrast to Saudi Arabia, has no formal mechanism to control or filter Internet content.[71] What Egypt did quite effectively prior to January 2011 was to harass and repress bloggers and other practitioners of online media. In fact the regime arrested more than 100 bloggers in 2008 alone.[72] Still, the lack of architectural control mechanisms means that individuals have still been willing to engage in activism online, and in many cases seem willing to suffer prison time. Thus, if digital activists could have an effect on authoritarian structures, that effect should have been visible in pre-2011 Egypt, which had a comparatively liberal Internet structure in the context of authoritarian practices. The Egyptian government, throughout the period of this study (2001–2011), still appeared to view the commercial and administrative potential of the Internet as greater than its potential for fostering political unrest and opposition coordination.

Perhaps no country in the region has seen a bigger impact from blogging and other forms of Internet activism than Egypt. Even prior to their spectacular success in January 2011, Egyptian bloggers – particularly those writing in English – had become important parts of the discourse in the West, and may have had an influence beyond domestic affairs. Many activists chose to remain pseudonymous because of security concerns in the repressive atmosphere of contemporary Egypt. But their ability to coordinate demonstrations and garner international attention to their causes has not escaped the notice of outside observers.[73] The country's bloggers and Facebook activists have been the focus of numerous journalistic accounts, but as yet the only systematic scholarly study – undertaken by Saleh in 2010 – took a dim view of the transformative potential of the Internet in Egyptian politics, arguing that the Internet had largely been captured and controlled by a nexus of state-corporate interests.

Early scholarly accounts of the Egyptian revolution disagree about the causal effects of the Internet. Lynch contends that online activism contributed to protest dynamics in a number of discrete ways, including increasing the costs of repression for authoritarian states and triggering information cascades (a dynamic which will be explored in depth in the following chapter).[74] While these accounts are important, and bring together some of the theoretical insights offered by other disciplines, none treat the phenomenon of Egyptian digital activism with both historical depth and theoretical sophistication. It is this gap in the literature that I hope to fill with this study. Snider and Faris have recently argued that digital media were tremendously important, but also dependent on a context of increased labour mobilization, press freedoms, and years of digital activism.[75] Khamis and Vaughn argue that social media helped the revolutionaries organize and reach local and global audiences. However, they caution that 'social media were not causes of revolution, but vehicles for empowerment'.[76] Hirschkind, meanwhile, credits the evolution of digital activism, starting with Kefaya in the mid-2000s, with 'paving the way to Tahrir'.[77]

Methodology and Case Selection

This book employs a single case-study design and focuses on political events in Egypt between 2005 and August 2011. This time period was chosen because it coincides with the decision of the Egyptian regime to hold multi-candidate presidential elections and was thus a time of increased expectations about levels of political openness. The end point of the study is the development of genuine, contentious politics following the January 2011 fall of the Mubarak regime. Given the difficulty in obtaining quantitative data about the use of social media networks, and the particular difficulty of conducting social network analysis in authoritarian countries where respondents are likely to be unwilling to provide data about their social networking activities, this study employs a qualitative research design. Open-ended interviews were conducted with dozens of prominent bloggers, journalists, human rights activists and others on a number of field visits to Egypt between October 2007 and August 2011. In addition to those interviews, I used the American University in Cairo's print media database, the Middle East Monitor, to conduct both qualitative and basic quantitative research in the Egyptian print media. On several occasions, I was able to conduct participant observation with the activists I was studying, most notably on April 6, 2008, during a general strike organized via Facebook group. On other occasions I was privy to meetings and conferences organized by online activists, and invited to share in their conclusions. Finally, I conducted process tracing through reading individual blogs and the websites of electronic media organizations.

The selection of individual cases for study in Chapters 3, 4 and 5 was also driven in part by circumstance. When I arrived in Cairo in August 2007, the project was primarily envisioned as a study of the Egyptian blogosphere, based on observations I made in the summer of 2006 while visiting Zamalek, the posh neighbourhood on the Nile in central Cairo. During the course of my first set of interviews with bloggers, beginning in October 2007, I kept hearing again and again that I needed to check out other new technologies that were being put to use by Egyptian activists, notably Twitter and the social networking site Facebook. Twitter at the time was a complete novelty to me, and it wouldn't be until the spring of 2009 that global audiences saw this application – which allows users to send short, 140-character messages to one another – used for activism in an authoritarian country. The ideas that came out of these interviews, in a 'follow-the-evidence' fashion, now form the core of my qualitative analysis, and changed the focus of this project from blogs to the larger world of networked social media. Those insights, quite literally, would not have been possible without the initial conversations with activists on the ground.

Many of the cases investigated in this study were uncovered via the interview process, by asking activists to explain the impact of social media technologies, and asking them to cite specific cases where they believed the technology had an impact. This process was in many ways haphazard, and open to the charge of selection on the dependent variable. However, in each case, I was able to investigate the record of the public sphere to test whether events were really being driven by the technologies, or by other factors.

Of course, some of these research decisions were made by necessity rather than choice. The reality is that a number of prominent bloggers were not willing to speak with me – whether because of interview fatigue or fear of my motives. In fact it took months to win any credibility at all in the tight social world of the Internet elite, and it was only after repeated calls, emails, and meetings that I was able to gain the trust of anyone at all. Furthermore, more quantitative investigations of social networks were simply not possible in Egypt, nor was an analysis of link structure between blogs, since Egyptian blogs are often structured very differently from their American counterparts. What this means is that ultimately, this is less a quantitative study and more an attempt to build theory about the effects of digital activism in authoritarian countries.

I chose to undertake a single case study analysis for a number of reasons. First, in Egypt alone, the rate of Internet usage skyrocketed during the past decade[78] and Wheeler notes that in all likelihood there are more users than estimated because of the widespread availability of Internet cafés.[79] Furthermore, as will be demonstrated below, Egypt may be unique in the region in terms of the degree of influence that blogs have had on events and public discourse – and this may be related to the absence of overt filtering or censorship. In this way Egypt can be thought of as a critical case for the idea that the Internet has placed new tools and resources in the hands of the political opposition. In other words, if the tools did not have an effect in an authoritarian but relatively open environment such as Egypt, we can be fairly certain that they will be of little use in stricter environments like China.

Additionally, Egypt forms a strong comparison to other authoritarian regimes and their regulation of the Internet. The response of authoritarian regimes to the Internet has run the gamut from total exclusion of most individuals from the Web (i.e. Burma) to the liberal encouragement of e-commerce and other online activities (as in the United Arab Emirates). The Chinese regime has cracked down hard on what it perceives to be online organizing by its chief opposition groups – notably the Falun Gong, whose e-activities have been almost totally curtailed by state strength[80] – and that these attempts at online regulation have been so successful.[81] In contrast, the Egyptian regime only went after a handful of prominent Islamist and secular Internet activists, and only when these figures had transgressed against very clear and significant rules of Egyptian politics. Why did Chinese and Egyptian authorities construct different architectures of control, and why did they appear to perceive the threat posed by online activism differently?

Finally, the ideas contained within this book started as part of a doctoral dissertation, one that argued for the capability of digital activists to spark or take advantage of a regime-level crisis in Egypt. The January 25 Egyptian revolution took place in the time between the completion of that project in April 2010 and the present moment. Thus, what began as a probabilistic prediction about the likely trajectories and uses of digital activism in Egypt has been transformed into an explanation of what actually happened, and an application of that theory to cases outside of Egypt. The penultimate chapter, on the Egyptian revolution, cannot therefore serve as a 'test' of the hypotheses generated in this book, since of course those hypotheses were driven by my research in Egypt from 2006–2009. It does, however, serve as a useful coda to the book's main body which was largely conceived and written between 2008 and 2010. Follow-up interviews were conducted in the summer of 2011 with leading digital activists and participants in the various youth coalitions that emerged in the wake of January 25. These interviews yielded new data, revealed tactical innovations unforeseen in my prior research, and largely confirmed predictions about how and why social media were so important in the Egyptian case.

Outline of the Book

The primary contention of this book is that what I call *Social Media Networks* (SMNs) can trigger informational cascades through the effects of their interaction with independent media outlets and on-the-ground organizers. They do so primarily through the reduction of certain costs of collective action, the transmission capabilities of certain elite nodes in social and online networks, and through changing the diffusion dynamics of information across social networks. An important secondary argument is that while states have become more adept at surveillance and filtering, SMNs make it impossible for authoritarian countries to control their media environments in the way that such regimes have typically done in the past. While SMNs cannot substitute for the difficult work of grassroots organizing, they can certainly make it easier, and enhance its effects. Finally, this book seeks to contest popular accounts of digital activism in Egypt that locates its origins in either the April 6 Youth Movement in 2008, or with the We Are All Khaled Said movement in 2011. In fact, as will be outlined in detail below, digital activism in Egypt stretches back nearly a decade. The work of these earlier blogger-activists was pioneering in the sense that it helped transform public debate about a number of issues that became focal points during the Egyptian revolution itself.

Chapter 2 provides the theoretical core of the book, and introduces its key terms. In Chapter 2, I explain how advances in our understandings of networks, as well as research into the link structure of the Internet, helps us explain how information can be diffused more quickly across SMNs, whether through blogs, text messages, social networking sites, or microblogging services, and how certain key nodes in networks are responsible for distributing information and influencing other members of their social networks. The chapter also argues that these diffusion dynamics can be instigators of 'informational cascades', or sudden and widespread shifts in preferences, attitudes or behaviors. These informational cascades can do two things – first they can make it difficult for regimes to maintain their control of information hegemony, and second, they can lead to the organization of collective action, by lowering the 'revolutionary thresholds' of individuals embedded in social networks.

Chapter 3, 'Agenda-Setters: Torture, Rights and Social Media Networks in Egypt', evaluates four case studies of blog-driven or blog-enhanced media events in Egypt to test the theories about media events and information control in Chapter 2. These four events are the sexual harassment scandal of October 2006; the torture scandal of January 2007; the Sudanese refugee crisis of 2006; and the Al-Qursaya Island takeover attempt of 2007–8. The chapter demonstrates the critical agenda-setting or story-breaking power of SMNs – particularly in comparison to the absence of media coverage of similar events in the past – and casts substantial doubt on the idea that SMNs have no substantial impact on authoritarian politics. Chapter 3 further argues that in a country like Egypt, where few are connected to the Internet, it is the presence of a robust independent media that is ultimately responsible for transmitting claims out of SMNs and into the broader public sphere. It thus revises our understanding of the causal pathways between the Internet and social or political change in authoritarian countries, particularly countries with low rates of Internet access.

Chapter 4, 'New Tools, Old Rules: Social Media Networks and Collective Action in Egypt', evaluates case studies of social media-driven mobilization to test competing hypotheses about the effects of SMNs on collective action. The two case studies are the general strikes of April 6 2008 and April 6, 2009. The two events, with similar organizers, goals, and execution, are strikingly close to a natural experiment. The chapter theorizes the April 6, general strike as an informational cascade and tests this theory against other possible explanations of the day's events. The chapter also tests theories of regime response to these activities and answers questions about their effectiveness. The chapter argues that while the April 6 2008 general strike constituted an informational cascade, its organizers misunderstood its relationship to the on-the-ground organizing done by the labour movement. This misunderstanding attributed more causality to SMNs than was warranted, and led to the failure of the follow-up strike. Important lessons were learned from this temporary failure – lessons that were applied successfully by organizers prior to the events of January 2011.

It is possible that SMNs had an additional impact on Egyptian politics and the Egyptian public sphere by creating and sustaining shared arenas or 'counter-publics' for marginalized groups like women and religious and sexual minorities. Chapter 5 evaluates the use of the Internet by Baha'is and Muslim Brothers. It explains the function of SMNs for these two groups, one socially and the other politically subordinated. The chapter uses evidence of blog-driven media coverage to evaluate competing hypotheses about the effect of social media. The chapter finds that while blogs and other forms of electronic media increased coverage of issues for both groups, this effect can largely be explained by the writing of the same group of elite blogger-journalists who helped drive coverage of the issues in Chapter 3.

Chapter 6 explains how the variables discussed earlier in the book converged to create a regime-level crisis for the Egyptian government. Earlier efforts against torture, for instance, produced a networked community called We Are All Khaled Said. SMNs were used not just to coordinate demonstrations, but to produce the time, place, demands and operating principles of the revolution itself. The chapter traces the development of the We Are All Khaled Said Facebook group, its usage during the revolt, and concludes with a look at how digital activists have transitioned to post-revolutionary Egyptian politics. It argues that SMNs were pivotal in sparking the protests and manufacturing the regime-level crisis, but that it was other dynamics – notably a general strike organized by a resurgent labour movement – that ultimately pushed the Mubarak regime out of power. This finding is consistent with the theory that SMNs can produce crises, but cannot necessarily determine their outcome.

Chapter 7 evaluates the SMN model tested in chapters 3–6 against outside-sample cases. It does so through a series of case studies which evaluate the use of the Internet in crisis mobilizations: in Ukraine, during the Orange Revolution of 2004; in Moldova, during the so-called Twitter Revolution of 2009; in Kenya, during the 2007–2008 election crisis; and in Iran, during the Green Revolution of 2009–2010. The chapter seeks to explain the role of the media environment in these cases. Chapter 7 confirms the findings of earlier chapters that SMNs contribute to informational cascades, that independent media outlets are critical transmission belts for claims made through SMNs, and that the outcomes of the crises in question depend not on the properties of SMNs but rather on local and international features of institutional politics in each case. As in the Egyptian revolution of January 2011, SMNs produced crises in very similar ways, but with disparate results.

CHAPTER 2

A THEORY OF THE NETWORKED REVOLT: SOCIAL MEDIA NETWORKS, MEDIA EVENTS, AND COLLECTIVE ACTION

In any case, there is an irremovable political obstacle to becoming sufficiently knowledgeable: vulnerable regimes can block the production and dissemination of information potentially harmful to their own survival.

(Timur Kuran)[1]

Introduction

The study of social media is becoming a subject of increasing importance for political science. Scholars are beginning to take seriously the claims that social media might lead to more collective action outcomes, and to consider the kinds of tools that may contribute to those outcomes. The study of networks is a critical factor in understanding the potential power of social media. The discovery of new laws governing networks in a number of different realms has led a small number of political scientists to investigate the relevance of network theories for their own areas of expertise. Some scholars have used advances in network theory to shed light on the mobilizing capacity of terrorist groups,[2] while others have used networks to enhance our understanding of globalization processes.[3] Slaughter uses networks to test theories about America's possible decline as a major power.[4] The concept of the power law (defined below) has been used to analyse the frequency and severity of wars in the international system.[5] And Elhafnawy argues that the existence of scale-free networks in complex societies poses important problems for the pursuit of security.[6] The relevance of certain properties of social media has been used to look at intelligence gathering and sharing.[7] Pedahzur and Perliger use social network analysis to examine the resilience of Palestinian terror networks, and notably argue that 'hubs' are critical for terror operations and that these networks indeed are scale-free and function according to power laws.[8] In this chapter, I explain how these network theories, and the Social Media Networks that operate by their laws, must cause us to revise our understanding of collective action outcomes, media events, and informational cascades.

Networks and Web 2.0

A flurry of scientific research in recent years has pointed to the importance of new discoveries about networks. Most importantly, this research emphasizes the idea that not all nodes or actors in a network are identical, and that certain kinds of nodes assume far greater importance in their networks than do others. A network, according to Watts, is merely anything that is connected to any other thing. Or as he puts it, a network is 'a collection of objects connected to each other in some fashion'.[9] Some networks are random, in that most nodes have about as many links as any other node – many scholars point to the US highway network as typical of this kind of network. No node in the highway network is substantially more important than any other, and even the most well-connected stretch of road has a limited number of links. Most US cities have a few connections to the interstate highway system, but none have dozens, and none have zero. Such randomness is how most scientists looked at networks until relatively recently.

But some networks operate according to different principles, which are called 'power laws' – the idea that certain nodes in these networks have virtually no limit on their potential size or scale.[10] The discovery of what this study will call *power law networks* was made when scholars tried to 'map' the Internet and found that while there are millions of web pages, only a few have more than a handful of links to other pages, while a select few have thousands and thousands. According to Watts, what distinguishes such a network from most of these ordinary networks is that they operate according to a *power law*: 'most nodes will be relatively poorly connected, while a select minority of hubs will be very highly connected'.[11] And these well-connected hubs operate according to the principle of the rich getting richer – they tend to attract more connections because they are already well-connected, transforming them from ordinary nodes into super-connected hubs. This is called the principle of preferential attachment and continues to apply so long as the network is growing. As Barabasi puts it, when new nodes enter a network, they are much more likely to link to the existing nodes with greater numbers of links.[12] New nodes in an existing network have great difficulty attracting links. Investigators intrigued by the results of the Internet mapping quickly discovered that power laws apply to diverse phenomena ranging from the spread of disease to the composition of terrorist networks.

What interests us here is not just the idea of networks themselves, but rather how the tools of Web 2.0 enhance those networks and are enhanced by them. To answer this question we must first agree upon an understanding of what Web 2.0 actually is, how it differs from Web 1.0, and the kinds of services, tools, opportunities and drawbacks

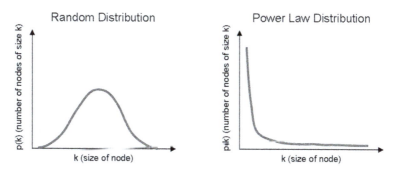

Figure 2.1 Power law distribution versus a random distribution.[12]

it offers to users. The Web has evolved over the past decade in ways that are theoretically meaningful. A definition is hard to come by, but O'Reilly argues that some of the critical components of Web 2.0 are participation (as opposed to simply publishing); 'radical trust', in the form of Wikis like Wikipedia; 'radical decentralization' and 'tagging, not taxonomy' in the form of the kind of user-generated sorting and rating that takes place on certain websites.[14] The typical transformation from Web 1.0 to Web 2.0 can be illustrated by the move from 'dumping' offline, print content onto the Internet, to the creation of online-only sites that utilize the new cooperative and collaborative capabilities of the technology itself. O'Reilly points to the contrast between the Web 1.0 site for the *Encyclopedia Brittanica* and the Web 2.0 site *Wikipedia*, where user-editors both create, edit, and police the content.

The rise of Web 2.0 has given rise to the creation of what some scholars have called 'social media', what Shirky refers to as 'social tools'[15] and what I will refer to as *Social Media Networks* (SMNs). *Social Media Networks* encompass weblogs (i.e. blogs), Social Networking Sites like Facebook, niche-networking sites like LinkedIn (for professional networking), crowdsourcing content like Digg[16] (a site that allows users to rank and control media content), text-messaging services (by which mobile phone users can send written messages to one another), micromedia services like Twitter (a many-to-many communications service that allows users to send messages to each other or post them to blogs), picture-sharing services such as Flickr (which allows users to mark or 'tag' their photos and self-organize the content), and event-planning sites like Meet-Up. Much of what these services offer people is the ability to share information and to form groups, at a very low cost, with a very large number of people. Power laws have also been applied to the study of blogs in addition to commercial websites.[17] Unsurprisingly, most of the blog traffic in the world is directed to a relatively small number of sites, whereas most blogs, like most websites, get somewhere between zero and a handful of hits[18] per day. The reality that blogospheres are governed by power laws helps explain the popularity of certain blogs and bloggers compared to others, and generate hypotheses about why certain events and stories receive coverage and others do not. Power laws should also lead us to be cautious about assuming, to paraphrase Hindman, that to speak in cyberspace is the same as being heard.[19] The reality is that not everyone has an equal voice on the Internet, and that Web 2.0 technologies have the effect of amplifying those inequalities.

In the political realm, information is of far-reaching importance, and therefore the speed and means by which information travels must be of equal importance. As Castells et. al. note, 'Control of information and communication has been a major source of power throughout history'.[20] This is particularly true of authoritarian systems, in which certain kinds of information – if shared by all citizens – might be damaging to the long-term viability of the system. SMNs perform a number of information functions that make them a desirable tool for dissidents in authoritarian systems. First, they facilitate 'many-to-many' communication, allowing individuals to share information instantly with large numbers of people – news of an arrest, the date and time of a demonstration, the impending arrival of security forces. This is increasingly true in the age of the 'mobile web'- when accessing the always-on Internet from mobile phones becomes at least as prevalent as doing so from a laptop or computer terminal. Second, they make it difficult for regimes to cover up news stories or events that are deemed threatening to government control. Third, they dramatically reduce the amount of time it takes for information to travel – both because of the nature of the technology itself and because of social media's ability to enhance standard social networks – while simultaneously increasing the geographic and spatial reach of that information. To explain the impact of social media, we must first understand how networks function and how the new networks being constructed and used are altering the social and political topology in societies that are adopting these technologies.

SMNs and Media Events

SMNs cause us to revise our understanding of the relationship between press freedom and authoritarianism in the developing world. By empowering non-professional actors and placing the tools of documentation and truth-telling into the hands of ordinary citizens, SMNs create linked activists who can contest the narrative-crafting and information-controlling capabilities of authoritarian regimes. In doing so, accepted interpretations of press freedom and its relationship to authoritarianism in the literature become subject to question. For instance, impartial rankings of press freedoms in the developing world may need to be updated to take into account the effects of SMNs and the feedback loop which generates coverage for issues that may have been previously ignored in the official press.

Drezner and Farrell claim that the effectiveness of blogs as sources of news and information is due to their consumption by political and journalistic elites. They write (in reference to the American context), 'There is strong evidence that media elites – editors, publishers, reporters, and columnists –consumed political blogs'.[21] There is no particular reason to imagine that this isn't also true in authoritarian societies with relatively free presses. In such societies, the universe of prominent bloggers is quite small, constrained by both the network structure of the Internet[22] and the still-limited Internet access for many ordinary citizens in less-wealthy parts of the non-democratic world. But this tiny elite of bloggers and journalists is able to have a disproportionate influence on public affairs, due to their interconnectedness with journalists. As Ajemian notes, '...the value of blogs as a form of new media is that they allow for individual grass roots political journalism and facilitate the creation of a counter-public sphere of discourse that has the potential to penetrate mainstream media.'[23] SMNs governed by power laws serve to create or amplify the social connections between journalists and elite bloggers, making it far more likely that certain bloggers will receive press attention, or that their work will be picked up or 'borrowed' by reporters.

SMNs have a number of structural advantages over the traditional media that make them quite different in their capabilities, and in some cases, able to report on subjects that other media outlets in authoritarian societies cannot or will not write about. First, SMNs have the advantage of instantaneity, in the sense that blogs can be updated instantly, either directly through laptops, or indirectly through SMS, Twitter, Jaiku and other manifestations of the mobile web. Maratea argues that the 'speed of transmission' available to bloggers and Web activists is more important than the lowering of cost barriers when considering conditions for entry into the media universe.[24] The fact that such individuals can make their claims without editors or interference from corporate entities makes it possible for them to reach diverse audiences instantly and to influence public discussion and debate. It also, of course, increases the amount of information available and thus concomitantly may decrease trust in its veracity.[25] For instance, mobile activists can update their colleagues and readers directly via a Twitter post about an arrest or demonstration, well before editors and writers at even the fastest newspapers can put stories online.

A large body of literature points to the importance of a free press to democracy[26] and the reverse side of that particular democratic coin is the importance of maintaining information and discursive control in authoritarian and semi-authoritarian governments. It is therefore not surprising that regime type plays an important role in the extent to which the Internet has penetrated a given society.[27] While semi-authoritarian countries may have some elements of a free press, those outlets are unlikely to have complete freedom of movement in the information market. It is therefore widely hoped that 'new media' – from satellite TV to the Internet – may provide an alternative source of information under such conditions, potentially leading to more democratic outcomes or allowing for more political space in the MENA region.[28]

What has been less studied is the serious effect SMNs have had on the effectiveness of these alternative media outlets and the scope of their reach, as well as the interplay between new media sources and professionals working in more traditional media. And by producing quicker informational cascades, SMNs may accelerate the transformation of certain kinds of discourses in the traditional media – they facilitate a process by which, as Somer writes, 'previously taboo terms and concepts are openly expressed'.[29] By serving as first-movers and accelerating the spread of certain memes, concepts, and ideas, the social media paves the way for the adoption of these discourses in the traditional media – and this might be particularly true for journalists who adhere to regime-sanctioned forms of discourse without having a firm conviction in favour of the government's position. Such individuals are particularly susceptible to the opinions of others (i.e. bloggers, journalists, and contacts maintained through social media).[30]

SMNs, Collective Action, and Informational Cascades

Power law networks force us to revise our understanding of collective action problems in social movements and revolutions. Networks interface with collective action problems by making communication, symbol-sharing, organization, and trust-building simpler and more efficient. SMNs directly impact three of the four pillars of social movement theory – by making organizing cheaper and faster, they affect the calculus of standard theories of resource mobilization. By affecting the spread of memes and symbols, SMNs make it easier to arrive at shared understandings of meaning. SMNs generate competing hypotheses about the generation and dissemination of frames. And by enlarging social networks and increasing the relevance of weak ties, networks might force a re-evaluation of the processes behind the formation of relative deprivation grievances.

SMNs reduce the costs of organizing collective action. Shirky has detailed how social media can create new networks and strengthen existing ones – both at lower costs than in the past.[31] The standard model of organization necessitates a headquarters and an elite structure of salary-drawing leaders, and may include the costs of holding real-world meetings and conventions, as well as the price of producing and disseminating literature in the pertinent media environment. However, SMNs allow groups to form, communicate, and 'meet' virtually for free, after the costs of Internet access and in some cases maintaining a highly-trafficked website are factored in.

Sunstein writes about the relevance of social media for communication practices in the business community, arguing that they effectively streamline a number of processes that once cost organizations a great deal of money.[32] For instance, contrast the model of advocacy presented by Amnesty International – which maintains a paid staff in a certain number of cities worldwide, and has a substantial budget – with an organization such as Global Voices, which operates for a fraction of that cost yet maintains reporters and staff in countries from Morocco to India. While Amnesty International is still the more prominent organization, the success of Global Voices – listed by the blog-ranking tool Technorati as one of the top 100 blogs in the world[33] – attained in a very short time period should provide evidence of the efficacy of their organizing model. If the costs of both organization and participation are much lower, then it would follow that participation is more likely by rational actors seeking to maximize their utility. Just as individuals are unlikely to participate in a collective endeavour whose benefits they can draw for free, organizers are unlikely to opt for models of organization that can be replicated and even improved upon for much less money.

Collective action theory also operates on standard assumptions about individual behaviour. Specifically, it assumed that individuals will not be willing to brave the considerable risks of revolutionary or oppositional behaviour if the benefits do not outweigh the costs. Of course, costs and benefits must be conceptualized loosely, as more than simply economic benefits for individuals. Perhaps the most important difference between pure rational actor theory and the way real-life collective action takes place involves the role of social ties.[34] Gould argues that in dense networks (like SMNs) the contributions of less central actors have a positive overall effect on the contributions of others.[35] Furthermore, as a number of authors have noted, different individuals have different thresholds of participation in mass political action. Moreover, they appear to have incentives, under certain circumstances, for fully or partially falsifying their public preferences.[36] Since much of this literature concerns itself with the fall of communist regimes, this preference falsification involves the penalties for expressing one's true feelings about a government or an opposition in contexts that involve serious personal risks for political action. As Kuran notes, theories of collective action are very good at predicting the non-occurrence of revolutions, but leave us still searching for theories of how, why, and where they *do* occur.[37] If individuals always have incentives to hide behind the revolutionary action of others rather than taking action themselves, then how do revolutions, or even mass political mobilizations, take place?

Networks facilitate the exchange of private information, which in turn makes political or informational cascades more likely – situations in which there is a widespread and sudden change in collective attitudes, beliefs, or behavior. SMNs also make it much less likely that hostile regimes can control the information environment to such an extent that this private information remains obscured or intercepted. As noted in the previous section, extensive SMN ties between activists and journalists assure that the stories documented and amplified by SMNs are also found in more mainstream press outlets. Under certain circumstances, the cascades triggered by this SMN activity might lead to rapid and spontaneous collective action of the sort that generates large protest movements and in some circumstances brings down governments. Cascades can also, of course, work in the opposite direction, suddenly dismantling or crippling a protest or social movement.[38]

The work on cascades originally grew out of frustration with theories of crowd behaviour which imputed irrationality to all participants in crowd behaviour.[39] The crucial divergence between theories of crowd irrationality and models that depend on rational individual decision-making is the idea that actors make decisions based in part on the behaviour and decision-making of others.[40] They do so in an environment of 'incomplete and unreliable information', a point that will be elaborated on below.[41] Berk also notes that collective decision-making calls for extensive communication between individuals. Later work, stemming from the research of Schelling, finds political cascade models using the idea of thresholds and focal points to suggest that certain social phenomena become widespread after reaching a so-called 'tipping point' that leads more and more actors to change their behaviour. Tipping models have been used to analyse everything from the dynamics of 'white flight' and changes in discourse to the spread of new fashion trends. As Somer writes, 'cascades explain how bandwagon effects and the strength of numbers can facilitate the occurrence of rapid changes in individual beliefs, expressions, and behavior during collective actions'.[42] The theory operates largely at the level of the individual, and assumes that actors are sensitive to the costs and benefits of participating in protests or rebellions.[43]

It also assumes that actors' thresholds are directly affected by the number of other people that they see participating in the activity.[44] As Granovetter writes, 'The cost to an individual of joining a riot declines as riot size increases, since the probability of being apprehended is smaller the larger the number involved'.[45] He posits that all individuals have 'thresholds' governing the point at which they will participate in a collective action, and that these thresholds are in some part dependent on the total number of other visible individuals participating in that action. Thresholds apply not only to collective action, but also to fads and trends, and are analysed with diffusion models. As Barabasi notes, 'Acknowledging our differences, diffusion models assign a threshold to each individual, quantifying the likelihood that he or she will adopt a given innovation'.[46] These thresholds are also context-specific, in that an individual does not have some abstract value assigned to the act of 'demonstrating', but rather adjusts his or her threshold according to the situation.[47] I posit here that Social Media Networks, by affecting the speed and scope of diffusion, are likely to powerfully alter the 'situations' of individuals, thereby changing the likelihood that and speed at which thresholds will be met.

Individuals are also dependent on pre-existing preferences that establish their thresholds to begin with. The more individuals join the protest, the more likely it is that individuals with higher thresholds for participating will in fact do so. This makes each individual decision *contingent*.[48] The tipping point, then, is that moment when the protest or activity becomes self-reinforcing, and increases without further direct organization or action by the leadership. This is because the action or trend will at this point be adopted by individuals who don't much care one way or the other but who generally prefer to be on the right – i.e. popular – side of things. For instance, many people aren't particularly interested in what happens on the runways of Milan and Paris, but they will adopt a trend, like Argyle sweaters, so they don't appear to be out of step with contemporary fashions. It is similar to the idea of network effects, which stipulate that a technology becomes more useful the more people who adopt it.[49] Ultimately this leaves only the small minority which is ideologically opposed to the now mainstream movement.

Work on cascades was given new life by the unexpected events that caused and followed the break-up of the Soviet Union. It is widely acknowledged that almost no one saw the break-up of the USSR coming far in advance. As Kuran argues, 'The evidence is overwhelming that virtually no one expected communism to collapse rapidly, with little bloodshed, and throughout Eastern Europe before the end of the 1980s'.[50] The sudden collapse of governments previously considered durable took the social science universe by total surprise. Similarly, few observers predicted or understood the swift break-up, along ethnic lines, of states like Yugoslavia. The descent of the Balkans into ethnic violence and genocide horrified journalists, social scientists, and policy-makers alike, who were left to rely on theories of 'primordial' or 'ancient' hatreds put forth by popular writers.[51]

It made seemingly very little sense for countries with thriving, multi-ethnic cities and traditions to suddenly implode and polarize along ethnic lines. However, using cascade models may help us understand the nature and causes of such a sudden and drastic shift. Somer argues that because of pre-existing uncertainties about the extent of ethnic tolerance, observers may have underestimated the amount of ethnic polarization already present in the former Yugoslavia, and thus a small shift in the amount of publicly-expressed divisiveness led to a drastic shift in support for the leaders and strategies of polarization. Specifically, Yugoslav society may have polarized privately during the 1980s without a general understanding of this polarization, making the collapse of the state and the bloody wars of succession far more surprising than they should have been had private preferences been known and available, both for observers and for the individual agents themselves.[52] The usefulness of these cascade models for understanding sudden, unexpected, and seemingly unpredictable shifts in collective behavior has obvious relevance for scholars engaging in Middle Eastern studies, a discipline which has long been accused of making inaccurate predictions about collective outcomes, or of not having foreseen the changes that have taken place.[53]

Lustick and Miodownik have defined a cascade as 'a radiating pattern of transformation in behavior across a large population involving an accelerating change in available information about the future condition of the population'.[54] The term is generally credited to Bikhchandani et. al., who defined informational cascades as taking place when '...it is optimal for an individual, having observed the actions of those ahead of him, to follow the behavior of the preceding individual without regard to his own information'.[55] Their model is sequential in the sense that every decision maker can see the decisions of all those who precede them.[56] However, it does make the problematic assumption that the ordering of individuals is 'exogenous and known to all'[57] – i.e. that everyone is aware of who the first-movers are and act sequentially, basing their own decisions on those of the first-movers and their followers. Firms and individuals react to the prior decisions of others, even when their own private information – preferences or beliefs known only to themselves and not to others – might lead them to do otherwise.

For Kuran, this concept of preference falsification is critical to explaining how the events in Eastern Europe unfolded in the last days of communism. The reason that few observers and academics successfully predicted the fall of communism has a great deal to do with the fact that until the very latest hour, many individuals either falsified their preferences for revolution, or maintained their support for the status quo. As Kuran notes, the trouble was 'imperfect observability'.[58] He defines preference falsification in the case of each individual as follows: 'Insofar as his two preferences differ – that is, the preference he expresses in public diverges from that he holds in private – the individual is engaged in preference falsification'.[59] Kuran's model gives individuals thresholds based on the information about others available to them. The size of the opposition affects an individual's payoff structure for supporting anti-government forces.[60] Kuran defines an individual's 'revolutionary threshold' as the point at which the potential benefits of joining the opposition outweigh the psychological costs of maintaining public support for a regime that the individual privately opposes.[61] He also emphasizes that very small changes in individual support for the regime can cause a cascade effect, as more and more individuals' revolutionary thresholds are crossed. Exogenous shocks, such as an external patron declaring its intention not to use force to prop up the status quo, can affect these thresholds, insofar as they affect payoff matrices for supporting the opposition or reduce the potential costs of revolutionary action. But as he notes, 'neither private preferences nor the corresponding thresholds are common knowledge'.[62] He notes that this makes it possible to arrive at the very brink of revolution without anyone knowing that the abyss is a mere step away.

In most of these models, too, the concept of private information is critical. Opposition to a particular regime or to particular policies of that regime may be widespread, but due to the possibility and cost of repression, that information is held and kept privately. Kuran argues that the costs of protest go down as the number of participants in widespread political action goes up. These kinds of analyses assume that changes in the percentage of the population supporting mass action will change the preferences of individual actors.[63] The problem where mobilization is concerned then becomes twofold. The first aspect of the problem is how to properly gauge and interpret the private information of potential revolutionaries; the second is how to ensure that said information, once transmitted 'publicly', reaches its intended audiences of both the regime and fellow potential revolutionaries. Lustick and Miowdownik argue that standard rational choice assumptions about private and public information falsely assume that individuals have perfect information about the behaviour of others. The authors claim:

> They assume that individuals do not receive information about their world from some subset of the population with whom they interact or in whom they place particular trust. Instead, individuals are modeled as learning about the state of the population as a whole by viewing the entire population or by making inferences from a random sample of it.[64]

Lustick and Miowdownik argue instead that individuals are greatly influenced by their 'neighbourhoods' – i.e. that subset of the population with whom they associate and about whom they have more information than about the general population. Schelling referred to these neighbourhoods as 'zones of knowledge',[65] whereas Lustick and Miodownik refer to the concept as 'spatiality'.[66] Somer prefers the terminology 'private zones of trust' in which individuals are comfortable expressing beliefs about the political system that they would not express in public.[67] Lustick and Miodownik point to research that suggests 'tipping' is 'more rapid and more common when the local neighbourhood of each agent is larger'.[68] They note that focusing on spatiality in fact makes tipping substantially less likely, and that 'an important determinant of their rate of occurrence is the size of the spatially defined neighbourhood'.[69] They argue that this finding accounts, in some part, for excessive expectations of collective action in certain contexts. If true, then private information stands in the way of collective action, and anything that serves to decrease the amount of privately-held information in tightly-controlled political environments would lead to a greater likelihood of a cascade.

For Kuran, the low likelihood of informational cascades ever happening makes the business of predicting (as opposed to understanding) revolutions a fruitless process. To his mind, acknowledging the human inability to predict the time and place of successful rebellion against authoritarian governance is not to be confused with abandoning the social-scientific endeavour: '...accepting the limits of what we can expect from science is not an admission of defeat'.[70] Kuran notes particularly the difficulty of obtaining accurate information about private preferences in non-democratic societies – during the 1980s, it was virtually impossible to undertake sophisticated opinion research in communist regimes, and even when research was undertaken, there was no way to really know if the information was accurate or if respondents were falsifying their responses because of potential state reprisals.[71] Furthermore, as Kuran himself notes, it is imperative for the regime itself to maintain its control over the flow of information – for according to his model, once it becomes common knowledge that the vast majority of citizens opposes the government, it is much more likely that individuals will be willing to take part in protest activity.

In that sense, informational cascades are not just about private information, but also about the perceived likelihood of revolutionary success. Individual assessments of this calculus are thus extremely dependent on individual cognitive processes. As Sunstein and Kuran note, human judgements about probability depend on what they call the availability heuristic – the human tendency to make assessments based on 'the ease with which we can think of relevant examples'.[72] They argue that those perceptions are often not empirically useful or correct – i.e. basing judgements about the kinds of conditions that lead to revolution solely on cases that an individual is intimately familiar with. The availability heuristic sometimes causes the spread of misinformation, leading to the adoption of sub-optimal responses by public officials, as in the case of the panic over the contamination of Love Canal – a perceived public health threat that was never proven as such.[73] As the authors note, far from being irrational, the use of the availability heuristic may in many cases be the best option for individuals operating in the real world, in which there are real obstacles to becoming the perfectly-informed actors of pure rational choice theory.[74] For our purposes, however, it should be sufficient to note the authors' larger point: that the availability of information leads actors to revise their own judgements about things that are normatively accepted, and gives them clues about the preferences and interests of others.[75] The role of social media in making information like this more readily available should lead us to think more about the conditions under which cascades take place. It also challenges the notion, advanced by Shirky, that social media merely helps bring together people who *already share preferences*, rather than changing preferences themselves.[76]

Sunstein writes about the information-aggregating potential of digital and social media. In Sunstein's analysis, what prevents groups from properly aggregating information is that certain members of the group will choose not to share their privately-held information – whether preferences or critical information or simply new ideas – for fear of ridicule or because of a willingness to go along with the group. Sunstein calls these wells of private information 'hidden profiles'[77] and defines them as 'the accurate understandings that groups could attain but do not'.[78] Groups arrive at sub-optimal decisions for a variety of reasons, among them the 'common knowledge effect', by which information shared by all group members takes on a much larger significance than private information held by one or more members of the group.[79] He also argues that lower-status members of groups are more likely to keep their hidden profiles hidden, and to be ignored even if they do speak up. According to Sunstein, and *pace* Bakhchandani et al., this actually makes cascades more likely since individuals in groups are liable to disregard their own private information and go along with the group.

SMNs have the effect of aggregating this dispersed, private information and revealing hidden profiles, either through the SMNs themselves, or by transmission from SMN activists to journalists. SMNs by their nature require users to share as much of their private information, political leanings, and activities as possible, and require deliberate action to make any of this activity private. What is new about SMNs is that, by default, *the actions of individual users are made public to that individual's entire network by automatically updating*. Bimber, Flanagin and Stohl have referred to this process as 'communality'. The authors argue that because the production of shared information resources involves taking information out of the private realm and into the public, digital technologies blur the line between the public and the private.[80] Blog postings are, by their very nature, public. Twitter posts, while not available to all in quite the same way as a blog, are also public for an individual's entire network. On Facebook, for instance, any change in an individual's 'status' (a short, updatable, two-line note that appears under your profile) can be seen by the dozens, hundreds, or thousands of other people in that network. So if Facebook had been around in Leipzig in 1989, the message 'Hans is heading to the square to demonstrate' would have been instantly transmitted to anyone in his network. While it is unlikely that Hans's close friends would have been particularly surprised by this decision – since actors tend to inform those closest to them of their political preferences – it may have been news to the weaker ties in his social network: distant cousins, acquaintances from work, old college buddies – the people commonly referred to as 'friends-in-law'. According to Gould, if Hans is a marginal actor – i.e. a non-connector – the marginal value of his contribution to the collective action might be very high.[81] These are precisely the kinds of ties that SMNs tend to 'activate' in the sense that, in the real world, such individuals are unlikely to interact or to exchange information on anything remotely approaching a regular basis. Of course, governments may use this practice as well, but because of the Friend of a Friend (FoF) nature of these sites, those messages are unlikely to be effective in reaching or changing the preferences of distant social clusters – in other words, there is a reputational component to SMNs that will be difficult for governments to fully overcome. Platforms like Twitter, of course, have even greater reach, since they enable complete strangers to 'follow' one another and to receive their updates. On Twitter there are two ways you might glean information from a total stranger: one is by following them – perhaps someone wrote an article you particularly enjoyed, and you want to follow them on Twitter. The other way is of course through Twitter's hashtag function. Users typically end their Twitter posts with a 'hashtag' that aggregates all the posts from anyone using that hashtag. So for instance, during the Egyptian revolution, users would end their Twitter updates with the hashtag '#jan25' – meaning anyone who typed #jan25 into the Twitter search field (or simply clicked on the hashtag itself) would be met with a rolling feed of *everyone* who ended a post with that hashtag.

SMNs create large, dense networks that effectively collapse the distinction between strong and weak ties. SMNs transmit information that was formerly 'private' – i.e. known only to a small subset of an indiviual's larger social network – and make that information 'public' in the sense of transmitting it to the entirety of that network (or at least the percentage of the network engaged in social media). For social scientists, a peek at this kind of data might allow for more informed classifications of regime popularity and legitimacy under conditions of incomplete or suppressed information – certainly an improvement over the kinds of information that scholars once used to judge the popularity of authoritarian regimes. As Kuran notes, in the 1980s, observers could only compare official, falsified data with the observations of travelers and dissidents.[82]

This discussion of public and private preferences points to a problem, firstly, with the traditional schema of 'public' and 'private' information. While information transmitted in this way may be known to an individual's entire network, it is still not necessarily 'public' in the way that Lohmann and Kuran would define the term – i.e. available as random, public information to *any* member of the general population. So perhaps the critical distinction is not between public and private, but between networked and un-networked information. What matters is not whether information is, strictly speaking, available to anyone, but rather whether preferences are open and well-known in individual neighbourhoods. And there can be little doubt that SMNs increase the volume and accuracy of information in an individual's network – even if it's also true that the amount of information available may be cognitively overwhelming. If only a small amount of formerly private information is transmitted, processed, and understood, it could drastically alter trajectories.

Making more private information available to social circles does not necessarily mean that this information will penetrate beyond an individual's narrow network. However, SMNs are likely to facilitate the transfer of information across social circles, reducing the 'small worlds' problem. Most people are familiar with the idea of 'six degrees of separation', in which you can connect anyone in six steps or less to any other person. Barabasi locates the first written instance of this phenomenon in the works of an obscure Hungarian short-story writer named Frigyes Karinthy, who speculated that there were no more than five degrees separating any two people in the world.[83] But most academic investigations refer back to the experiments of the controversial social scientist Stanley Milgram, who wanted to see if randomly-selected individuals could forward a letter to certain 'target' individuals, and attempted to count the number of intermediaries needed to get the letters across the country.

Although the study itself seems beset with difficulties in retrospect,[84] Milgram found that the median number of stops made by the letters on the way to their targets was 5.5. If there are so few degrees separating any two individuals, then we indeed live in what can be termed a 'small world'. Other discoveries include the idea that people tend to sort themselves into social 'clusters', with small groups of well-connected people clustered around common interests or locales. Instead of all people having an equal number of social connections, in actual social networks, small clusters are connected by a few people with a high number of connections – those whom Gladwell called 'connectors'[85] and whom others term 'influencers'. Furthermore, weak ties – i.e. acquaintances – are just as important as strong ties in bridging these clusters.[86] This is because even a single connection bridging two distinct social groups has the effect of 'shrinking mathematical worlds'.[87] It is worth quoting Barabasi in full here to obtain a full understanding of the importance of these links:

> The surprising finding of Watts and Strogatz is that *even a few* extra links are sufficient to drastically decrease the average separation between the nodes. These few links will not significantly change the clustering coefficient. Yet thanks to the long bridges

they form, often connecting nodes on the opposite side of the circle, the separation between all nodes spectacularly collapses.[88]

The implications of this 'spectacular collapse' of social distance are only now becoming widely understood. But if the above finding holds true, then social networking tools may help solve one of the conundrums of small-world social reality – the limited cognitive ability of most people to sustain more than a few hundred connections at a time. In some ways, Facebook turns *all* of its users into connectors – people with dozens of instantaneous social connections that span social clusters and build bridges between distinct social groups. Not only does Facebook collapse social distance within clusters, it collapses social distances between them.

SMNs like Facebook thus might have an important role to play in amplifying weak ties, making them transparent and usable, and simplifying the process of activating them. Expanding on Gould's conclusions about the role of social ties in collective action, SMNs empower peripheral actors in very dense networks, whose contributions become more valuable. SMNs help build what Shirky calls 'bridging capital'[89] between diverse groups of people who might not otherwise think to work together for a common cause. Therefore, again, theories that operate on assumptions of randomness might be of less use in coming to a true understanding of the dynamics of informational cascades. Cascades take place in Small Worlds and so studies that start from an assumption of social randomness are at a serious disadvantage.

Assuming that individuals base their preferences not on a random subset of the population, but on their local neighbourhoods, any change in the ratio of private-to-public information about those neighbourhoods would have a corresponding effect on preferences and revolutionary thresholds. SMNs reduce the amount of truly private information for individuals in any network – leaving only falsified public information (saying on your information page, for instance, that your political views are 'very liberal' when in fact they are the opposite). Concomitantly, any increase in the amount of public information decreases what Sunstein calls 'hidden profiles',[90] and may lead to more optimal outcomes in cases of group action or deliberation. Users of these forms of media tend to make information public without a great deal of discomfort about the potential ramifications. In revolutionary or potentially revolutionary situations, then, the amount of what Sunstein calls 'dispersed' information[91] is greatly reduced. This makes it both easier and more likely, all things being equal, that collective actions can be successfully organized. D'Anieri notes that later protest movements in Serbia and Ukraine were successful, whereas earlier movements, undertaken under similar circumstances, were not. He allows that the later movements were 'clearly stronger, more organized, and better funded, than their predecessors' and avoids a discussion of why this might be *at the level of group organizing*, arguing that it was pre-existing divisions at the elite level that explain the divergent outcomes.[92]

Network Effects and Authoritarian Responses

Authoritarian states are likely to recognize the threat posed by SMNs and to respond accordingly. The properties of SMNs, however, are likely to mediate the effectiveness of authoritarian response. SMNs are not invulnerable to destruction, but they do present unique challenges to anyone seeking to undermine them. As Matthew and Shambaugh argue, such 'networks are easy to access but difficult to destroy'.[93] For activists seeking to oppose the state, the networking capabilities of SMNs make it both more difficult to take out hubs, and lessen the consequences of doing so. A large number of nodes need to be removed from the system before the network itself will cease to operate properly. To put it more directly, while the state can conceivably shut down any one human rights organization, it cannot erase the accumulated experiences, knowledge, and wisdom of its members, which exists independently of their physical headquarters and is situated in a larger, denser (online) network. On the other hand, it is exceedingly easy for the state to reach out and use repression on individual members of the network. The fact that many prominent activists in authoritarian societies are linked to transnational activist networks also makes it costlier for regimes to systematically engage in this kind of repression.

However, a focus on the individual neglects more systemic variables that might affect a state's effectiveness in combating SMNs. Firstly, the more powerful authoritarian states are moving toward a strategy of stripping SMNs of their power, by partnering with corporations to make 'non-generative' and 'tethered' technologies.[94] Tethered technologies reserve to the corporation, and thus the state, the ability to remotely track, alter, or destroy the devices upon which all SMN activity so critically depends. Powerful authoritarian states can also force SMN companies, like Google, Facebook, or YouTube, to capitulate to authoritarian demands – whether those demands are for filtration, blocking individual users, or altering software to suit local repressive needs.

Authoritarian states that nevertheless possess functioning parliaments, quasi-independent press outlets, active parties, and at least mildly competitive elections are most vulnerable to pressure from digital-based dissidence at moments of extreme tension and crisis. This conclusion is drawn from the lessons of the various 'colour revolutions' of the past six years, discussed in more detail in Chapter 7. In Serbia, Lebanon, Georgia and Ukraine crucial turning-points revolved around elections and electoral competition in long-standing, authoritarian regimes. Mass mobilization in these situations was aided significantly by widespread technological usage, particularly mobile. SMN technologies like Twitter and SMS are tools that make these kinds of meetings and networks possible, in part because of their own unique technological characteristics and in part because states have been unable to entirely clamp down on users' activities. We should expect authoritarian regimes to engage in increasingly sophisticated attempts to control the use of SMNs, and for those responses to vary by regime. Strict authoritarian regimes are more likely to engage in strict control of the Internet's architecture – filtering, censoring, and surveillance – whereas semi-authoritarian regimes are likely to allow for greater debate but then respond to actual provocations with traditional repression.

Hypotheses

If the expectations and theories outlined in this chapter are correct, they lead to a series of hypotheses about the relationship between Social Media Networks and media events, and political mobilization. The first and most obvious is that, *ceteris paribus*, an increase in the density of SMN usership should lead to an increase in group formation and political mobilization in any given society. Specifically, we should expect that under similar structural conditions, mobilization should be expected and observed whereas in the absence of social media, mobilization did not occur. We should expect to see, at the least, attempts to mobilize what Olson called 'the forgotten groups' – groups that in the past may have remained unformed. These are groups that may share common interests but that previously lacked the capacity to organize themselves into politically relevant entities. Of course this causes something of a methodological conundrum, since there is no way to establish cause-and-effect for absent social phenomena. Absence of evidence is not evidence of absence.

Some scholarly work contradicts this hypothesis. While Calfano and Sahliyeh found that increased access to the Internet has not led to increased political freedoms in the Middle East,[95] a simple tally of Internet connections does not lend insight into the full spectrum of applications and services offered by Web 2.0, many of which are specifically geared toward organization and mobilization. Since the MENA region has been late to adopt the Internet generally, it should also be expected that the region will lag behind other parts of the world in the pace of its adoption of social media. Therefore a more comprehensive approach would take into account not only Internet connections, but also mobile phone users, members of social networking services and so forth. Comparative, global statistical analysis is badly needed for political scientists to properly understand the role of social media in political change – and more importantly we need to leave behind the monolithic conception of 'the Internet' as an explanatory variable, and come to more nuanced understandings of what takes place online, who is doing it, for what purposes, and to what effect.

Secondly, if SMNs facilitate the movement of information, it follows that we should expect semi-authoritarian regimes (which operate under some constraints) to have an increasingly difficult time managing the information environment (as opposed to strict authoritarian regimes, as noted above). SMNs turn individuals into reporters, photojournalists, and documentary filmmakers, requiring nothing more than a standard mobile phone. The topology of such networks suggests that the work of individuals is likely to be found, cited, or borrowed by traditional media sources, and thereby will be disseminated to the mass of un-networked individuals in societies with relatively free press environments. Therefore, the more SMNs active in a particular society, the more likely it is that government will be unable to quash stories that it finds threatening. On the other hand, in societies with little to no press freedom, SMNs are unlikely to be nearly as effective. This can be directly measured by the appearance of stories in the independent press as compared to the traditional press, in paired comparisons with previous instances of similar events and coverage. As manifestations of this prediction, we should expect to see similar news events receive disproportionately greater coverage in networked societies as opposed to un-networked societies. For the purposes of this project, the coverage and outcomes of labour demonstrations (increased ancillary activity in addition to on-the-ground labour mobilization), sexual harassment movements (increased NGO and street mobilization), and torture incidents (increased NGO activity, mobilization, and at least cosmetic changes in regime torture policy) should be considerably different between the pre-social media and post-social media age. Inasmuch as collective action is driven by events and grievances, this element alone should lead to greater organization around certain key issues, as will be seen most clearly with respect to the prior three issues in Egyptian politics.

These phenomena of SMN-driven coverage in the press and SMN-driven collective action are mutually reinforcing. SMNs may generate press coverage, the existence of which enriches the information environment, and in tandem with SMNs lead to informational cascades. Therefore our final hypothesis is that increased usership and density of SMNs should more easily trigger information cascades in authoritarian regimes.

CHAPTER 3

AGENDA-SETTERS: TORTURE, RIGHTS AND SOCIAL MEDIA NETWORKS IN EGYPT

The internet means geography isn't so important, so if you can find the 1,000 or 5,000 or 50,000 people out there who want to make a certain kind of change and can connect them and show them a path, they want to follow you.

(Seth Godin)[1]

Beyond their momentous effects, protest waves are intrinsically fascinating. The phenomena of ordinary people struggling to preserve their honour and dignity, organising to make forceful demands on those who control their fates and livelihoods, activating their citizenship, this is an awesome thing to behold.

(Baheyya)[2]

Introduction

Until very recently, conversations about the impact of the Internet in Egypt (and most parts of the Middle East) proceeded from a caveat: the limited access of most Egyptians to the Internet stands in the way of any real impact. Not only that, but even cursory observation makes it clear that most Egyptians still get their news and information from print media and satellite television. The primacy of more traditional media forms is true not just in Egypt, but in comparison to other countries as well.[3] With these largely-uncontested caveats, the study of New Media in the Middle East has been considered marginal in comparison with that of long-standing institutional, economic, and social realities. While there may be widespread admiration for the work and courage of SMN activists, enthusiasm about their impact has been largely limited to popular accounts[4] rather than academic inquiry. Even those studies that postulate a link between New Media and outcomes typically fail to identify causal mechanisms. However, outright dismissal of New Media fails to explain the way that Social Media Networks have generated coverage of previously taboo subjects, from sexual harassment to the Baha'i faith. Sceptics are right to insist on the primacy of traditional forms of media, but miss the SMN-enhanced social connections between journalists and activists.

As argued in Chapter 2, one of the ways that SMNs generate traditional press coverage is through electronically-enhanced social networks. SMNs have the effect of extending an individual's social 'neighbourhood' by transforming weak into strong ties, and non-existent ties into weak ones. Journalists in general tend to be better-connected than the average individual, and in Egypt, prominent SMN activists are either former journalists (Wael Abbas, Nora Younis) or double as either print or electronic activists (Hossam El-Hamalawy). The ties between this small set of individuals and the large number of traditional journalists in Egypt means that the work of SMN activists has a significant chance of getting picked up by the press and written about or broadcasted. This does not necessarily mean that SMN activists will be credited for their work, although their work may convince traditional journalists that a particular issue or event should be covered. In the American context, Drezner demonstrated that journalists regularly read a small number of blogs, giving those bloggers an immense amount of influence and credibility.[5] Egyptian journalists also routinely mention the same small number of bloggers as influential, particularly in the areas of most interest to this project (human rights activism).

Expecting SMNs to cause macro-level change in stable authoritarian regimes may be asking more than the technologies by themselves can deliver; a focus on the state level also misses the most important effects of SMN activism. Theorizing from the failure of SMN-led organizing or protest leads to conclusions of inefficacy, under circumstances in which few political or social forces have successfully mobilized for macro-change across the region. Success under such conditions needs to be defined much more narrowly. This chapter argues that SMNs have had a very clear, if politically limited, impact on several issue-areas in Egyptian politics, under conditions in which the opposition is fragmented.

As Mosahel argues, 'Mubarak's opposition hums with disparate voices....'.[6] Often the failure of opposition forces to come together provides ample evidence for theorists who argue for the efficacy of Mubarak's divide-and-rule strategy. Unsurprisingly, these successes all fall under the umbrella of issues on which the opposition forces in Egyptian politics have found broad agreement. Rutherford argues that a 'convergence of political alternatives' has taken place, in which Islamist and secular opponents of the regime agree on a small set of substantive human rights and rule-of-law reforms.[7] It is SMN activism which focuses on this narrow area of convergence that is likely to be successful, and has been successful in the past.

This chapter will trace the emergence of the relationship between blogs and other forms of electronic media, on the one hand, and the traditional Egyptian print media, on the other. In particular, it will be argued here that SMNs, by breaking some major stories, and reporting in unique ways on others, contributed to the overall climate in which the pre-2011 Egyptian regime was unable to control public discourse and enforce its dictates without opposition. Yet while SMNs add essential elements to public discourse, they are still very dependent on the existence of the independent press to publicize their findings and to create an environment in which the general public has access to the discourse of the blogosphere and the issues raised by web activists. The methodology will compare these cases of SMN-driven coverage against past coverage or non-coverage of similar events in the Egyptian political system, to determine the impact of both SMNs and the emergence of independent press outlets in 2003–2005.

The Birth and Maturation of Egyptian Blogging

Boas and Kalathil note that Egypt during this period, in contrast to Saudi Arabia, had no formal mechanism to control or filter Internet content.[8] The Mubarak regime appeared to view the commercial and administrative potential of the Internet as greater than the potential for political unrest and opposition coordination, although a branch of the police now known as the 'Internet Police' was formed in 2004.[9] With the inauguration of the National Project for Technology Renaissance in 1999, the regime set itself on a course of using information technology and the Internet as a way to streamline government and improve efficiency, as well as to attract international capital.[10] Thus the regime, having committed itself to the positive externalities of e-commerce and e-government, defined for itself a path which would make it very difficult to substantially filter the Internet.

It was in that free-flowing context that one of the first 'blogs' in Egypt was formed, Cairo Live.[11] It began operating in 1995. At the time, Internet subscribership was miniscule in Egypt, and most web content was in English. Cairo Live's owner was Tarek Atia, who says that he was 'blogging before blogging was invented'.[12] Cairo Live began as a news aggregation service, which summarized articles and featured an interface similar to The Drudge Report. Atia, presaging much of the rationale for later bloggers, argued that:

> The key function is to reengineer or reestablish news priorities. It's basically a window for readers to see that the news priorities that traditional news authorities present to them is not the paradigm that they have to function on. It's an attempt to explain to people that politics should never only be limited to this concept of foreign policy or domestic policy. Politics is much wider than that, it's the stuff of everyday life. Our newspapers and our traditional media have limited what people think is newsworthy.[13]

Egyptian blogs thus from the beginning provided an alternative to official discourses. Many bloggers consider themselves guardians of a kind of objectivity that they do not find in any of the newspapers or other media outlets in Egypt. However, with the exception of Cairo Live, this activity had to wait for the emergence of more sophisticated publishing platforms – as well as the right political moment. In the meantime, chat rooms, Yahoo groups, and email listservs (mailing lists) played important roles in the development of the Egyptian public sphere, particularly with respect to Egyptian reactions to the second Palestinian Intifada. These now-outdated forms of discourse emerged in Egypt around the turn of the century. As Hossam El-Hamalawy recalls, 'I was being spammed left and right by people who have the boycott lists, updates about the Intifada, pictures of the dead, pictures of the atrocities – these were being emailed, and Yahoo groups[14] were like the hip thing back then'.[15] In the early part of the decade, Blogger – one of the world's foremost blogging platforms – began offering its services in Arabic, and the Egyptian blogging scene grew more vibrant. There was also a deep and intimate connection between the emerging blogosphere and the nascent protest movement that emerged in Egypt after the beginning of the Iraq War. The movement was known as Kefaya (literally: Enough!) and was conceptualized as a broad-based protest and political movement opposing corruption and the continuation of the authoritarian regime of Hosni Mubarak.

As Radsch writes, 'A natural symbiosis between Egypt's early core bloggers and the emerging protest movement helped popularize the Egyptian blogosphere as a site of protest as *Kefaya* grew in popularity during 2005'.[16] Radsch terms this period 'the experimentation phase'.[17] As more and more politically-interested individuals formed their own blogs over this period, they made the platform of blogging itself increasingly relevant to Egyptian internet users since, according to Reed's law, the value of a communications network increases the more people use it. The most prominent Egyptian bloggers of this period still blogged in English – sites like The Arabist,[18] as well as the still-anonymous Baheyya, the Sandmonkey,[19] Big Pharaoh[20] and others. Some of these bloggers were notable for their pro-Western positions, which together with their choice of language placed them well outside of the political mainstream in Egypt and led some to dismiss blogging as the niche tool of an Americanized elite. This early period was also when the relationship between bloggers and journalists – before the maturation of the independent press – was most toxic. As Wael Abbas says, 'The relationship between the blogs and the newspapers was not really good from the beginning. As I told you we had like exclusive material and exclusive footage, in the beginning they used to steal it without even crediting us...but it gradually grew into a cooperation between newspapers and blogs.'[21]

As noted in Chapter 2, strong evidence from other contexts indicates that journalists read and borrow stories from bloggers.[22] Every journalist I interviewed in Cairo mentioned at least a handful of blogs that they read on a regular basis – typically this included Wael Abbas's influential blog,[23] as well as people like Malek Mustafa,[24] Hossam El-Hamalawy[25] (who writes about labour issues and human rights) and Nora Younis.[26] In fact the universe of prominent bloggers is quite small, constricted both by the network structure of the Internet[27] and the still-limited Internet access for most Egyptians. But this tiny elite of bloggers and journalists is able to have a disproportionate influence on public affairs, due to their interconnectedness with journalists; in fact many prominent Egyptian bloggers are or were journalists. As Ajemian notes, '...the value of blogs as a form of new media is that they allow for individual grass roots political journalism and facilitate the creation of a counter-public sphere of discourse that has the potential to penetrate mainstream media'.[28] Digital media serve to amplify the social connections between journalists and elite bloggers, making it far more likely that certain bloggers will receive press attention, or that their work will be picked up or 'borrowed' by reporters.

Observers are split about the relationship between bloggers and the press. 'My own theory is that bloggers want to replace old media,' says Atia. 'Any new media wants to become old media.'[29] As even the activists themselves acknowledge, there is an element of competition and jealousy between members of the traditional media and the blogosphere, with each side asserting its primacy and in many cases questioning the authenticity and legitimacy of the other. However, this competition does not negate the idea that the electronic media – spearheaded by SMN activists who are grounded both in citizen journalism and activism – has taken its place in the Egyptian media and discursive environments and irrevocably altered both. In some cases

Egyptian SMN activists see themselves as the only unrestrained and reliable sources of political information, while the journalists view the bloggers as sensationalist and unprofessional. These accusations are leveled repeatedly at and by both sides, but at the same time most participants in this discourse understand that they are situated in a particular media environment and that they are each playing distinctive and important roles.

What SMNs accomplish in Egyptian politics is to expand the public sphere to accommodate new 'claims-makers'. As Maratea argues, the traditional press serves a 'gatekeeping function', restricting access to the media and controlling the content which reaches the mass public.[30] Citizens have traditionally had very little control over or input into the content of mass media, serving largely as recipients of information and consumers of entertainment and news.[31] However, the rise of digital media has created an environment in which individuals have the opportunity to interrogate the social and political worlds, and to influence the content of news coverage.[32] There is also, undeniably, an aspect of the Internet that has consolidated the interests of commerce,[31] but the reality of commercial domination of the Internet does not exclude the potential for the promotion of alternative discourses. As Maratea writes, '…the Web makes it feasible for average citizens to disseminate their own commentaries on mainstream media coverage, political events, or any other issue of relevance'.[33]

SMNs and the Egyptian Press Environment

In Egypt, while there is certainly a strained relationship characterized by invective between these two groups, the relationship is actually much more complicated and cooperative than one might be led to believe. Egypt's press environment can best be described as 'somewhat free'. Rugh classified Egypt's press environment late in the Mubarak era as 'transitional'; he elaborates: 'these systems were quite complex, containing strong elements of government control and influence, alongside elements of freedom and diversity'.[35] Rugh argues that while journalists had much more freedom in such countries than in the past (he includes Tunisia, Jordan and Algeria in this category) the government still retains certain privileges, and that there are 'red lines' that journalists dare not cross.[36] In a practical sense, this manifests itself as what appears to be a lively press environment, with copious criticisms of regime practices and policies – even in the government-owned papers – but with a great deal of self-censorship occurring still. In Egypt, the process of obtaining a license to publish a newspaper is a daunting obstacle to any entity or individual who wishes to pursue one. Black details the ordeal endured by the would-be publishers of *El-Badeel* in 2007, who were forced to wait month after month for their license.[37]

Prior to 2011, there were, generally, five kinds of newspapers in Egypt: the government-owned dailies, the opposition dailies, the party newspapers, the regional papers, and newspapers published from abroad.[38] The most-read and most important government papers were (and still are) the dailies *Al-Akhbar*, *Al-Ahram*, and *Al-Gumhuriya*, while other government-aligned newspapers of note included *Rose Al-Yusef*. These papers, while not averse to carrying criticism of the government at times, generally toe the editorial line of the ruling National Democratic Party, and are known for ignoring stories that are unfavourable to the regime, or at least initiating coverage much later than other media. It is generally agreed that the Egyptian press environment was energized with the founding of the daily opposition paper *Al-Masry Al-Youm* in 2004, as well as the re-issuing of *Al-Dustur*, first as a weekly, and then in 2007 as a daily. Their publication followed changes in the press laws that ended the government's monopoly on news information inside Egypt.

During the final years of Mubarak's rule, these two newspapers were by far the most important and influential opposition newspapers in Egypt. These independent papers were willing to carry frank and often direct criticism of the Mubarak regime, and tended to cover stories that the government papers won't touch. The existence of this independent press then and now calls into question the routine lumping of Arab media systems together under the umbrella of 'unfree', and ignores the values that Arab journalists may share.[39] This independence tends to confer a certain legitimacy not possessed by the government dailies, even while they seem to have a reputation for sensationalism that was only further reinforced in the summer of 2007 when *Al-Dustur* in particular headlined concerns about the health of President Mubarak and relayed rumors of his death. *Al-Dustur* Editor-in-Chief Ibrahim Eissa paid a steep price for these decisions, after being sentenced to six months in prison with hard labour.[40] In this environment it cannot be argued that blogs and new media were the only available forms of dissent available to Egyptians – one needed only to turn to the op-ed page of any major or minor opposition or party paper to see direct criticism of the state – although of course there continued to be red lines, such as calling for regime change or insulting the president or his family, which are not always observed online.

Instantaneous communication, as noted in Chapter 2, is very important in Egypt. Such was the case in 2008, when an imprisoned American journalist used Twitter to get himself out of jail after covering a labour demonstration.[41] One major newspaper editor admitted that on the day of the events in question (April 6, 2008), he did not turn to *Al-Ahram* or even his own paper, but rather to the blogs for information about what was happening and where. He argued:

> I've been working on Sunday until the late evening for the first edition or the second edition, so this was my day off, so I've taken Monday [as] a vacation. When I wake up in the morning I didn't turn on my TV or [start] wandering around the papers, I've just opened the blogs and Haraka Masria site, and opened my email. There is a very famous mailing group called al-Mahroosa, and I found many, many news entries for my knowledge. I want to know what's happening all night, and this is the first source I visited to know what's happening at night.[42]

This was due both to the reliability of the bloggers in question – earned the hard way over a period of years – and to the structural advantages enjoyed by blogs and mobile media.

As noted in Chapter 2, (some) SMN platforms offer the possibility of remaining pseudonymous to their writers and activists, particularly in a state whose security services do not appear to be terribly sophisticated technologically. The roster of pseudonymous Egyptian bloggers is long, from the caustic right-wing Sandmonkey to the reflective Baheyya and the critical Zeinobia,[43] but the fact remains that the medium gives these writers the option to remain anonymous to the security services.[44] The Egyptian government in 2008 deployed new identity-tracking software in Internet cafés, but with constantly-evolving and freely-available masking software the state was unable to clamp down on the kind of activity it wanted to see stopped. And as Shapiro notes, activists increasingly migrated to sites that are dual-purpose, like Facebook – commercial in purpose, but able to be used cleverly by regime opponents to advance their claims.[45] This is very much in keeping with Ethan Zuckerman's 'cute cat theory' of digital activism, which argues that authoritarian regimes will ultimately be undermined by activism on sites they regarded as frivolous or non-threatening.[46] The regime, in turn, grew increasingly successful at infiltrating those sites and forcing activists to move to still other applications, as we will see in Chapter 4.

SMN activists were willing to violate the red lines of the Egyptian media environment and to risk extreme consequences – punishment, arrest, imprisonment or worse – therefore allowing them to report on issues and events that might go unreported in the state-aligned, opposition, or party presses. It is not that bloggers have never been arrested – on the contrary nearly every activist can tell stories of harassment, intimidation, arrest, and in some cases even torture – but rather that few were sentenced, and even fewer stopped writing and organizing due to these efforts, and thus many bloggers expressed a willingness to risk arrest for the sake of truth-telling and dissent. The fact that these individuals do not have to report to editors or institutions who might be wary of having their entire operations shut down by the state only makes it more likely that SMN activists will cross the boundaries which ordinary journalists will not. This absence of institutional oversight and control – something that has been criticized by observers[47] – actually means that the element of caution present in established relations between the regime and the opposition press is completely absent in the blogosphere. Bloggers report to no one but themselves and their readers, and they openly express their commitment to taking this responsibility quite seriously. As Mina Zakry of the Arab Network

For Human Rights Information (and the blog Egypt Watchman)[48] put it in conversation with me, 'Through my blog I was defending freedom of expression, freedom of religion, practicing political and social criticism.'[49] Another activist for the Muslim Brotherhood, who infiltrated the show-trials of the organization's senior leadership, remarked: 'Of course I am afraid, but I don't care, because it's my life in this country. I have been arrested two times.'[50] This lack of reticence about the repercussions of activism is widespread in the small blogging and human rights community.

The content provided by SMNs increasingly resembles traditional reporting in terms of its emphasis on communicating hard news, often about arrests, reports of torture, violations of human rights, and other abuses by the regime. In many ways, the development of citizen journalism has led to a bifurcation of Egyptian blogging, one path leading to Wael Abbas and his style of first-hand reporting, photography, video-taking, Tweeting, and commentary, and the other to what most people imagine when they think of a blog – an often acerbic, individualistic take on the news and other people's writing – the style pioneered in Egypt by the Sandmonkey. In fact these citizen journalists function effectively as their own news agencies, and have developed a following that makes them respected and trusted. The influence of bloggers on the public sphere takes place through social network connections between bloggers and journalists – connections that are strengthened (or created) by the capability of SMNs to bridge social clusters. Even when claims advanced in the blogosphere are not immediately picked up by journalists who may have other stories to cover, they provide what Maratea calls 'a database of available claims' that can be drawn upon during lulls in news coverage.[51]

The more 'traditional' type of blogging was pioneered in Egypt by the Sandmonkey, of whom Hossam El-Hamalawy caustically notes of that blog, 'He represents himself and like ten other people in the whole republic.'[52] While both styles of blogging have their utility and their role in the Egyptian media environment, it is becoming increasingly clear that the individuals who have the most influence are those who practice the former – those who perform all of the functions of traditional journalist but are willing to cross lines and violate taboos where professional Egyptian journalists are typically unwilling to do the same.

Generally, the impact of blogs on the media in Egypt can be broken down into four categories. The first is *breaking* stories, when SMN activists either report original information not carried anywhere else in the news universe, or when an activist is actually present to provide the first-hand reporting. The second is *documenting* stories, when a SMN activist is present to provide unique textual, photographic, or video evidence of stories that were already present or would have been reported on in any case. The third is *transmission*, when SMN activists post or share videos, stories, or photos of something that has already happened, via a third party. Finally, there is *red-lining*, the practice of SMN activists crossing traditional media boundaries in a case or cases in which traditional media practitioners are unwilling or unable to say or print certain things. The remainder of this chapter will detail one instance of each of these phenomena.

Breaking Stories: Sexual Harassment in Downtown Cairo

In the spring of 2005, Egyptian blogs began to attract international attention, as they served as a platform for coordinated protests against a proposed Constitutional amendment.[53] However, perhaps the defining moment of Egyptian blogging took place in October of 2006, during the Muslim holiday of Eid al-Fitr. Downtown Cairo witnessed a string of mob-like sexual assaults on women – assaults that initially went unreported in the Egyptian press. By coincidence, two of Egypt's more well-known SMN activists, Wael Abbas and Malek Mustafa, happened to be on the scene at the time. A clearly horrified Malek (who blogs as Malek-X), detailed the assaults in all their grotesque gratuity on his blog. Amira al-Husseini of Global Voices[54] provided this translation of Malek's initial report:

> We saw a large number of men whistling and running in the direction of Adly Street. We went with them to see what was happening. I was surprised to see a girl in her early 20s falling on the ground and a mob of men gathering around her, feeling up her body and tearing her clothes off her. I didn't understand or rather

I couldn't comprehend what was happening. The girl got up and ran into a restaurant and hid inside. Some boys surrounded the restaurant and wouldn't leave until one of them shouted that there was another one coming. All of them ran towards Talaat Street again and there I saw a girl who was completely surrounded by a mob of hundreds of men trying to touch her body and take off her clothes. This girl was rescued by a taxi driver, who pulled her into his taxi. But the boys would not allow the taxi through and formed a circle around the car, he said.[55]

Despite the presence of bloggers and the pictures and videos circulating on the Internet, the press remained completely silent for days. However, the first penetration of the official silence came via a report on Dream TV on October 28, with talk show host Mona El Shazly and other reporters confirming the allegations with other witnesses and shopkeepers.[56] Then with a series of press articles, the official silence began to crack. The first paper to run a report was *Al-Fagr*, by the journalist Wael Abdel Fattah. Other outlets of the independent press soon followed suit, including *Al-Masry Al-Youm* and the still-weekly *Al-Dustur*. The November 1 issue of *Al-Dustur*, 'borrowing' pictures straight from Abbas's blog, ran no less than eight articles directly or indirectly addressing the incident.[57] Articles and criticism followed in all the major independent and party newspapers, eventually trickling into the official press. The regime denied that anything untoward had happened downtown, while the official press was largely silent. Typically when that silence was broken, it initially took the form of attacking Abbas himself, a pattern that would become sadly familiar in the years to come.[58] However, the protests, coordinated by bloggers such as the Sandmonkey, forced a debate that eventually reached even the government press. Activists called for the resignation of Interior Minister Habib El-Adly, which of course did not happen. However, the more details leaked out about the case, the more it appeared that sexual harassment on Eid enjoyed the official or unofficial support of elements of the regime, particularly security forces who either participated in the assaults or tolerated them.[59]

With both video and photos, taken on mobile phones, the event was difficult if not impossible to credibly deny. What made the story even more poignant were the first-hand accounts from women that day, some of whom were apparently inspired to begin blogging by what happened that day. The short-lived blog Wounded Female From Cairo[60] provided the following account:

> We, girls, had our butts, breasts, and every inch of our bodies grabbed. I end up slipping into a car that was parking on the road side when I tried to catch one of the [profanity omitted] who insisted and never gave up on grabbing my butt. So, I end up with a deep cut in my right hand palm and another one on my thumb of the same hand as I slipped into the car's headlight that broke and cut my hand. 6 stitches on my hand palm cut and 3 on my thumb – still my anger is pretty fresh in the deep inside of me that makes want me [sic] to put all Egyptian men on fire right now for what they have caused...Don't you have sisters who can also face the same thing as we did?[61]

The story was another instance of SMNs providing undeniable evidence of a social or political trend that many people may have preferred to ignore. Blog entries like that from Girl4Cairo cited above also provided indispensable platforms for the coordinated protests that followed (including protests on November 9 and November 14, 2006), a subject that will be returned to in Chapter 4. While of course many Egyptians were aware of the prevalence of sexual harassment, most were untouched by it or had never witnessed it first-hand. The videos and pictures that made it out of the Eid harassment story forced individuals to confront the reality of sexual harassment, much like the torture scandal in 2007 – also propelled into the press from the blogosphere – forced Egyptians to confront another unpleasant aspect of their government. While the two incidents may not have led to a regime change or substantial legal revisions, they did change the context of the relationship between the regime and its people.

Several factors propelled the sexual harassment story out of the blogosphere and into the mainstream discourse. First, the assaults exposed the prominence of sexual harassment in Egypt, and deeply embarrassed the regime. Second, the assaults appeared to dovetail with two major social problems in Egypt – the continuing delay in the age of marriage and the mounting sexual frustration of the country's young men (and women, although of course discourse focused on the former). Third, elements of the emerging SMN sphere contributed to the viral effectiveness of the story, such as the existence of digital videos which could be passed around through email and hyperlinks, and the ubiquity of pictures and first-hand accounts that the regime was unable to quash despite a total press blackout for the first week following the events. In short, blogs, mobile videos and the Internet made it possible for this story to persist in a way that, while not impossible in the past, would have been phenomenally unlikely. Finally, the story was almost instantly picked up by international observers and organizations like Global Voices, which provided further extensive coverage and amplification of the events and drove the shaming of the Egyptian government for its total inaction, particularly when it appeared that sexual harassment might interfere with the booming Egyptian tourism industry. This was a story that the activists refused to allow to die.

Crucially, however, the online writing and dissent moved into the real world, with protests that were organized in part by the Sandmonkey.[62] And when the independent press started covering the story, they did so with vigor, forcing the government finally to acknowledge that something was at stake. That press attention culminated in a series of protests and a still-ongoing campaign against sexual harassment, spread across the blogosphere and a number of human rights organizations. Blogs had officially become a force to be reckoned with. Wael Abbas, who witnessed the events and wrote about them on his blog, argues:

> Now with flocks of young people harassing and molesting girls, in groups, in a religious feast, in downtown [C]airo, or in the absence of the police or the police [who] were there but didn't interfere, it brought to light the issue of sexual harassment in general in workplaces and families, and it made it to be discussed in TV talk shows, even in the official newspapers they couldn't ignore it. The only thing that pissed them off was that we exposed that the police were negligent for what was going on.[63]

The jump to international outlets was an acute embarrassment for the Egyptian government and society, which relies heavily on tourist receipts – not only from the United States, but from elsewhere in the West and the Middle East. For Egypt to develop a reputation as a place that is unsafe for women to travel would be devastating for the tourism industry. Still the state-run press dismissed the story, smeared the people propagating it, and denied any official culpability. As Ehab El-Zalaky, Deputy Editor of *Al-Masry Al-Youm* in 2008, says:

> It was a big shock for the whole society for that matter. You know that it happened on Eid al-Fitr after the holy month of Ramadan... so it was an explosive story for the blogs for two or three days, the first things came after that period of silence, it was being circulated as a story, and many were talking about what was happening. People in all of Egypt were talking about it, and there was pure silence from the mainstream media, and there was a statement from the interior ministry that no such thing happened at all. The first thing was published in *Al-Ahram* and denied what happened, and talking about things on their sites from their imaginations, some of the independent newspapers started to write about the issue, at the same time – blogs were trying to back each other, so some of the blogs published some blurry pictures taken with mobile phones, so it wasn't very clear what was happening, after about a week, one of the Egyptians who was living in the States sent Wael Abbas a video shot taken a year before that, which detailed another mass sexual harass-ment in Cairo streets, he take the shots and took it back to the States and never thought about publishing it.[64]

El-Zalaky's last point makes it clear that this sexual harassment dur-ing Eid was not something new in 2006, but rather something that had happened in the past but remained an undocumented rumour.[65] The tools of SMNs made it possible for distant contacts to pass videos through enhanced social networks, and the credibility of the blog-gers in the streets allowed them to establish the veracity of the events in question. The way that the story went from rumour to full-blown media event in a matter of days calls to mind the kind of informational cascades discussed in Chapter 2. And the way it called attention to previously subordinated events recalls both El-Zalaky's claim that blogs provide 'a voice for the voiceless'[66] and serves as evidence for the efficacy of SMNs in breaking news.

The linkages between SMN activists and independent journalists continued to give the story increasingly wide play. *Al-Dustur* ran a series of hard-hitting articles that December, not just about that particular incident, but about sexual harassment in general. The number of articles about sexual harassment in the Egyptian press– hardly a new issue in Egyptian politics – jumped from 33 stories in 2004 to 173 in 2006 and 171 in 2007. Other Arab print outlets picked up on the story, as did regional papers and outlets like Al-Jazeera. The Egyptian Center For Women's Rights launched a campaign against harassment in Egypt that continues to this day, in coordination with grassroots organizations like The Street Is Ours. The point is not that harassment has been eliminated, for such a deeply-rooted phenomenon is difficult to change in such a short period of time, and after all women are harassed not just in Egypt but all over the West and elsewhere in the Global North. The point is that a cross-political coalition was forged, with the work of SMN activists, to contest the issue of sexual harassment in Egypt. In fact, Eid harassment has continued. In the autumn of 2008, there was a very similar incident that took place downtown; however, in contrast to the 2006 incident, when security services did finally arrive the harassers were arrested. As the Egyptian Center For Women's Rights argues, while it is unfortunate that such incidents still take place, a climate in which the perpetrators are punished does at least represent progress.[67] As Gamal Eid notes, 'There are some official coalitions between some groups, but when these cases are finished, every group will be on its own.'[68] El-Zalaky believes that this was the moment that bloggers gained domestic credibility: 'This is one of the major hits and major turns of the blogs to be known by ordinary people and I think after this incident blogs gained a huge amount of credibility.'[69]

Documenting: Sudanese Refugees and the State

Even before the widely-reported genocide in Darfur, Cairo has played host to thousands upon thousands of Sudanese refugees fleeing the country's endemic violence, particularly the civil war between the north and the south. The refugees themselves are in a particularly precarious position in Egyptian society, since many do not speak Arabic, cannot work, are very poor to begin with, and must contend with endemic racism. Overall there are upwards of one million refugees in Cairo. The Egyptian and Sudanese governments signed an agreement in 2004, guaranteeing Sudanese refugees the right to live, work, own property and move about freely, but critics argued that the agreement was never implemented and that life for the refugees was very difficult in Cairo.[70] Most refugees sought resettlement in a third country, not wanting to stay in Egypt where their plight was grim, but equally unwilling to return to the endemic violence of their homeland. The UNHCR had offered voluntary repatriation for the refugees on a case-by-case basis, but the threat of mass deportation loomed and in any case Sudan itself remained manifestly unsafe in many places. The Egyptian government, its resources already strapped by trying to provide for its swelling population, had been very reluctant to grant asylum to the refugees, believing it might lead to more refugees, more asylum applications, and more responsibility that the government did not seek or want.

On September 29, 2005, hundreds of asylum-seeking Sudanese refugees began a sit-in that lasted for months at Midan Mustapha Mahmoud, near the Cairo offices of the UNHCR.[71] Both the Egyptian government and the UNHCR maintained that the refugees were economic migrants who would not have been in any immediate danger if they were to return to Sudan. Whatever the merits of this claim, the refugees, all in danger of deportation, staged the sit-in to draw attention to their plight. The only attention they drew, however, was from residents and merchants who considered their day-and-night presence to be a nuisance. As the months dragged on, it became increasingly clear that the regime was likely to break up the sit-in by force.

On New Year's Eve, the journalist and blogger Nora Younis was near Mohandisin, an upscale neighborhood near downtown Cairo. Younis had been on her way home when a friend told her that 'the police presence in Mohandisin is incredible'. She quickly made her way to the square, and when she arrived, public buses were being prepared to take the refugees to an undisclosed location. Younis had her camera with her, but her battery was low, so she began to document what was going on with her cell phone camera and SMS messages. Younis was apopolectic with rage. 'I realize that I'm there to document, nobody can stop this at the moment what we can do is not let them get away with it. I was so angry. I was freaking out and I was crying.'[72]

Younis snuck into an adjacent building and camped out on the tenth floor, where she had an unimpeded view of the goings-on. What she saw was appalling: police had turned water cannons on the astonished and terrified refugees, herding them toward the buses. The security forces deployed force against the refugees, beating many of them, and it was clear even to Younis from her tenth-storey vantage point that a number of people were going to lose their lives. December 2005 was pre-Twitter, but Younis sent texts from her cell phone, took pictures with the phone's camera, and her heretofore largely-unknown website later became a clearing-house for information about the incident. Younis was unquestionably the first journalist on the scene, and the government press barely mentioned the incident at all. Her account of the evening's events – which turned into a massacre – was widely linked, reported, and cited by media organizations as a definitive version of the evening's events came together. Below is an abridged version of her account, as much an indictment of the racism of the Egyptian observers as it is of the police themselves. She called her account 'Ashamed to be an Egyptian', and it detailed the confrontation between the police and the refugees in painstaking detail; Younis even followed the refugees after they were taken away in buses to a detention facility in Dahshur.

Younis' presence at the atrocity allowed for coverage by blogs, independent media, and non-Egyptian international press outlets. In fact, the account was cited as evidence for where the refugees were taken. As Ehab Zelaky argues, 'No one wrote and took pictures of what happened like Nora Younis.'[73] As Younis herself notes,

My coverage of the Sudanese refugees, it got covered by the independent media and the blogs. People translated it into I don't know how many languages, it was weird, people were picking

it up, translating it, and I was getting comments from different places, but the mainstream media did not cover my coverage. The mainstream media commented on the human rights
report, there was no report that was issued that did not make
reference.[74]

The regime and its press allies predictably tried to pin the blame on
the refugees themselves. Notably, the refugees (who were Christian)
were said to have been drinking, attacking the police and having sex
in public.[75] There was little to no evidence for any of this, but the
rumours were calculated to diminish any potential public sympathy
for the refugees themselves. The tourism ministry claimed, absurdly,
that the refugees were tourists.[76]

Word leaked out that the surviving refugees were to be deported,
which generated a firestorm of criticism in the Egyptian press, and
attracted the attention of legal forces who sought to prevent the deportation. Younis's story ignited a debate in the press about the refugees themselves, their treatment, and the issue of racism in Egyptian
society. It is important, of course, that Younis was on the scene that
evening. Without the documentation from her cell phone, press outlets would have had no credible source, aside from eyewitness reports
(of which there were many), for the stories that later ran about the
massacre.

Coverage of refugee issues did not change much after the massacre,
going from 15 articles between 1998 and December 29, 2005[77] to 21
between December 29, 2005 and January 1, 2007. So the immediate
upshot of the furore appeared to be that the Egyptian government
relented on its plans to deport 654 refugees from Mustapha Mahmoud.
In the aftermath of the incident, the regime had announced plans to
deport the refugees. However, in the wake of a series of protests, as
well as intense international press attention (which appeared to be
more effective than anything that appeared in the Egyptian press)[78]
the government relented and agreed to review the status of the refugees. While of course no direct cause and effect can be ascertained
here, it would be something of a coincidence that the regime agreed
to review long-standing plans for the refugees – plans that had been

hatched before the massacre in the Midan – just as activists mobilized protests, rights organizations combined on behalf of the refugees, and the regime was receiving negative press attention, both at home and internationally. The regime also saw nascent cooperation between liberal and Islamist opposition forces, as the action was widely condemned and the refugees were supported by the Brotherhood bloc in Parliament. This might have been what frightened the regime most of all. It was perhaps a minor concern for the regime, but a concern nonetheless.

Transmission: Torture and the Fate of Emad El-Kabir

In January of 2006, a 21-year-old microbus driver named Emad El-Kabir was arrested for attempting to break up a police assault on his cousin. The allegations against El Kabir, even if true, were relatively minor. However, during his detention, he was subjected to torture by the police officers interrogating him, who beat and raped him. El-Kabir himself was nearly powerless to do anything about his brutal treatment by the police; while he could file a complaint, torture is widespread in Egypt, something that most individuals realize is taking place, but that until 2007 received little press attention. However, by 2006 the mobile web had arrived in Egypt, and one of the officers engaged in the practice of taping El-Kabir's torture with his cell phone, and then passing the video around to others.

The video, taken in January 2006, apparently passed around Cairo social networks for nearly a year before it arrived in the hands of bloggers like Demagh MAK[79] and Wael Abbas. The video itself is graphic and devastating, as El-Kabir pleads with his captors, whimpering 'Ma'lish ya basha!' ('Forget about it, Pasha!'). The naked El-Kabir is savagely sodomized with a nightstick – the video was so graphic that YouTube, where it was eventually posted as well, briefly suspended the account of Wael Abbas, who had posted it. Social Media Networks have the ability to accelerate the transmission of information – including messages, videos, and frames – out of target networks, and this appears to be what eventually happened in this case as well. The officers who were supposed to share the video instead forwarded it along to someone – it is not clear who – who then passed the video on to the blogger Wael Abbas. Abbas posted the torture video to his blog in December 2006, and generated interest on the part of traditional media practitioners; while torture is widely acknowledged, it is rarely discussed, and it is even more rare for it to be documented so graphically.

El-Kabir himself apparently played no role in the dissemination of the video; in fact, when Abbas published the video on his blog, no one knew who the victim actually was. As Abbas says, 'I didn't know who he was and where, and what were the circumstances and when, and so an independent investigative journalist was able to find the microbus driver and interview him.'[80] The journalist, Wael Abdel Fattah, was from the independent newspaper *El-Fagr*,[81] further underscoring the importance of cooperation between SMN activists and traditional media practitioners.[82] Other media outlets quickly piled on the case, with *Al-Masry Al-Youm* claiming to publish the first photo of an officer responsible for the torture of El-Kabir.[83] *Al-Masry Al-Youm* credited *El-Fagr* for breaking the story in its first piece on El-Kabir.[84] The publication of the story in different independent press outlets (none of which had anywhere near the circulation of government dailies at the time) contributed to a kind of critical mass. Columnists denounced the torture and wrote about the venality of the practice, while newspapers covered the case in depth as it made its way through the court system. El-Kabir's torture and the subsequent focus on torture as a practice constituted a kind of informational cascade. El-Kabir put himself at great risk when he decided to step forward and push for the prosecution of the officers themselves.

Perhaps more offensive to public sensibilities than the initial, undeniable torture was the fact that El-Kabir was subsequently sentenced to three months in prison for 'resisting the authorities'.[85] The re-arrest of El-Kabir signaled to observers that the authorities were unrepentant and bent on maintaining total hegemony. However, because the case had broken in the media, the regime was no longer able to keep the story hidden, and unable to convince anyone that El-Kabir had resisted the authorities, not with such graphic evidence on display for everyone to see. The idea that torture is widespread in Egypt became an accepted truth, and press outlets became increasingly outspoken critics of Egyptian torture practices – with some even denouncing Mubarak himself in addition to El-Adly. Mohamed Baghdadi wrote that the videos were not evidence of the reality of corruption, since 'everything is corrupt'.[86] Corruption was so pervasive in contemporary Egypt, so much a part of everyday life, that no single piece of evidence, no matter how incontrovertible, could make it any more true. *Al-Masry Al-Youm*, in particular, provided ongoing coverage of torture in Egypt, documenting torture complaints,[87] publishing op-eds, and following the El-Kabir case as it progressed. The paper also went into unusual, and gory, detail about conditions inside the stations.[88] The independent press also provided close coverage of other torture and abuse scandals, such as the slapping of a man named Ahmed Gad and the abuse of a female murder suspect who was interrogated while suspended from a stick, like meat being cooked on a spit.

The El-Kabir case wound its way through the Egyptian court system, finally resulting in sentences for the officers involved on November 6, 2007.[89] While the sentences were light considering the overwhelming evidence in the case, it was a small victory for human rights activists. The years since 2007 have seen the solidification of a de facto alliance against torture.[90] Ultimately the significance of the El-Kabir case goes far beyond the prosecution of three individual police officers, though that in and of itself was an accomplishment for the opposition. Abbas and his fellow bloggers succeeded in making torture a serious issue in the Egyptian public sphere, and the controversy appears to have ignited a kind of coalition against torture – a coalition that reaches beyond traditional political left-right boundaries and encompasses everyone that is interested in seeing more serious implementation of the rule of law. Actors appear to have recognized their mutual interest in seeing practices of torture abolished or abated, and are acting rationally in that self-interest. The Egyptian Human Rights Organization, for instance, was supported by the Muslim Brotherhood faction in parliament, and together they publicly oppose the practices of the Mubarak regime with regards to torture – uniting under the guise of international legal conventions.[91] This not only suggests an emerging coalition, but also points to the power of international rights activism. Rights activist organizations who had long written about and documented torture in Egypt also noted the importance of the El-Kabir case.[92] They were not the first groups to agitate against torture in the Egyptian context – the Egyptian Association Against Torture (EAAT) was formed in 2003 and issued important reports in 2005. But it was Social Media Networks that helped transform torture from a niche issue largely neglected by the pubic into something that became a burning issue in Egyptian politics – one that eventually led to the formation of We Are All Khaled Said and the downfall of the Egyptian regime.

Of particular note in the context of Egyptian anti-torture activism is the development of documentary activist blogs dedicated to writing about and eliminating torture. Noha Atef started a blog about torture in the spring of 2006, but quickly found that she had no readership, and thus no power. Atef contacted the veteran digital activist Alaa Abdel Fatteh, the creator of the Egyptian blog aggregator at Manal and Alaa's Bitbucket.[93] Knowing the importance of getting buy-in from the power-bloggers, Atef sought Abdel Fatteh's help, and asked him to mention her blog on his site, to increase potential traffic. As Atef tells the story, the power of the digital activist network becomes very clear:

> It cost us almost nothing. We chose open source software, and assumed that people will contribute. Manal (Alaa's wife) is now hosting the web site for free, and Alaa (Abdel Fatteh) is doing the maintenance, and Amr (Gharbeia) told me how to use it, and Ahmed (Gharbeia), if I wanted anything regarding security or anything, he helps me for nothing.[94]

Atef's blog became Torture in Egypt.[95] Unlike Misr Digital, Torture in Egypt became more of an archive related to torture, rather than a running news archive of instances of torture. If you went to the Torture in Egypt site, Atef says, 'you'd find a picture related to a police officer and a list of his crimes, what I call a criminal record. In the year x he tortured this person, and you find this person and the hyperlink to this person's testimony.'[96]

Atef's project led directly to the creation of another, more open-source project, called Piggipedia,[97] led by Hossam El-Hamalawy.

On Piggipedia, any member can upload pictures of officers accused of torture, and as of this writing, there were over 500 such pages on Piggipedia, hosted on El-Hamalawy's pre-existing 3Arabawy.

Other Egyptian activists soon followed suit. Mohammed Maree was a veterinarian with little concrete political experience in Egypt. On April 6, 2008, he participated in the workers' action in Mahalla (see Chapter 4 for details), where he was arrested and sent to Borg Al-Arab prison in Alexandria for 17 days. As he describes the experience:

> Before they arrested me I thought that Egypt took many steps for reform, that they have no torture inside the prisons, and that this only happened during the Nasser period, the Sadat period... When they released me, you know, I became so strong, and I felt that I had a battle with this regime, with the security of this country, I launched my blog, at blogspot.com. I started to write about torture inside the police stations, inside state security, I make documentation for the victims, and make connections between them and the human rights organizations in Cairo. I tried to create marketing for these cases by social media, Twitter, to create a scandal for the Mubarak regime.[98]

Maree and his blog, EgyTimes,[99] became part of a small digital community working on these issues, along with Wael Abbas, Noha Atef and Hossam El-Hamalawy. Like Atef, Maree often did his own documentation about particular cases of torture – traveling to villages, taping video interviews with victims, and then publishing those documents on his site. Like other activists, he often worked closely with independent media practitioners, as well as with human rights organizations. Maree echoes other activists when evaluating the utility of traditional media for digital activists:

> We and other bloggers and activists, help each other in marketing. To make a certain case, we have to deal with journalists and the media. Someone asked me before, whether traditional media or new media is more important. I said that the new media can't

live without traditional media, and now traditional media can't live without new media. They both complete each other.[100]

Through their network connections with independent journalists, Abbas, El-Hamalawy, Atef and Maree were able to bridge the divide between the digital haves and have nots in Egypt, and to become new and respected 'claims-makers' in Egyptian politics. Their work created the foundation upon which was ultimately built the We Are All Khaled Said campaign, and the latter would not have been possible without the former.

Red-Lining: The Case of Al-Qursaya

In late 2007, one of the biggest political controversies in Egypt involved a tiny island on the Nile in Cairo called Al-Qursaya. Home to some 5,000 largely impoverished Cairenes,[101] the island was suddenly inundated with the regime's armed forces in the spring of 2007. The exact purpose of the takeover was the subject of intense speculation, but the effort was eerily similar to another attempted takeover by the regime of Al-Qursaya and another Nile island, Gold Island (Jazirat Al-Dhahab) in 2001. The most common, and plausible, explanation was that developers wanted to get their hands on the island, and that the Egyptian army was financially implicated in the takeover. Even with the independent press involved in the fight, however, it seemed like a David vs. Goliath situation. The army is a 'red line' in Egyptian politics and journalism, and any public discussion of the armed forces was forbidden. No matter the outcry, in all likelihood the army would be able to do as it pleased to the island, regardless of the wishes of its marginalized residents. However, within a year the regime's plans for Al-Qursaya would be in tatters, defeated in two courts – the Egyptian legal system and in the court of public opinion.

The Al-Qursaya Island case presents a different kind of challenge to entrenched power. Unlike the sexual harassment and torture cases, the Al-Qursaya Island incident does not appear to have begun on the Internet or in the blogosphere, instead breaking initially in the independent press. The general outlines of the Al-Qursaya case remain somewhat murky despite considerable press attention to the subject. This murkiness is rooted in the involvement of the Egyptian army in the proceedings, meaning that ordinary press outlets writing in Arabic have been incapable of telling the true story of what went on between September 2007 and the spring of 2008. It is also true that officials involved in the takeover of Al-Qursaya adamantly deny the idea that residents were to be evicted so that Al-Qursaya could be turned into some sort of neoliberal tourist paradise. However, because the government made a similar attempt on another Nile island earlier in the decade, the regime's credibility on this issue was low to begin with. The murkiness surrounding the takeover of Al-Qursaya is given emphatic life in the signs posted all over the island after the army's arrival, announcing that Al-Qursaya '... belongs to the army. No photography.'[102]

The island of Al-Qursaya itself is a small outgrowth in the middle of the Nile, home to a population of fisherman and other hardscrabble Egyptians, and a place that has so far resisted the Westernized development that now characterizes other parts of Cairo. There had been rumours about the impending takeover in the Egyptian press as far back as the previous spring, but nothing concrete emerged until the army arrived, treating the island and its citizens like occupied territory. However, many of the residents have ownership deeds on their houses that in some cases go back 150 years, giving the lie to regime propaganda that the residents are squatters impeding the development of tourism and the Egyptian economy.

Almost immediately the independent press pounced on the story and began muckraking, turning Al-Qursaya into a virtual cause célèbre for the country's opposition. In June 2007, stories began to appear in independent press outlets like *Al-Dustur* warning that a vast crime was about to be committed against the indigent inhabitants of the island. At the time the story fed into a general atmosphere in the media of contempt for the Mubarak regime's lawless venality, and the press used its more sensational style to play up the story for its hungry audiences. Coming immediately on the heels of months of rumours about Mubarak's death, the trial of prominent editors, and a burgeoning economic crisis, the Al-Qursaya Island takeover represented to many the total venality of the Mubarak regime and its contempt for ordinary citizens.

One blogger who wrote about Al-Qursaya was former physician Mina Zakry. As he tells the story, 'The government with some businessmen wanted to take over. Armed forces from the army went down to the island and intimidated the people, pushing them to sell the land, or even to just evacuate it.'[103] Zakry acknowledges that newspapers were covering the story, but insists that they were unable to tell the entire tale. In the carefully-honed tradition of self-censorship, the news stories would skirt around the issue of an army takeover. As Zakry argues, 'They [print reporters] would even say something like "a dominant body" or a "high entity" – the law prevents anything.'[104] This impression is widespread, as is the idea that outside of *Al-Dustur* and *Al-Masry Al-Youm* no one wanted to touch this story. On November 13, 2007, weeks prior to Zakry's story, the Sandmonkey asked himself why the media wasn't reporting on the island takeover. His answer was: 'Because critisizing [sic] the army in any way can land you for at least year in jail. Plus, whatchu gonna do? Call them thieves? Can't really steal what you already own, and they own all of our asses.'[105] The AFP story that Sandmonkey links to makes this same point – 'Emergency laws in place for decades mean that any Egyptian will think twice about reporting on military activity, and the few media references to what is happening on the island studiously avoid mentioning the army.'[106]

Research confirms the allegation that even the independent press was unwilling to print the truth about the island's takeover. Typical of this reticence is Fahmy Howeidi's December 27 *Al-Dustur* op-ed 'Ghazwat Al-Qursaya'. In his acerbic piece, in which he criticizes the island's takeover and lauds the efforts of the islanders, he refers to the perpetrators as 'armed soldiers'. While this may seem like hair-splitting diffidence, it is in fact a deliberate semantic choice to avoid fingering the army, despite it being a well-known fact that reporters were well aware of the identity of those sending forces into the island and causing trouble between the regime and its residents. Howeidi even went to the trouble of writing a follow-up column for *Al-Dustur*, 'Hidden Realities of Al-Qursaya' in which he writes about 'armed forces' being behind the takeover, but refuses pointedly to direct attention to the Egyptian Army. Some realities in Egypt must remain hidden. This was a pattern followed by nearly all other reporters and columnists at the time.

According to Zakry, an *Al-Masry Al-Youm* reporter dropped the Al-Qursaya Island file into his lap one day, claiming that the newspaper couldn't print the truth about what was really going on. Zakry, understanding the risks involved in telling the truth, decided to proceed anyway.[107] On December 3, 2007, Zakry published a story on his blog about the army takeover of Al-Qursaya. The entry was entitled 'Video: The army conquers Al-Qursaya Island'.[108] The entry contains an embedded video that depicts the unmistakable signs of the Egyptian armed forces (*al-quwat al-musaliha*). Soldiers on a boat are captured on video by an intrepid cameraman, and those soldiers, as the commentary indicates, are clearly not from other organs of the Egyptian security apparatus.[109]

In the entry, Zakry claims that other than one story in *El-Badeel* (at the time a new paper with an extraordinarily limited circulation) he was the only person willing to go on record with the allegations about the army. To his surprise he was not arrested – suggesting that perhaps the so-called 'red lines' are more perceived than actual, or that crossing them is indeed possible in Egypt's new press environment, through a process of challenge-and-response. It is also possible that he got away with it because no one connected to the regime actually noticed. But perhaps once a new red line has been violated, other journalists and bloggers look to the transgressor to see whether he or she is punished. SMN activists are taking the lead in this process. Zakry's story was one small piece of a very large campaign on behalf of Al-Qursaya's residents, which unfolded over the course of the year. In November of 2008, the regime was finally defeated in court, and the army takeover was halted.[109] While it is still possible that the army will resume its plans for the island once the furore has passed, activists can legitimately claim this as a substantial victory for the residents.

In addition to Zakry's reporting, digital media gave activists and citizens other tools for pooling their resources. The reporting on

Al-Qursaya falls under the umbrella of awareness-raising. As Fenton writes,

> The internet has become home to mediated activity that seeks to raise people's awareness, to give a voice to those who do not have one, to offer social empowerment, to allow disparate people and causes to form alliances, and ultimately to be used as a tool for social change.[110]

Dozens of other bloggers took up the cause. The blogger Ahmed Al-Hiwari wrote a post, typical of the blogging response to the crisis, on December 3, 2007 entitled 'Al-Qursaya: Island of Fear'.[111] The article, which clearly editorialized against the takeover, featured original reporting and gave first-hand insight into the lives of the islanders. This period of early December was one of great import for electronic resistance to the takeover; the prominent left-wing blogger Hossam El-Hamalawy, co-founder of the influential English-language blog The Arabist,[112] made a number of posts on the issue. On December 4, for instance, he posted three videos of the island, one depicting islanders resisting the armed forces, and another a documentary by the filmmaker Mohamed Abla.[114] Hamalawy's story (and another story that same day on the main Arabist page by Issandr El-Amrani) was the catalyst for a Global Voices story on December 5, which placed the island takeover in the context of increasing regime incursions into civil society.

The photo-sharing site Flickr, furthermore, was used to coordinate the upload of photographs of the island and its people. Bloggers reported the times and dates of demonstrations, and contributed to an environment in which the Al-Qursaya takeover was becoming a PR nightmare for the Mubarak regime. Facebook also became a site of dissent and resistance, presaging the site's role in the April 6, 2008 general strike that brought widespread notoriety to the social networking site. Shortly after the publication of Zakry's story – which was widely linked in the small Egyptian blogging community – a Facebook group was formed called 'Anqidhu ahali jazirat al-Qursaya' (Save the People of Al-Qursaya Island). It quickly boasted hundreds of members, and its wall featured links to outside stories and the times and dates of demonstrations.[115] In November 2007, over 600 people gathered for a press conference to promote a documentary about the residents.[116] Prominent human rights lawyers – including Amir Salim, who represented jailed opposition leader Ayman Nour – filed a case on behalf of the residents,[117] drawing on a 2001 Prime Ministerial decree which allowed the residents of nearby Gold Island to stay in their homes. Egyptian celebrities got into the act, staging a protest on New Year's Day to draw attention to the plight of the islanders. The pace of press coverage picked up, and the government press was forced to provide some grudging coverage. Protests were arranged, including one at the journalists' syndicate downtown.[118]

Ultimately, the government – which had been stonewalling the press for months – was forced to admit that it had drafted plans for the island. On January 4, *Al-Dustur* columnist Ibrahim Monsour reported that the government had admitted that it had planned to turn the island into a tourist resort.[119] Simply getting the government to admit to this can be considered a minor triumph, considering the murky relationship between the executive and the army. The fact that residents ultimately triumphed is remarkable. Zakry's account also coincided with an increase in the density of coverage of the Al-Qursaya case. Between May 2007 and December 3, 2007, 85 stories appeared in the Egyptian print media on the crisis – mostly in the independent newspapers *Al-Masry Al-Youm*, *Al-Dustur* and *El-Badeel*.[120] Except for a handful of stories, the state-controlled press largely ignored the story or printed accounts of ministerial defenses of government conduct.[121] Between December 3, 2007 and December 1, 2008, however, that number jumped to 194 stories. While the majority of these stories appeared in the independent press, the official press was forced to confront the issue as well, with substantive articles describing the conflict appearing in *Rose Al-Yusef*, *Al-Ahram*, *Al-Gumhuriya*, and others.

The relevant comparison for the Al-Qursaya takeover is not difficult to discern – the regime had in fact made multiple attempts to seize the island, as well as others on the Nile. A similar attempt failed in 2001, when the government was once again opposed in court.[122] However, the specifics of that case are difficult to come by, since not a single article was published in the Egyptian or Arabic press about the case.[123] Since the government did not successfully take over the island in 2001, we can assume that press attention and digital media are not the only causal variable at work here – clearly the government does not control the judicial system to the extent that some observers imagine.[124] And certainly the heightened atmosphere of protest that existed in 2007 thanks to Kefaya played a role as well. However, the outcry caused by the 2007 edition of the case far and away eclipsed anything that occurred in 2001. The evidence of a similar attempt in 1998 puts Al-Qursaya in the same category as Qurna, a settlement in Luxor that the government tried for 50 years to clear of residents – finally succeeding in 1997. In other words, the Nile islands around Cairo are clearly coveted by the regime or elements in the regime, and activists and residents should expect repeated and continual attempts to push them out in the name of progress or tourism.

Conclusions

In evaluating the evidence presented in the above cases, several hypotheses from Chapter 2 are supported. The first is that Social Media Networks transmit information through critical nodes. When looking at the Sudanese refugee case, it is striking that Nora Younis is herself a journalist and has extensive contacts in the Egyptian press community, making her not just a credible source, but a node in the broader SMN in which she is situated. Her contacts allowed both for her presence that day, which was anything but serendipitous – it was rather orchestrated via a text-messaging network in which activists who knew her and knew of her interest in such matters were able to 'activate' her and get her quickly to the scene – and for the seemingly instantaneous way in which the information she gathered made its way to the press outlets. While any ordinary Egyptian with a cell phone could have taken pictures and posted them to a blog, it was Younis – a highly-connected and highly-read journalist-blogger – who was able to turn that hypermedia footage into more than an interesting entry on a little-known web outlet.

The same connection can be made with the sexual harassment and torture cases – in both cases information was first provided by a former journalist whose blogging and SMN activism was trusted and credible. Younis has trained as a journalist, and her presence on the scene mitigated the concerns expressed by a number of professional journalists that bloggers don't know what they're doing, are willing to report rumour as fact, or who can't or won't actually get out in the street, do interviews, and perform the difficult work of a paid journalist. As *Al-Ahram* journalist Amira Howeidy noted about another blogger, Hossam El-Hamalawy, 'First of all, I know Hossam personally, I think that's an important factor, I know he is an honest person, and he's connected in his field, and he's into labour activism and he's a socialist and so on and he's very devoted to his cause, when there are events related to these issues, I find him credible.'[125] It is this sentiment that drives the credibility of certain bloggers for journalists in the field. This is the difference between a dead end in cyberspace and a SMN with capabilities – with *power*. It is not the power to put an end to refugee crises, racism, or the lawlessness of authoritarian regimes, but the power to set the agenda of public debate.

Corroborative evidence is also found for the hypothesis that authoritarian regimes will have increasing difficulty controlling the media environment. The El-Kabir case points clearly to a shift in public discourse, and the willingness of Egyptian journalists to write about torture in the wake of the case. No one has argued that torture became more widespread between 2007 and 2009 – if anything police might have become somewhat more reluctant to torture given the consequences for the officers caught torturing El-Kabir. This does not mean, by any stretch of the imagination, that torture has been eradicated or that it is no longer a problem. It does, however, mean that in 2007 it no longer took place under a shroud of secrecy. The success of the El-Kabir story and the widespread use of cell phone cameras to document police abuse outside of police stations means that the watchers are being watched by the citizenry, and that individuals are increasingly emboldened to document cases of police abuse. This is particularly surprising given that a general scholarly consensus emerged between 2006 and 2011 arguing that Mubarak's regime had become increasingly emboldened to commit renewed human rights violations with the retreat of the Bush Administration's mid-decade democracy promotion initiatives.

A close reading of the Al-Qursaya case offers further understanding of how SMNs function in Egypt. First, not all cases of blogging's relevance involve breaking stories that would otherwise have gone unreported. This can be seen especially in the case of the recent Israeli invasion of Gaza. Blogs, of course, did not 'break' this story, but along with other forms of digital media, they greatly amplified the activist response. Second, it is clear that the Mubarak regime cared about and was sensitive to its press reputation and the international repercussions of its actions. The regime appeared to be most vulnerable on populist issues – salaries, working conditions, the plight of the poor – and on human rights issues that are capable of drawing the broad-based support of Islamists, leftists, and liberals – issues like sexual harassment, torture, and due process. This is not to say that activists had the upper hand, but rather that everyone involved would benefit from knowing which issues they are likely to be able to promote successfully from *within* the system. Aside from a handful of developers and whoever was going to benefit directly from the conversion of Al-Qursaya into some kind of magical tourist paradise, few would publicly argue for the dispossession of some of Cairo's poorest citizens.

This discussion of the cases should not lead us to believe that digital media *necessarily* have a democratizing effect in authoritarian countries. Notwithstanding Howard's optimistic account,[126] the quantitative evidence linking the Internet with democratization is spotty at best.[127] Rather, under certain circumstances, digital media can serve as tools in the repertoire of dissidents. They also create alternative public spheres – which some have theorized as counter-publics.[128] These alternative public spheres function through the empowerment of individuals whose ability to express themselves and participate in politics in other ways is severely limited. As Al-Saggaf writes, 'The Internet not only allows people to discuss and debate issues of utmost importance to them, it also makes them authors of media content rather than a passive audience'.[129] Regardless of whether such places qualify as Habermasian public spheres in the strict sense, they certainly operate as focal points of dissent and allow individuals

– particularly those from repressed minorities like Baha'is, Coptic Christians, or others – to articulate their needs, desires, and dreams. In the uncoordinated chaos of the Internet, these focal points allow for the production of commentary and agreed-upon narrative frames and calls to action.

Wael Abbas, the internationally-recognized Egyptian blogger and citizen journalist, told me: 'We are recording history so that in the future no one will dare to lie about it.' Abbas argues that Egyptian media (and Arab media generally) have a long tradition of deceiving citizens about the true nature of news events and social and political developments. He cites the Egyptian media's cover-up of the country's devastating loss to Israel in the 1967 War and the way that press organs cooperated with the Nasser regime to downplay the terrible losses suffered by the army and airforce. While it cannot be said that regimes have lost all control over information, one of the lessons of the cases presented above is that SMNs greatly complicate the efforts of authoritarian regimes to craft and control narratives about politics. The four cases presented above are illustrative of the new media environment in which authoritarian regimes must operate. They highlight the effects of cooperation between embattled reporters at independent media outlets and their digital media critics. Finally, it suggests that tactical victories are within reach of determined and digitally-mediated activists, under the right circumstances.

However, these battles are not simply one-off struggles, in which SMN activists sometimes win, and sometimes lose; nor is this simply another tale of regimes allowing for 'safety valves' for the harmless release of pressure. The growth of SMN activism is an expression of dissatisfaction with the structural alignment of political forces in Egypt, and the way that big decisions – economic, social, political – have been made without the input of actors outside of the NDP or the military. As Castells argues,

> sociopolitical forms and processes are built upon cultural materials and... these materials are either unilaterally produced by political institutions as an expression of domination or, alternatively, are coproduced within the public sphere by individuals, interest

groups, civic associations of various kinds (the civil society), and the state.[130]

SMN activism contributes to a public sphere in which politics is *co-produced* with the state by other actors, particularly independent journalists and human rights organizations. While the state may still be the dominant actor in Egyptian politics, SMNs make it possible for other actors to contest that domination and occasionally to subvert it. The role of the public sphere in these developments– in theoretical terms – will be addressed in Chapter 5.

The importance of the independent press holds true not just for the advancing of claims, breaking of stories, or introduction of marginalized actors into the public sphere, but also for the mobilization of collective action. The question of whether or not SMNs facilitate the organization and execution of collective action in authoritarian contexts is the subject of Chapter 4.

CHAPTER 4

NEW TOOLS, OLD RULES: SOCIAL MEDIA NETWORKS AND COLLECTIVE ACTION IN EGYPT

Introduction

Since their development in the early part of this century, activists all over the world have seized on the tools of Social Media Networks as they organize opposition to authoritarian regimes and practices. From the text-messaging armada that descended on Epifanio de los Santos Avenue in the Philippines in 2001, to text-messaging protestors and electronic journalists in the Orange Revolution, and now today to Iranian protestors Tweeting the news of mass protests, arrests, and intimidation, activists have proven that under the right circumstances, SMN activism can be powerful and effective. However, scholars have yet to identify the kinds of circumstances under which SMNs can be effective, and why. This chapter, through the evaluation of case studies in Egypt, seeks to explain the circumstances under which SMN activism can successfully mobilize collective action in authoritarian contexts, and the circumstances under which such mobilization is likely to lead to political change; arguing that one does not necessarily lead to the other. In so doing, the chapter contributes a critical piece of theory-building as scholars seek to understand the impact of technological proliferation in the developing world. The chapter evaluates competing hypotheses about the mobilization and collective action potential of SMNs under conditions of authoritarianism. The null hypothesis is that, especially in low-connectivity societies like Egypt, SMNs have little to no role to play in mobilizing dissent, because so few individuals have Internet access and because social movements are built and sustained by persistent frames, concrete demands, and organizational ties within communities. This hypothesis would expect that thriving social movements like the Muslim Brotherhood and the Egyptian labour movement will have a much greater role to play in the Egyptian collective action environment. The alternative hypothesis advanced here is that SMNs reduce the costs of collective action, and thus should lead to more protests, demonstrations, and strikes, the standard manifestations of dissent in authoritarian societies. Consistent with Lust-Okar's expectations that included groups are less likely to involve themselves in protest and dissent activities,[1] it also seems a reasonable expectation that excluded groups like the Muslim Brotherhood will invest more heavily in the tactical tools of SMNs.

Mona El-Ghobashy posed a critical question for scholars of Egypt: if authoritarianism had in fact deepened and stabilized in Egypt through the institutional choices of the regime, or become 'durable' in the popular language, as many scholars argue,[2] why has there been a massive increase in the number of civil society organizations, and an organized effort on the part of the judiciary to exert its power vis-à-vis the regime? Her answer involves the internationalization of Egyptian politics in the form of routine connections between international NGOs and governments and domestic Egyptian actors, as well as the 'mobilization of the constitution' by which opposition forces, including the judiciary and ordinary citizens, seek the enforcement of the actual laws on the books in the country as opposed to more arbitrary forms of state power. El-Ghobashy, however, whose argument will be explored in more depth below, fails to conceptualize or seek to explain precisely what has enabled those international connections or the increased ability and willingness of civil society forces to agitate on behalf of constitutional issues in Egypt.[3] In this chapter, in addition to testing hypotheses about the causes and consequences of new information technologies and their relationship to collective action, I will seek to fill the gap in El-Ghobashy's argument by arguing for the critical role of Social Media Networks in internationalization and mobilization in Egypt – even while remaining sanguine about the potential of these technologies for truly large-scale mobilization. As we will see with the Judges' Club ferment, the April 6 movement and the reaction to the Israeli invasion of Gaza, SMNs are the missing variable in recent accounts of Egyptian civil society, and understanding how they operate, as well as their possibilities and limitations, is critical to a proper understanding of contemporary politics in Egypt. In so doing, I hope to explain the salience of SMNs in Egypt, and to situate the changes that have taken place in Egyptian politics within a larger narrative of authoritarian persistence.

This chapter will proceed first by looking at the collective action environment in Egypt and the ways that SMNs have changed the incentives and possibilities for organizers. It then proceeds to explain the contribution of SMNs to four discrete events: the struggle over judicial independence in 2005–2007, the April 6, 2008 General Strike, the 2009 General Strike, and the protests against the Israeli invasion of Gaza in 2008–2009.

Mobilizing Protest in Egypt

Khaled Al Khamissi's non-fiction best-seller *Taxi* related the author's experiences travelling around in Egypt's ubiquitous black-and-white taxis, often operated by men just barely getting by, and in many cases, not getting by at all. Anyone who has been to Cairo has had the experience of getting stuck in one of these taxis, which are to all appearances often held together by glue and paper clips. For their drivers, though, these cabs are their lifeblood. In one of Al Khamissi's tales, a driver lampoons a Kefaya demonstration by comparison to the protests of days past. 'In the old days,' says the driver, 'we used to go out on the streets with 50,000 people, with 100,000. But now there's nothing that matters.'[4] The driver identifies the enormous and regime-rattling bread riots which greeted Sadat's decision to slash subsidies for staple goods in 1977 as 'the beginning of the end' of Egyptian protest. But after those riots, which the regime successfully quelled, few Egyptians had dared challenge the government publicly. 'And since then the government has planted in us a fear of hunger. . . . They planted hunger in the belly of every Egyptian, a terror that made everyone look out for himself or say "Why should I make it my problem?"' Al Khamissi, stunned that the driver remembers the exact dates of the bread riots and melancholy about his cynicism, ponders why 'the end' came about.

One could argue that this protest lull ended with the Second Intifada in Palestine, and culminated in the January 25, 2011 uprising. Most activists with whom I spoke during my research indicated that it was indeed the Palestinian uprising which first galvanized Egyptian resistance to authoritarian rule. But it is certainly true that before that uprising, there had been relatively few broad-based protests that threatened the regime itself, and that, as with most Kefaya demonstrations, protests were usually limited affairs, with small numbers of protestors surrounded by riot police and the plainclothes thugs known as *baltagiyya*. Al Khamissi's taxi driver inadvertently identifies the fundamental collective action problem – the 'rebel's dilemma' in Lichbach's memorable formulation[5] – that prevents citizens from uniting against the tyranny of the state.

Beneath the surface though, conditions were converging in Egypt in the 2000s to produce a moment of peril for the Mubarak regime. The neoliberal reform programme pursued relentlessly by the Mubarak government may have been superficially improving the economy, but it had been devastating for industrial workers, and had increased the gap between rich and poor.[6] The Bush Administration and its Freedom Agenda argued that it was political tyranny that had produced Islamic terrorism, and had thus begun to place pressure on the Mubarak government to reform – at least until the Iraq debacle and the trauma of the Hamas victory in Palestinian elections caused the administration to reverse course. In the midst of this pressure, the Mubarak government allowed the flourishing of new and independent press outlets (see Chapter 3), and held multi-candidate (if far from free) presidential elections in 2006. The announcement of those elections came in 2005, which coincides with the largest recorded number of yearly protests. The role of SMNs in mobilizing demonstrations during this period is well-known and has been written about at length,[7] but it is worth exploring how exactly it worked and why it represented such a change.

It was exceedingly difficult, if not impossible, to organize a demonstration in the 1990s. Groups had to obtain permits and then embark on the difficult process of drumming up support and participation. This meant paying for leaflets, finding somewhere to assemble and then carrying out the protest successfully, which rendered groups vulnerable to regime harassment and surveillance at every turn. The regime's dirty war against the Islamists had created such a climate of fear and repression in Egypt at the time that most Egyptians feared taking part in any political activity whatsoever. Hossam El-Hamalawy elaborates:

> in order to organize a demonstration in the 1990s there was so much secrecy, you can't talk over the phone, you would meet people, you would chat, and how would you publish for a demonstration, you had to print out something.[8]

During this time period, as well, the regime held what amounted to a monopoly on news, information and events in Egypt. As El-Hamalawy argues, if someone showed up at a demonstration in the 1990s with a camera, demonstrators would turn away and hide their faces, since they could be fairly certain that the journalist was from one of the three major government dailies, *Al-Akhbar*, *Al-Gumhuriya*, and *Al-Ahram*. Reporters from those newspapers were believed to feed information and pictures directly to the security services, making it very dangerous to have your picture taken at any kind of demonstration. Beatings, arrests, and other forms of rights abuse all took place with little scrutiny from the press or international observers. The costs of organizing this kind of collective action were then exceptionally high, and the odds of those protests, even if the organizers managed to pull them off, being reported inside or outside of Egypt were low. A confluence of circumstances – largely related to relative calm in the Israeli-Palestinian conflict and strong domestic economic growth rates – combined to make protest a relatively rare thing in the 1990s. Protest waves clearly depend as much on external and internal circumstances as they do on the means that demonstrators might deploy to execute their plans. However, the advent of satellite television in the 1990s introduced a competing news source into the Egyptian news environment,[9] even if that source was typically focused more on international relations and Arab-Israeli conflict stories than it was on local Egyptian stories. Hossam El-Hamalawy explains:

> The outbreak of the Palestinian Intifada [in 2000] – this marked the beginning of internet activism, that took the form of email lists, yahoo chat groups. I was being spammed left and right by those who have the boycott lists of updates about the Intifada, pictures of the dead, pictures of the atrocities. These were being emailed, and yahoo groups were like the hip thing back then.[10]

The primary function of SMNs during this time period was coordination and information-transmission. Bloggers posted, texted, and emailed the times and dates of demonstrations or other actions, and SMN technologies like SMS messages were used to find agreed-upon places for demonstrations, to adjust those locales on the spot, and to communicate information about the results and any arrests. As Hossam El-Hamalawy says:

> With the crackdown on the judges movement, I was mailing continuous updates, at the same time I had 50 plus numbers on my mobile that I had in a group, that I used to text updates, we would be running around in downtown, and seeing people kidnapped, and sending SMS and then running home, uploading emails and photos, and Issandr would post the pictures.[11]

SMNs like blogs, especially during this time period, also played a role in transmitting information to outsiders, and challenging the boundaries of public discourse. SMNs were important sources of information transmission and dissent during the clash over judicial rights in 2005–2007. The struggle over judicial reform and the role played by SMNs helped set the political context in which the April 6 Movement –

which forms the core of this chapter – developed. Understanding how that first struggle played out is critical to understanding where and how the April 6 Movement succeeded and failed.

The Judges' Club and the Protest Wave of 2005

The Egyptian judiciary has been engaged in a struggle with the regime since at least the Second World War.[12] The struggle has primarily centered around the function of the judiciary as a check on the power of the executive. Since Nasser, the executive has tried repeatedly to undermine the judiciary's capacity for independent action. Sadat's initial draft of the Supreme Constitutional Court law in 1977 would have left the organization toothless and subordinate to the regime.[13] Opposition from prominent judges led the Sadat regime to agree to a far more invasive and powerful SCC than had originally been conceptualized. And because of that power, the SCC has again and again challenged the arbitrary power of the state, such as in 1985, when it ruled against Sadat and his attempts to use the emergency law to amend the Law on Personal Status.[14] Rutherford concludes, 'The SCC and the administrative courts have accumulated a large body of rulings that seek to limit state power and render it more accountable to the law'.[15]

Especially since Hosni Mubarak took over after Sadat's assassination in 1981, the judiciary has repeatedly struggled to carve out victories vis-à-vis the state – for the right to form democratic syndicates and political parties, property rights, and freedoms of speech, in particular. The long-standing involvement of the courts in questions of multiparty politics in Egypt stretched across a number of national elections. And when, seemingly under pressure from the United States to democratize, the regime announced it would hold not just parliamentary elections, but a multi-candidate election for the presidency, the stage was set for different political forces to converge in opposition. The 2005 presidential and parliamentary elections were thus formulated as the perfect opportunity for a very public struggle between the regime, which wanted to rig the elections for the NDP, and the judiciary, which was constitutionally tasked with overseeing the fairness and legality of the elections themselves. The looming battle pitched the rhetoric of democracy and pluralism against the continued reality of the Mubarak regime's use of the threat of 'terrorism' and the Muslim Brotherhood to uphold the state of emergency that has been in place since 1981.[16] But compared to the decades-long struggle between the regime and judiciary, rather than against the exigencies of the moment in 2005 alone, it was clear that both sides saw the elections as a pivotal battle. Truly free and fair elections could potentially threaten the core of Egyptian authoritarianism.

The elections themselves split the Judges' Club between those who believed they should take no part in what would likely be fraudulent elections, and those who argued that they should exercise their power, even taking into consideration the institutional limits placed on judicial freedom. After the elections, Mahmoud Mekki and Hisham Bastawisi, vice-presidents of the Court of Cassation, very publicly declared the parliamentary elections rigged and presented evidence of their claims, igniting what Wolff calls 'a huge civil society movement'.[17] The judges themselves were arrested, along with hundreds of activists and leaders from the Muslim Brotherhood and Kefaya. The streets of Cairo became sites of contestation between these opposition forces, who sought transparent and fair elections, and forces of the regime, which hoped to quash them. The outcome of these struggles was, and remains, unclear. Most observers agree that there has been a retrenchment in political rights since the heyday of the Kefaya movement in the mid-2000s. And it is certainly true that the regime won an important victory when the judiciary was essentially stripped of its election-overseeing component in 2007, as Article 88 of the constitution was amended to create an electoral commission to oversee future elections.[18] The regime's victory highlights the important difference between successful mobilization and successful political change.

On May 25, 2006, The Arabist, at the time one of the leading English-language blogs in the Middle East, published what it called a 'recap' of the demonstrations planned for that day. The author (Issandr El-Amrani) wrote that he was just 'passing along the info'.[19] The post contained the times, places, and messages of the day's various protests, which were not just in solidarity with the Judges' Club, but also included an anniversary demonstration for Black Friday, May 25, 2005, in which female journalists were assaulted by the security services.[20] The Arabist itself had long served as a depot for information, pictures and analysis about the demonstrations that were taking place in Cairo against the usurpation of the judiciary's power. These posts often included links to Flickr accounts, where amateur photographers gathered documentary evidence of the day's events, building shared meaning through exchanging and linking to pictures. This lent the blogs themselves both a pre- and post-demonstration utility – before the demonstrations, they served to provide information to the select minority of Egyptians who got information like this online, and after the demonstrations, they constructed and deconstructed the demonstrations themselves, calling for more action, criticizing the treatment of the demonstrators, and attempting to bolster the movement. Many posts, such as the one that appeared on The Arabist on May 18, 2006, depicted police brutality, particularly by the so-called *baltagiyya*, the plainclothes police often hired by the regime to break up demonstrations.[21] Demonstrations themselves took place over a long period of many months, leading up to the passage of the constitutional amendments in 2007.

The struggles of the Judges' Club are arguably representative of the kind of democratization that was taking place in Egypt just under the surface prior to the events of January 2011, in spite of the fact that in many respects authoritarianism has worsened in recent years. El-Ghobashy calls this 'mobilizing the constitution' – i.e. framing and organizing contention around the actual written document of the 1971 constitution, and challenging the state on the basis of its legal precepts.[22] It would not be the first time that 'flawed constitutions' were used to bring about democratic reform – as El-Ghobashy notes, the same strategy was used in Poland.[23] Many constitutions, even in authoritarian countries, promise rights that are not delivered in real life. In Egypt, it was the ferment created by the announcement of multi-candidate presidential elections in 2005 that made this strategy the default mode of the Judges' Club and the various NGOs organizing in support of them.

Once again, though, independent media and its relationship to SMNs played an important role in the mobilization process. With only the state press on the scene, it's unlikely that the kind of debate about the elections that occurred would ever have taken place. And the blogs would have had no one to link to. As Issandr El-Amrani put it,

> The 24-hour cycle in Egypt in terms of breaking news, didn't really exist [in 2005]. The official press is often vague about what's happening, it didn't have a lot of serious competition. That changed in 2004 with the new independent dailies that came out...it really created a wonky discussion about what was taking place in the political arena. It's not that it didn't exist before, it didn't get updated at a daily pace. It forced the issue of election fraud on the agenda, election fraud is nothing new, it's just that there are these outlets available and the right political atmosphere.[24]

As the protest movement continued its actions in 2005–2007, blogs became sites of discussion and documentation – of the demonstrations themselves, and also of arrests. Leading Arabic-language blogger Amr Gharbeia, on October 26, 2006, wrote about central security forces surrounding the Judges Club, and about the arrests of fellow bloggers – in real time. 'Central security forces are surrounding the Judges' Club,' he wrote, while also posting the names of arrested activists and bloggers.[25] Wael Abbas, on his blog Misr Digital, posted a detailed description of the protest events planned for May 25, 2006, both in Egypt and abroad.[26] The posting of dates and times of protests was common during this period, particularly since the movement to oppose the constitutional amendments was led by Kefaya, which had (and still has) a strong web presence. Sympathetic activists in the blogging community helped spread the word about these protests. One such blog was Manal and Alaa's Bitbucket, one of the oldest and more well-known Egyptian political blogs, which was published sometimes in English and sometimes in Arabic. A typical post would list the time, date, and place of an upcoming demonstration, along with the organizers. They also included short descriptions of the events' *raison d'être*, such as the demonstration in Midan Tahrir on March 15. 2007, which saw the constitutional amendments as designed to 'continue dictatorial rule and eliminate judicial supervision of elections'.[27]

The protests continued through March of 2007, including demonstrations – generally neglected by the international press – on university campuses across Egypt. One such demonstration on March 25, 2007 drew thousands of protestors across Egypt, not just in Cairo but in universities across the country, including in secondary cities like Tanta.[28] Still, constitutional amendments were passed over the objections of this movement. The Judges' Club and their political allies lacked the grassroots organizing capabilities that might have put more people on the streets, while international pressure on the regime proved incapable of changing its course. And while SMNs contributed to coordination and globalization, they were not the fundamental driving cause of the events of 2005–2007. However, the political context created by the struggles of 2005–2007 helps us understand the environment in which later organizing took place. To assess the impact of SMNs on collective action in Egypt, we must look at the April 6 Youth Movement, and the strikes organized on April 6, 2008, May 4, 2008 and April 6, 2009 – strikes that were organized in large part online and the outcomes of which can tell us much about the conditions under which SMN-driven collective action might succeed or fail. In terms of theory testing, these strikes were conducted by the same group of activists, under virtually identical political conditions, with widely divergent results. More than the Judges' Club organizing, the April 6 Movement is a kind of natural experiment, so rarely possible in comparative politics – an experiment which will assess the possibilities and limitations of mobilization conducted through Social Media Networks.

Informational Cascades and the April 6 Movement

A sandstorm was en route to Cairo on the morning of April 6, 2008, but a tight-knit group of young digital activists was engaging in preparations for an entirely different disruption. Another activist friend had kindly arranged for me to spend the day with these activists, telling me he thought something really big was going to happen and that these were the people who were going to be doing it. As we skipped from Internet café to Internet café, it became clear that the group believed themselves to be monitored by state agents, and that they hoped the events they were monitoring and coordinating from their laptops would turn Egypt upside down, at least for the day. The morning took me from the garish coffee houses of Mohandisin and Zamalek to the Judges' Syndicate downtown, where organizers had mounted an anti-Mubarak demonstration that was surrounded by the typical moat of riot police, plainclothes thugs (the *baltagiyya*) and the occasional European or American 'disaster tourist'. While in the cafés, the activists busied themselves collating reports of demonstrations, arrests and other incidents from across Egypt. When a friend or associate was arrested, a hush fell over the group for a moment, but the collective quickly surged back into action. It was no accident that this mixed-gender group of activists was gathered in these Western-style cafés (as opposed to traditional male-only cafés). As De Koning notes about such cafés, 'These are the spaces, and for many upper-middle-class women, the only spaces, where social life outside the family takes place'.[29] All of the activists were multi-tasking – taking cell phone calls, updating their webpages and sending out Twitter updates through phones and laptops, engaging in what one observer once dubbed 'continuous partial attention'.[30] One of these activists told me: 'With the Internet you can get online anytime, wherever, so like now we are publishing all the same news the same minute. If someone got caught now, arrested now, we can write about it now, rather than the old style.'[31] The 'old style' of news gathering meant the traditional media, where a natural time-lag for editors and publishing prevented precisely the sort of instant news gathering and coordination made possible by social media.

Some of this activity appeared to be facilitated by the Internet. SMNs have little to nothing to do with broadcast news media, the traditional focus of academics studying Arab media, almost to the exclusion of all else.[32] The day's events also had little to do with the kind of blogging we had come to associate with the form – the airing of opinion and analysis by non-professionals, or angry people in their pyjamas railing against the media or political forces. These were blogger-activists, or 'citizen journalists' in the new lingo of the field. The reason that April 6, 2008 received so much domestic and international attention was because of the actions of a Ghad party functionary named Esraa Abdel Fattah and a handful of her friends (all of them also veterans of Kefaya's Youth For Change), who decided to create a group on the increasingly popular social networking site Facebook. She and her fellow activists turned April 6 from a localized labour protest into an international event. The Facebook activists, as they came to be called, triggered an informational cascade, as outlined in Chapter 2.

Abdel Fattah started the Facebook group in mid-March of 2008, although it had its origins in the Youth For Change movement (*Shebab min agl at-tagheer*), an outgrowth of Kefaya which, despite its reputation for futility, ultimately served as a catalyst for all other kinds of protest activity. According to Ahmed Saleh, another founder of the movement, discussion had been taking place for quite some time in Youth For Change circles about how activists outside of Mahalla could show their support for the labour uprising taking place in that industrial city just north of Cairo. The Facebook group was devoted to striking with the textile workers of Mahalla al-Kubra, in the Delta. Mahalla workers had selected April 6 as the day to go out on strike as a protest against stagnant incomes and inflation. Due to other factors affecting Egypt at the time, the strike had the potential to develop into something much larger than an isolated labour protest. For months the prices of basic commodities had been rising in Egypt at the same time that official figures on the economy continued to look rosy, and the regime didn't seem terribly interested in helping ordinary people out of trouble. Inflation was making it increasingly difficult for poor Egyptians to eke out their already-subsistence lifestyles, and yet the regime appeared committed to pushing forward with its campaign of insider privatization and state retreat.[33] And to add to that already significant discontent, citizens were dismayed by the regime's campaign of revenge and intimidation against senior leaders of the Muslim Brotherhood, designed to help discredit the organization before the local elections on April 9.[34] Finally, the state faced widespread disgust with its complicity in the brutal siege of the Gaza Strip by Israel.

On April 6, Cairo was a city transformed by this struggle. Many shops and businesses were closed (though certainly many remained open) and there was a general atmosphere of tension and confrontation.

At this point I had been in Cairo since August of 2007, and I had seen nothing like this during my nine months there. But the scene in Cairo paled in comparison to what was happening in Mahalla itself, where workers clashed violently with police for days. As the *New York Times* describes Mahalla:

> In Mahalla al-Kobra, the center of Egypt's textile industry north of Cairo, a melee broke out late in the day as the riot police fired tear gas and workers threw stones. Officials said there were more than 200 arrests around the country, including at least seven people arrested for their efforts to use the Internet to promote the call for a day of unrest.[35]

Clashes in Mahalla would continue throughout the week before the regime regained control of the situation. While the day's events did not constitute, at the time, a threat to the regime's existence, they did demonstrate the possibility for the first time in decades that Egypt's fractured oppositions might unite around a small set of issues to mount a full-scale challenge to the regime's authority. In essence, the regime regarded every closed shop to be a threat to its legitimacy, and for the first time saw digital activists as a constituency that might develop into a more important threat in the long run.

Just two weeks after it was nothing but a title on a Facebook page, Esraa and her friends' new organization boasted 70,000 members, which is amazing given that only approximately 790,000 Egyptians were even members of Facebook at the time.[36] The organization called on its members to stay home on the day of the strike, and to wear black if they did go out. But in the heavily policed state of Egypt, organizing demonstrations was technically illegal, and calling for a general strike particularly so. Strikes took place anyway, but citizens became accustomed to the almost ritualistic dance between the small Kefaya protests and their regime tormentors – so much so that the site of demonstrators on the streets of Cairo and other cities became routine. It may at first seem puzzling that organizers moved their operations to a social networking site, but when we examine the scale-free Egyptian blogosphere and the innovations in network theory explored in Chapter 2, the choice to migrate to Facebook from the blogosphere makes much more sense.

The development of Facebook as an organizing tool in Egypt tracks nicely with Ethan Zuckerman's 'cute cat theory' of digital activism.[37] State elites generally don't want to shut off popular (and presumably frivolous) websites, like Facebook, or websites that involve creating captioned pictures of the aforementioned cute cats. The state itself certainly (and belatedly) recognized the power of these social tools and the threat that they represented to the state's control of information.[38] Shortly after the strike, the regime undertook a campaign of delegitimization against Facebook and other Internet sites deemed a threat to regime authority.[39] Esraa herself was arrested the day after the strike and kept in prison for more than two weeks, in the process becoming a minor celebrity within the country. And on an individual level the state's intimidation worked briefly, since she emerged from prison telling reporters she would not be getting involved in any more online organizing.[40] Yet she later returned to organization and to her involvement with what became the April 6 Youth Movement, and today remains one of the group's most important members. The state's campaign of insinuation and accusation against the group and even the medium of Facebook itself, however, did not convince the Egyptian intelligentsia. In one of his post-April 6 columns, Fahmy Howaidy, one of the leading lights of Egyptian letters, referred to the Facebook organizers as 'hope for the future in Egypt'.[41]

Why wasn't the April 6 strike organized on one of Egypt's 160,000-odd blogs? To begin with, a certain cynicism and exhaustion with blogging had descended over the activist community, which helped push organizing and activism to other platforms. Even some of Egypt's foremost blogger-activists seemed to believe that the 'blogging moment' had come and gone. As future parliamentary candidate Mahmoud Salem, then known only as the Sandmonkey, told me about the on-the-ground impact of blogs: 'It's rare. We're talking three stories in three years.' Salem was referring to the major news events discussed in Chapter 3, and which were spearheaded by the efforts of the bloggers, who he referred to as 'pushers'.[42] Even observers who believed in the utility of blogs tended to follow only a tiny number of online writers – Hossam El-Hamlawy, Wael Abbas, Nora Younis and a small group of other elite bloggers. In an interview, El-Hamalawy referred to them as 'power bloggers'.[43] These power bloggers become even more influential as time goes on, since fellow bloggers tend to read and link to their articles. Together with the attention paid to the elite bloggers by international news organizations (and scholars), the elite bloggers became, in network terms, 'hubs'. Hubs prove their utility by 'providing routing, coordinating, and information functions that increase the ease and efficiency of navigating the network'.[44] While their work was courageous, their fame and popularity made it more complicated for new voices to gain any kind of traction in the Egypt blogosphere. The network architecture of the Internet created a small group of power bloggers in the United States beginning in the late 1990s, and that small (mostly male, mostly elite) group had the effect of excluding most aspiring bloggers from the online public sphere.[45] This dynamic can be seen most clearly in the case of the left-wing community blogging site Daily Kos, whose traffic greatly exceeds that of even reasonably well-trafficked sites in that community, like Firedoglake.[46] The enduring popularity of sites like 3Arabawy or Misr Digital is best explained by the fact that they are so much more popular than their competitors that the properties of the network make it difficult for other parties to achieve similar results.

Despite the heavy readership of many Egyptian blogs, there are a number of important reasons why the April 6 Movement was launched on Facebook rather than Blogspot. Most Egyptian blogs at the time were solo affairs, rather than participatory communities like Daily Kos. While such sites boast large readerships, and can attract dozens of comments to a post, they lack the ability of readers to contribute unique content to the site via a 'diary' function. As Karpf argues about Daily Kos, 'Community blogs are designed to enable collective action'.[47] Individual blogs give the owners so much power that it is difficult to coordinate any kind of action, resolve disputes or formulate effective calls to action. Further, while blogs can help create ad hoc communities around issues of interest, they do not fundamentally operate on the basis of an individual's social network (because they are open to anyone), and blogs are not natural places to start large groups. Finally, the initial readership of a blog is the blog's author. Family members and friends have to be told about the blog, and then must make the decision to click on the link and actually go there. On the other hand, a Facebook audience begins with the number (on average, 130)[48] of friends that users have made on the site, and can then multiply quite quickly if shared by friends-of-friends. The way that information can be relayed through social networks is probably the most important reason why activists took to Facebook beginning in 2008.

The April 6 Facebook group was the most important focus for the creation of calls to action and resonant frames for the general strike. The day's events also lent credibility to the idea that Twitter and Facebook might serve as important tools of coordination and on-the-ground adjustment during moments of crisis. It was this realization, not the somewhat limited impact of the strike itself, that led activists to turn increasingly to Twitter and Facebook in the years prior to the uprising on January 25, 2011. This is because Twitter is particularly useful for short-term organizing and on-the-fly coordination and adjustment. As El-Hamalawy argues,

Let's say we had a demo scheduled in the square, the initial scouts show up, they see they are detaining people already, they say, let's move the demo to the press syndicate, then we receive the updates, then we communicate it.[49]

The blogger-activist Mohamed Khalid (whose blog handle is 'Demagh MAK', or 'the brain of MAK', argues

I've moved to Facebook because Facebook is easier to write and more popular. Everybody's on Facebook all the time. I started 6 months ago, I posted on my blog and the same time I posted to FB, the comments and the feedback on the Facebook more than the blog, but I still love my blog, it's my main thing I do first every month. You can write a note in the Facebook, then you tag 30 people and it's like a message and this 30 people and [sic] open their Facebook in the morning.[50]

The April 6 organizers, as well as the medium of Facebook itself, garnered a great deal of press attention in the aftermath of the strike. Foreign reporters also gave a great deal of column inches to these Facebook revolutionaries and the havoc they helped create in Cairo. There were, however, critics who believed that the role of Facebook in the April 6 drama was vastly overblown. Hossam El-Hamalawy, the author of the well-trafficked 3Arabawy site, and who played a crucial role by writing about the events of the general strike from California, argued that the April 6 organizers and the events in Cairo were merely distractions from the main event in Mahalla. Critics like El-Hamalawy cautioned against assuming that the strike was successful, and urged activists to instead focus on the more difficult work of grassroots organizing. When the organizers of the movement tried to follow up their success a year later with an anniversary strike, it seemed that El-Hamalawy would be proven right.

April 6 Redux and the Limits of Online Organizing

The April 6 organizers, seeking to capitalize on their success the previous year, plotted a follow-up strike for the one-year anniversary of the strike. In doing so they united with many factions of the opposition, including Kefaya and the Muslim Brotherhood, who signed onto the action. Having been caught flat-footed the first time around, Mubarak's regime was prepared for this iteration of the strike, waging a weeks-long press campaign against the group and the strike, and scaring Egyptians into not participating. Even press outlets that had worked in many ways with the blogging community and the activists since their founding deemed the day's events a resounding failure. The success of the first strike and the failure of the second leaves observers with a puzzle – if the same activists using the same set of tools performed similar actions on different days, what explains the divergent trajectories of the two actions?

One explanation involves the connection of the strikes to existing grievances in the labour community. The first strike had been tied to the wage demands of the striking workers in Mahalla, as well as to the general rise in prices throughout Egypt in the period preceding April 6, 2008. No such organizing principle was to be found in the anniversary strike. As Amr Shubaki put it,

> If we remember last year's General Strike, we will find that some of us forget that it was called by textile workers in Mahalla, not political activists or party members, to demand improved working conditions and to raise wages.[51]

Shubaki argues that by undercutting the demands of the movement, the regime was able to kneecap its broader appeal by depriving the elite Cairo activists of the grassroots energy they so desperately needed. Shubaki's insights are consistent with the findings recorded in the literature of social movements, which regards motivations and opportunities much more highly than any technological innovations that might have been pioneered. Ironically, though it would take another year and a half, the April 6 organizers, and their allies in the digital activist community more generally, would learn the lessons of this failure all too well, as we will see in Chapter 6.

The very success of the April 6 organizers in drawing media attention may have led the regime to regard them as a threat, and to crack down accordingly. As Hossam El-Hamalawy argues, 'They scared the regime about what was going to happen that day. The April 6 guys came into the picture – around that time that had 70,000 plus members – and the newspapers dealt with it very sensationally.'[52] El-Hamalawy believes that it was that press attention which diverted the group's focus from the real grievances of Egypt's labour community and led them astray. The regime test-drove its strategy of disruption and fear by interfering with the April 6 organizers more immediate follow-up to the initial strike: a strike on May 4, the president's birthday. The message of that strike, though, did not seem to resonate with ordinary Egyptians, and the regime was able to score an early victory. It also did not hurt that the regime had already started harassing and imprisoning the April 6 organizers themselves. What were the exact strategies used by the regime to disrupt the momentum of the April 6 movement?

First, the regime employed the full weight of Egypt's enormous repressive apparatus to harass, detain and deter the organizers and founders of the movement.[53] The first victim of this campaign was the group's public face, Esraa Abdel Fattah, who had helped found the organization and was the lead administrator of its Facebook page. Abdel Fattah was snatched from her home and held incommunicado for two weeks, after which she told the press that she would not be organizing anymore (although she would later return to activism). Abdel Fattah's public humiliation set precisely the tone of remorse, repentance and fear that the regime wanted to establish with the group's main constituency: Cairo-based digital elites. Prominent April 6 leaders Ahmed Maher and Mohamed Adel were also arrested and imprisoned, though not for a particularly long time. How were these individuals treated in Mubarak's torture gulag? The novelist and essayist Alaa al-Aswany describes the 2010 interrogation of April 6 members by a police official named Amr Bey:

> After that Amr Bey settled down in his office, where he interrogated two young men from the April 6 Movement who had been inviting people in the street to come and welcome Dr. Mohamed ElBaradei at the airport. The interrogation was easy because the men had arrived in his office completely exhausted after detectives beat and whipped them through the night.[54]

This 'beating and whipping through the night' was de facto regime policy with anyone it wanted to browbeat into submission. Activists became so afraid of being arrested and disappeared that they started to keep typed SMS messages in their phones, to be sent to human rights attorneys, families and friends should they be captured by the police and sent off to a police cell, or worse, to Tora prison or one of many similar facilities throughout Egypt. This is not to say that the campaign against the April 6 organizer ever became quite so violent and widespread as that against the Muslim Brotherhood, but it was systematic nevertheless. More importantly, many Cairo elites were probably deterred from joining political groups in the first place. A closer look at the actual dynamics of the two strikes might shed some light on the failure of the April 6, 2009 strike, and also anticipate the reasons that the organizers were able to reverse their failure so spectacularly on January 25, 2011.

First, the regime simply made a decision to meet the wage and conditions demands of the striking Mahalla workers who were, as the Sandmonkey argued, the central actors of April 6. 'As for the real heroes of April 6th, the poor underpaid and courageous workers who took a stand that day? Well, they were never interviewed by the media, or the satellite news networks, never were invited to a conference, or were the focus of a news piece. What they were the focus o[f], was the government's vengeance.'[55] Mahalla was only one skirmish in a larger and longer struggle between the Mubarak regime and the labour sector, which saw the number of workers' protests between 2006 and 2007 escalate to 650.[56] At the time, Egyptian organized labour was all under the aegis of the Egyptian Trade Union Federation (ETUF), which was, rather than representing workers' rights, part and parcel of the regime's power structure. Some scholars argued that even under such conditions, labour had been able to wring concessions from the government, but overall the labour movement under Mubarak was repressed and suffered from a lack of autonomy.[57] Starting in 2006, the labour movement attempted to construct trade federations outside the structure of the ETUF, most recently illustrated by the successful campaign of the tax collectors. However, while the movement has seen its fair share of victories, the state made concessions to forestall the kind of national movement that the Mahalla strike seemingly threatened. The government announced a 30 per cent wage hike shortly before the May 4 strike, which seemed to successfully forestall mobilization.[58] Targeted salary increases were also used with certain professions (like doctors) to defuse potentially serious labour disagreements.[59]

Labour organizing and protest, however, would increase even more in the years 2009 and 2010.[60] As Lesch notes, by 2011 '...nearly 2 million workers had participated in organized protests at 3,300 factories or in front of the People's Assembly since 2004'.[61] In the fall of 2008, the regime surely believed that it had diffused the labour crisis. However, considering the role played by organized labour in finally pushing Mubarak out of power between February 9 and February 11, 2011, it is safe to conclude that the regime's strategy ultimately failed even more spectacularly than the April 6 organization's 2009 anniversary strike.

The Limits of Facebook Activism

In the build-up to the April 6, 2008 strike, Facebook accelerated the transmission of the strike meme, because the site connects people with similar interests. SMNs helped construct shared understandings of meaning and action by facilitating easy communication between members of Facebook groups, and by making even passive communication the norm between friends and acquaintances on the site. The original April 6 Facebook group and call to action allowed a large number of Egyptians to participate in meaningful dissent at a very low cost to themselves – bordering on no cost at all. Thus the regime itself was suddenly and unexpectedly confronted with a broad challenge to its legitimacy and ability to control social forces. However, it is unclear whether Egyptians stayed home because they felt solidarity with the workers in Mahalla, or whether they were simply afraid of what might transpire in the streets.

Whatever the truth of what happened that day, the April 6 organizers were given a significant share of the credit by international reporters, and by regime elites themselves. That credit, however, did not translate into a successful follow-up strike in 2009. The idea of an anniversary strike apparently did not persuade potential participants that taking action was worth the risk of the very substantial repressive penalties that could be meted out by the Mubarak regime. In terms of messaging, it also wasn't terribly clear whether the organizers were commemorating Mahalla, or the April 6 action, or both. In the face of both muddled messaging and the sustained regime campaign against the April 6 organizers, most young Egyptians probably took the rational route and chose to let others do the work for them. Social Media Networks certainly do allow diffuse individuals and groups with common interests the opportunity to come together,[62] but those same tools cannot necessarily create the common interests themselves.

On April 6, 2009, organizers once again asked Egyptians to stay home and not buy anything, and to wear black if they left the house.

The *raison d'être* of the strike was to voice opposition to the injustices perpetrated in Egypt since the 2008 strike; against workers but also against the April 6 organizers themselves, which gave the action an almost self-referential vibe. Organizers claimed four primary goals for the April 6, 2009 strike, each of which was problematic in its own way at the time. Organizers sought a new national minimum wage to improve the fortunes of Egypt's poorest workers, asked for prices of staple goods to be indexed to inflation, demanded elections for a national constituent assembly to write a new constitution, and finally wanted the regime to halt all natural gas exports to the Israelis.[63] While these same organizers would, a year and a half later, succeed in starting protests that would lead to a new constitution, at the time the goal was far beyond the group's capability to rally support. The group's campaign for a national minimum wage was also certainly undercut by the regime's success in temporarily buying off sectors of the labour movement and diffusing anger by raising wages in certain sectors. Finally, while the demand to end gas exports to Israel probably expressed a widespread societal consensus, it also served to confuse the central message of frustration with inequality and authoritarianism. It was only when other actors collaborated with the April 6 movement to produce a clear, unambiguous and resonant message in 2011 that digital activists were able to resolve this problem.

Regime Interference with Mobile Activism

The April 6 movement can be said to have awoken the Mubarak regime to the dangers of digital activism in a way that years of dedicated blogging by activists like Nora Younis and Wael Abbas never quite had. The regime instituted a registration and tracking system that made it harder for users to stay anonymous and easier for regime censors and authorities to follow their activities. The state also used its influence over Egyptian telecom companies to ensure that there were no unlimited texting plans at the time, making it extremely expensive to conduct on-the-go coordination and adjustment of protest plans via cell phone. In 2009, the state successfully prevented activists from sending bulk SMS messages to rally supporters and coordinate strategy. Mohamed Adel, at the time one of the main leaders of the

April 6 movement, argued, 'In 2008, we used SMS, we used mobile technology to contact all the people.'[64] In 2009, though, the government was able to block SMS messaging on April 6. This meant that only those organizers and participants who could access relatively new platforms like Twitter were able to send and receive messages, which greatly interfered with organizing and coordination efforts.

Beyond problems of cost and technology, the organization at the time boasted only about 2,000 participating members, according to co-founder Ahmed Maher, which was substantial given the country's repressive context but still far short of the numbers needed to execute a broad-based strike.[65] Foreshadowing what would happen to the April 6 movement after the 2011 uprising, there were already splits between co-founder Ahmed Maher and other groups who wanted to take control of the organization – likely regime elements looking to execute one of their patented hostile political takeovers, similar to how regime functionaries wrested control of the Ghad Party from Ayman Nour in 2007–2008.[66] In rumours that would resurface in 2011, Maher himself was alleged to have accepted $20,000 in cash from the American NGO Freedom House, a group that promotes global democracy but that has often been quietly linked to the American intelligence community. The soft link between the group's co-founder and an American democracy promotion outfit undercut the organizers at a key moment in the organization's development. Activists repeated to me the idea that no matter how well-intentioned, the public connection of Egyptian organizers to American democracy promoters can be poisonous to their efforts in Egypt itself.[67] As the Tunisian activist Sami Ben Gharbia argues, this is due to the perceived hypocrisy of American democracy promotion efforts. He argues:

> There is a strong focus on the Internet control in countries posing serious geostrategic challenges to the Western Interests, with a preferential focus on Iran and China and a near omission of allied states or 'friendly dictatorships' which maintain close ties with the West, such as Egypt, Saudi Arabia, and the Gulf States.[68]

Even after the revolution in January 2011, such accusations and counter-accusations resounded with a public tired of the perceived hypocrisy of American policy, succeeding in splitting the April 6 movement in half.

Egyptian telecoms also began offering, between 2008 and 2009, Internet access through a USB device.[69] For many, this allowed them to circumvent the cumbersome process of having broadband hooked up at home, an uncertain procedure that can take weeks. Via the USB device, connections are excellent, reliable and possible more or less anywhere in Cairo. But the regime instituted a policy of collecting names, addresses and mobile phone numbers for those who sought to obtain these devices. Those devices were thus capable of being tracked by regime authorities through the service providers, with whom they coordinated closely. The regime also began to enforce a policy of requiring Internet café owners to collect information about individuals using their computers – which was problematic because at the time so few Egyptians had Internet connections at home, and the mobile web was only just then becoming widespread. While Internet sellers and café owners were known to cooperate with activists by allowing them to use fake addresses, names and phone numbers, it still presented another hurdle to ordinary users, which is the ultimate goal of most state interference with the Internet. Activists will typically find workarounds, because they are not that difficult to find, and because they have the motivation to do so; ordinary users, however, may be deterred from taking part in risky activity knowing that the regime might be monitoring them. While no single hurdle may be successful, the cumulative effect of these small measures of harassment against ordinary Internet users might frustrate them and prevent them from doing the things the regime fears. Particularly in the context of a small Egyptian digital activist community, removing any number of nodes from that network can ultimately cripple it or at least reduce its capabilities.

Mobilizing and Coordinating during the Gaza Campaign

On December 27, 2008, Israel launched an invasion and bombardment of the Gaza Strip. The Israelis had removed its civilian settler force in 2005, as well as its military forces. However, tensions remained high, particularly after the victory of the Islamist movement Hamas in the 2006 parliamentary elections. As a result of the organization's position on the Israeli-Palestinian conflict, and because of accelerated rocket fire from the Gaza Strip into Israel, a blockade of the Strip was enforced by the Israelis and the Egyptians since June 2007. This blockade was controversial from the outset, and engendered widespread resentment in Egypt as well. It was in this environment that the incursion took place, 11 days after the expiration of a six-month ceasefire between Hamas and Israel that had been brokered by Egypt.[70] The war generated substantial criticism in the Egyptian and global press, and led to the mobilization of protests against the Israeli incursion and the perceived complicity of the Mubarak regime. Such mobilization reflects the same kind of widespread anger that led to protests against the Lebanon War in 2006, or against the Israeli-Egyptian blockade of Gaza in 2008. But the battle between protestors and the state also, in many cases, reflects the success of the state in shutting down protest against the regime's policies, which had been causing resentment ever since the government agreed to help the Israelis conduct a blockade of the Gaza Strip.

SMNs also became important tools in the building of shared meaning. One of the most prominent activities on Facebook was the changing of both profile names and pictures to a first name of 'Gaza'. Doing so was a simple and powerful gesture of solidarity, in many cases reaching out into a social network of friends with mixed or hostile feelings about the cause of the Palestinians. Blogs and video-sharing websites also remained important sites of documentation and functioned as workarounds for a press reluctant to write about the protests. YouTube, for instance, provides powerful documentation of protests in Alexandria on December 28, 2008, in which engineering students organized against the Israeli incursion. Thousands of protestors can be seen.[71]

The government, however, was loathe to admit to this unpopular policy. The Egyptian official press cleverly disguised the prohibition against street demonstrations against Operation Cast Lead. *Al-Ahram*, on December 31, 2008, printed a story with the headline 'Angry responses sweep the streets of Arab capitals'.[72] The story detailed the protests taking place across the Arab world in response to the Israeli incursion. The section dealing with Egypt came first, but instead of details about street protests and mobilizations, the story talked about an announcement from the Lawyer's Syndicate, hardly evidence of an angry response sweeping the streets of Cairo. The Muslim Brotherhood was able to mobilize some protests across Egypt, including ones in Mounifiya, Dimyat, and Fayoum, but overall the security prohibition against protests was effective in Cairo. Even when protestors did manage to take to the streets, such as after Friday prayers on January 2, 2009,[73] their success was short-lived in the face of sustained repression from the regime. Outside of Cairo, though, protestors met with more success. In Alexandria, a demonstration on January 9 was participated in by as many as 50,000 people.[74] Reports indicated that security forces backed off from confronting the demonstrators because of the numbers involved. As a direct result of this protest, the regime arrested 21 members of the Muslim Brotherhood in Alexandria and charged them with organizing the protests.[75] Dozens of Brotherhood members were arrested across Egypt during Operation Cast Lead, as the regime sent an unmistakable signal that the protests had crossed the line.

Even these limited protests mobilized against the Israeli incursion into Gaza cannot be said to have taken place because of SMNs. It is impossible, in fact, to evaluate the actual contribution of these media to the mobilization itself, except by comparison to similar mobilizations that took place in the past. While SMNs have been used to mobilize protest against Israeli policies on many occasions in the past, including the invasion of the West Bank in 2002, the war in Lebanon in 2006, and the ongoing blockade of the Gaza Strip, it remains unclear whether those who attended the protests did so because of SMNs or for some other reason. Large protests against Israeli policies have also been organized by, for instance, the Muslim Brotherhood, an organization that has been quite prominent in its opposition to the Mubarak regime's perceived complicity with Israeli policies. Most media reports of Gaza protests during Operation Cast Lead credit the Brotherhood with their organization, and the group was also behind the January 2008 protests against the Gaza blockade. While SMNs certainly contributed to these protests – Brotherhood members were active bloggers, Twitterers, and emailers – the group remains a grassroots organization whose strength is derived from on-the-ground organizing and face-to-face contact. Another large protest was organized in Mahalla Al-Kubra, the site of the labour unrest that led to the April 6, 2008 general strike.

The evidence from the Gaza episode tells us two important things about the mobilization potential of SMNs in authoritarian regimes: first, while SMNs lower certain collective action costs, it is not at all clear that they lower the most important costs in Egypt and in places like Egypt. While communication, frame-building, and coordination carry substantial costs for any organizer, they are much smaller impediments to large-scale organizing than heavy repression. The precise conditions under which opposition groups might be most successful is a subject which will receive greater scrutiny in Chapter 6. Even a determined state, however, cannot stop activists from transmitting information, frames, and calls for solidarity to international audiences, where they may create pressure on the Egyptian regime. And the Gaza campaign, while ultimately unsuccessful in forcing the government to change its policies vis-à-vis the Palestinians, further emboldened protest forces in Egypt, gave critical organizing experience to thousands of volunteers and further changed the dominant culture from one of acquiescence. The April 6 Youth Movement may not have been successful in its 2009 strike, but their efforts contributed to an atmosphere of confrontation with the regime. The results were not clearly apparent at the time, but additive in nature. Again, just as with Kefaya, while no single instance of mobilizing may have been decisive, they all contributed to a discursive and activist environment that by 2011 allowed for a large-scale and successful mobilization.

Internationalizing but not Mobilizing

This mobilization and activation of international networks of human rights activists can also pressure the governments of authoritarian regimes like Egypt and lend solidarity to strikers, protestors, and prisoners of conscience. Many of Egypt's top bloggers travel frequently to Europe, have contacts in IFEX (the International Freedom of Expression Exchange) and the global human rights community, and either work for or are otherwise active in local Egyptian rights organizations like The Arab Network For Human Rights Information (ANHRI), the Egyptian Center For Women's Rights (ECWR), the Egyptian Organization For Human Rights (EOHR), and the Hisham Mubarak Center. The networked contacts developed by this relatively small cadre of SMN activists reaches far beyond Egypt and into the West, in ways that are sometimes productive and sometimes unproductive (as we have already seen with the April 6 Youth Movement). The blogger and rights activist Mohamed Khaled, who was the first major blogger to post and disseminate the Emad El-Kabir video to a wider audience, is also the program coordinator for ANHRI. He claims:

> We have connections with all the NGOs about specially freedom of expression, we are a member of IFEX this is the biggest network in the world concerning freedom of expression, we have a lot of contacts with other NGOs inside of Egypt and outside of Egypt, we can make a statement and send to the NGOs friends and sign it and campaign with us, we campaign with them, it makes a big media pressure on the government that the government doesn't listen to us anymore, so you get some international pressure on the government that would be more useful.[76]

The Internet thus becomes a crucial piece of local and international NGO activism, since the regime did not have either the capacity or the will to engage in sustained filtering or blocking of NGO Web sites themselves. This means that the sites themselves have become accumulated stores of knowledge and communication between activists and the international community, available to Egyptians with an Internet connection and to anyone in the world interested in what's happening in Egypt. As Mohamed Khaled argued, 'it's opened the door for us, like if you wanted to speak or talk to the people through the newspaper, this can be cut from the newspaper from the government, but there is no censorship on the Internet, we can write about whatever we want.'[77] These organizations now as standard practice compile yearly reports and compilations of documentation of rights abuses. Some of these are only in Arabic (that produced by the Hisham Mubarak Center for instance) and some are produced and translated into English as well (ANHRI provides some of its reports in both English and Arabic, like its yearly report on Freedom of Expression in Egypt).[78]

Scholars noticed this increased internationalization of Egyptian public life. Ghobashy defines it as:

> ...the bargaining and interaction between Egyptian politi-cal actors and two specific sets of international actors: foreign governments and transnational nongovernmental organizations (NGOs) and advocacy networks encompassing the international press and media.[79]

Activists on the ground echo this scholarly appraisal. Nora Younis argues:

> I realized there was a gap between the activism and the media. Most of the activists don't speak English in a way or another there is a communication link that's broken somehow, so I started, I had already some of the numbers of the reporters, and I was SMSing news of who was being released and suddenly it was this list of 800 reporters and human rights activists, cameraman, lawyers and other activists and I was sending mass SMS's. The cell phone and the charger became the most important thing.[80]

This is true whether the goal is labour reform or freedom of expres-sion. SMNs facilitated the transmission of information to global labour networks during the campaign for an independent union of tax col-lectors, for instance. Ties between networked activists like Hossam El-Hamalawy and the global labour movement produced statements of solidarity and individual letters,[81] like the one sent by a branch of the Northern Ireland Fire Brigades Union: 'We totally support the efforts of the Higher Committee for Strike (RETA) in trying to estab-lish a free, independent and democratic trade union structure, to prop-erly represent the rights and interests of ordinary workers and will do all we can to help make your voice heard.'[82] While the tangible benefit of such displays might be limited, anything that globalizes the campaign of internationally marginal workers in Egypt has the potential to raise the profile of the labour movement, which appears to be happening: *Time* magazine's August 2009 story on Egyptian labour unrest details the struggle for an independent labour federation and features an interview with El-Hamalawy himself.[83] Support from abroad may also galvanize workers and organizers struggling to maintain the morale of campaigns.

Conclusions

In evaluating the evidence from all of these cases, one thing becomes very clear: there is a substantial methodological difficulty in attempting to explain the impact of SMNs on protest and collective action in a single-case study of Egypt. There is simply no way to isolate the influence of blog and Twitter posts or Facebook groups on any individual protest that took place in Egypt between 2005 and 2009. These difficulties are why the comparison between April 6, 2008 and April 6, 2009 is so illuminating. It is, methodologically, as close to a natural experiment as you might find in qualitative social science. In each case, the demonstrations, in addition to being publicized, written about, documented, and coordinated online, were also organized by existing political forces on the ground in Egypt, most notably Kefaya and the Muslim Brotherhood. It is clear that the Muslim Brotherhood has consistently put together much larger demonstrations with little help from the toolbox of Social Media Networks. Organizations with deeper social ties to local communities and an interest in the issue at hand will continue to have a mobilizational and organizational advantage over SMNs organized principally around 'issue ad-hocracies' in the sense that the elite, blog-driven protest movement centered around the issues in question coexisted with a much more organic and well-organized protest drive by either the Brotherhood or by the labour movement, both of which possess organizing capacity far beyond the capabilities of even the most well-connected bloggers or SMN activists. This is because, during the period in question, the demands of the Egyptian SMN core were quite diffuse and dependent on day-to-day developments in Egyptian politics and society, whereas Muslim Brotherhood organizing does not depend principally on daily developments, but rather on its core of enthusiastic and risk-taking supporters which it has developed through painstaking organizing over the course of decades. This conclusion is only reinforced by recent events, where it was SMN activists who instigated the January 2011 protests, but it was the Brotherhood and the new Salafist Nour Party that inherited the power once elections were held post-revolution.

The data presented in this chapter supports the contention that SMNs can mobilize short-term protest activity and build linkages between groups and individuals seeking to contest extant issues in Egyptian politics. Data and interview work also support the hypothesis that certain SMN technologies – particularly Twitter posts and SMS messages – have great tactical utility for activists seeking to plan and execute demonstrations, as well as to contest and avoid arrests. This is true even in collective actions organized primarily without SMNs. SMNs reduce certain costs of collective action, including communication and tactical coordination. In rare instances, they may spread information and frames rapidly enough to instigate an informational cascade, but this possibility remains to be demonstrated on a scale which would indicate the clear support of ordinary citizens beyond the educated, urban, Internet-savvy elite. SMNs also facilitate linkages to international groups and organizations who can lend their voices to public discourse and agitate for governments and NGOs to contest arrests, human rights violations, and structural economic and political policies.

The final conclusion drawn from the data presented in this chapter is that SMN-mediated protest and opposition movements must be complemented by grassroots organizing that takes place offline. The April 6 organizers did eventually learn this lesson, as online organization prior to January 25, 2011 was complemented by painstaking on-the-ground preparations, as we will see in Chapter 6. Successful micro-level mobilizations – such as those that took place around the constitutional amendments (2005), the Lebanon War (2006), the sexual harassment problem (2006) and the Gaza war (2007) – demonstrate that is possible to mobilize elite support and contention around issue ad-hocracies, and that the tools of SMNs are critical in raising both domestic and international awareness for these causes, as well as for the coordination of the demonstrations and dissent themselves. Such movements may have been ephemeral, but they contributed to an overall erosion of trust for and support of the Mubarak regime over the past decade. Despite the relaxation in the media environment detailed in Chapter 2, and notwithstanding the very real challenge presented to regime autonomy by the judiciary, other opportunities within the Egyptian political system were quite limited prior to 2011. Those limitations on formal openings drove people again and again back to the power of Social Media Networks. The fallout from the failed strike in April 2009 also had the unexpected effect of revivifying the April 6 Movement itself. Freed from the shackles of staging a demonstration at an inopportune time, the movement was able to refocus its energies on building membership and motivation, and regrouping for a time when a confrontation with the regime might gain more participants and yield greater dividends.

The material presented in this chapter supports the theory that both the mobilizing and political potential of SMNs are context-dependent. In Chapter 6, I will address how those contexts converged to create a moment of true danger for the Mubarak regime, and the ultimate triumph for the activists. However, social media had an additional impact on Egyptian politics and the Egyptian public sphere by creating and sustaining public spheres or 'counter-publics' for marginalized groups like women, religious minorities, and sexual minorities. This chapter argues that the context for the April 6 Movement was generated by political struggles which took place earlier in the decade. Chapter 5 will argue that by creating virtual counter-publics for marginal groups, SMNs can potentially lead to successful mobilizations. It is to those issues that this study now turns.

CHAPTER 5

(AMPLIFIED) VOICES FOR THE VOICELESS: SOCIAL MEDIA NETWORKS, MINORITIES, AND VIRTUAL COUNTER-PUBLICS

Introduction

Chapter 4 explained both the possibilities and limitations of digital mobilization through Social Media Networks. They diffuse information quicker and more efficiently than traditional modes of organization and communication, thereby lowering certain costs of and barriers to collective action, Social Media Networks themselves cannot bring about the revolution unless aided by on-the-ground planning and organizing (as we will see in Chapter 6). If Chapter 3 explained the impact on the media environment, and Chapter 4 explained the impact on mobilization, Chapter 5 aims to explain how both the collective action and media effects of SMNs can combine to impact public discourse. The chapter will explain how, even taking the limitations outlined in previous chapters into consideration, Social Media Networks can impact public discourse and serve as channels for mobilization for marginalized groups in Egyptian society. These effects are realized, as in Chapters 3 and 4, through digitally-enhanced networks of journalists, elite bloggers, and the properties of information diffusion explained in Chapter 2. Again though, as in Chapters 3 and 4, changes in discourse or even mobilization do not necessarily lead to changes in policy. This chapter is crucial for building theory about SMNs, since Chapters 3 and 4 largely detailed the efforts of individuals who can be considered elites (i.e. bilingual international journalists, and educated Cairo-based student activists). Arriving at a theoretically-informed explanation of the impact of SMNs on marginalized groups and individuals will help construct a generalizable theory of Social Media Networks under authoritarianism.

Prior to January 25, 2011, the Egyptian public sphere was dominated by state-owned or state-affiliated sources of media, like the venerable daily newspaper *Al-Ahram* and various Egyptian television outlets including Dream TV. This is not to say that criticism of the government never appeared in the pages of *Al-Ahram* but rather that there were certain red lines that were observed by journalists, as we saw in Chapter 3. Independent newspapers certainly enlivened the Egyptian public sphere beginning in 2003–2004, but their circulation figures were still dwarfed by the state outlets. Even the newest outlets, like the *Youm 7* and *Al-Sharouq* newspapers, as much weight as they may have carried with the activist community, were not widely read by the broader Egyptian public. This set-up made it very difficult for some groups and individuals in Egyptian society to have *stable access* to the public sphere. Some groups were excluded for religious reasons, like Egyptian Coptic Christians and particularly the much smaller community of Baha'is, or it may have been political in nature, as with the Muslim Brotherhood. Since activists began using digital tools for real-world political mobilization in the 1990s, scholars have offered different theoretical explanations for how they might impact politics. Oftentimes they have employed the concept of the 'public sphere' as pioneered by Habermas.[1] Such scholars argue not only that digital technologies offer access to public spheres via 'counter-publics' but also that such access may provide a crucial nesting ground for identities and movement-building. As Palczewski argues, 'Social movement and counterpublic sphere theories have recognized the importance of identity creation and self-expression to the disempowered'.[2] Earlier chapters suggested that these 'voices for the voiceless' are only heard or amplified through critical nodes of elite journalists and bloggers.

Below I will describe how these counter-publics interface with the power-blogging and independent media communities, and how these forces converged prior to January 2011 to produce changes in Egyptian politics – building movements that would provide a preview of the ferment that would sweep Egypt during the revolution.

The findings of Chapter 4 indicate that while Social Media Networks can be important tools of coordination and mobilization, they cannot mobilize in the absence of grassroots organizing. What they can do, however, as noted in Chapter 2, is connect diffuse actors with common interests. To test this proposition, this chapter will explore the role of SMNs in two prominent cases of mobilization and movement-building for marginalized groups in Egyptian society: the case of ID cards for Baha'is; and the growth of websites and blogs dedicated to Muslim Brothers. The chapter will offer answers to the following important questions: 1) Do SMNs create counter-publics for marginalized groups in authoritarian societies; and 2) Can those counter-publics have any impact on actual policy-making decisions in closed societies? The hypothesis advanced here is that SMNs transmit information from electronic public spheres into larger spheres, either national or global, and thereby impact perceptions of subordinated minorities and under certain circumstances lead to mobilizations. They do so, once again, through critical 'nodes' of elite blogger-activists and their connections to the mainstream Egyptian media. The competing hypotheses will be evaluated against the evidence presented below in the hopes of arriving at an explanation and building theory.

Politics in the Online Public Sphere

Inquiries about the role of the Internet in providing access to the public sphere are typically derived from Jurgen Habermas and his seminal *The Structural Transformation of the Public Sphere*. Habermas defined the public sphere as 'A domain of our social life in which such a thing as public opinion can be formed'.[3] As it evolved in Europe in the eighteenth and nineteenth centuries, the public sphere was a space for citizens to come together to debate public affairs; it cultivated an interest in politics among ordinary people, as well as an awareness that those politics could be affected by mobilization and coordination.[4] However, Habermas included some limiting variables – ways that public spheres might fall short of the ideals he outlined in his theory. It is according to Habermas's third principle that online public spheres appear to have the most trouble meeting: that 'ideas presented in the public sphere were considered on the basis of their merits, and not on the social standing of the speaker'.[5] While blogs, chatrooms and Facebook groups are in theory open to anyone, in fact the limited access to the Internet in many developing societies (and even in some economically prosperous states) means that many people are de facto excluded from participation in these public spheres. This is known in the Internet literature as 'the digital divide'.[6]

Dahlberg offers a compelling argument as to why online public spheres fail to meet the criteria originally set out by Habermas. He argues that the penetration of the digital world by corporate entities, the tendency of online deliberation to degenerate into *ad hominem* attacks and the challenges in verifying the truth-value of claims advanced online means that these sites are not truly 'public' in the sense that Habermas intended.[7] To Dahlberg's arguments it makes sense to add Hindman's finding that the American blogosphere is dominated by Ivy League-educated elite men.[8] As Chapter 3 demonstrated, however, such elites, through the dynamics of networks and power laws, can be the critical nodes in the dissemination of information into the wider public sphere.

Still other scholars, despite the shortcomings of online public spheres, describe these sites as either 'virtual counterpublics' or 'cyber-movements'.[9] Nancy Fraser characterizes counter-publics as 'parallel discursive arenas where members of subordinated social groups invent and circulate counterdiscourses to formulate oppositional interpretations of their identities, interests, and needs'.[10] Asen and Brower argue that not only are counter-publics sites of resistance, identity-building and discourse, they can also be critical training grounds for activists seeking to actively contest repression, rather than just talking about it.[11] In Egypt, both Baha'is and Muslim Brothers (as well as other groups like women and Coptic Christians) are challenging received notions of identity and exclusion which have been foisted upon them by the state and its allies.

For marginalized groups, blogs and other forms of SMNs can offer the kind of literary public sphere outlined by Habermas. According to his theory, there can be both literary and political public spheres. As the form of the novel developed out of letter-writing in early modern Europe, citizens were able to glimpse the 'interiority' of other human beings – to see their habits, fears and dreams as similar to their own. As Edgar argues, the development of the novel reconfigured 'the intimacy of the private realm', which rather than an opaque space, become instead 'the authentic space of human existence'.[12] Like Facebook groups, no one with the appropriate financial means could be excluded from reading novels. And in contemporary Egypt, it is the purview of bloggers and Facebook organizers to humanize the Other and to offer citizens a glimpse of the inner lives of marginalized political or social minorities. But these sites offer not just opportunities to see others as human, but also for those others to come together and contest their exclusion. As Edgar notes,

> ... the truth of the public sphere, is realized in the critical examination to which the public sphere subjects government policy and law.[13]

Just as it was difficult for ordinary people in seventeenth-century Britain and France to influence matters of state, it was difficult in pre-2011 Egypt for minorities like Baha'is or persecuted groups like the Muslim Brotherhood to influence public affairs.

In Egypt, these counter-publics are both literary, in the sense that personal blogs allow access to the interiority of marginalized groups, and political, in that they offer diffuse participants the opportunity to collaborate and coordinate on solutions to the problem of their exclusion from the public sphere. For marginalized Egyptians, SMNs 'bypass political or business control of communication' and create 'autonomous process[es] of social and political mobilization that do not rely on formal politics...'.[14] In Egypt prior to 2011, this was critical because normal politics offered so few opportunities for even non-marginalized citizens to influence public affairs.

SMNs may have increased what Maratea calls 'the carrying capacity' of the public sphere in authoritarian Egypt. He argued that 'the emergence of social problems results from a competitive process in which claims-makers vie for public attention by promoting problem claims in public arenas'.[15] In Egypt this process was closed to most people, because of the restrictions on free media described in Chapter 3. SMNs, however, were able to introduce what Maratea would call new 'claims-makers' into the Egyptian public sphere.[16] Bloggers were able to provide traditional media practitioners with 'a trove of available claims'.[17] Because of the limited access available even to existing media in Mubarak-era Egypt, SMNs were particularly critical in their ability to transmit claims from Baha'i and Brotherhood activists to the journalistic elite. It is those linkages between marginalized bloggers, power bloggers and the independent media that this study posits as being of paramount importance in understanding their ultimate impact.

Baha'is and Virtual Identity-Formation

Tiny religious minorities in Egypt have very few ways to protect themselves under Egyptian law. Copts and the few remaining Egyptian Jews can claim some protection as *Ahl Al-Kitab* (People of the Book) but no such special status exists for the Baha'is. The Baha'i faith was purportedly founded in present-day Iran by a man now known as Baha'ullah. Baha'is began to appear in Egypt around 1895, when a religious scholar named Mirza Abu'l-Fadl Gulpaygani was invited to lecture at the venerated Al-Azhar. A very small number of conversions to the Baha'i faith took place, and the community has remained small ever since.[18] In 1924, the National Spiritual Assembly of the Baha'is was established in Egypt, where they were always seen as heretical by mainstream Sunni Islam. Because of their tiny numbers, Baha'is have been quite susceptible to both institutionalized and informal persecution. The Egyptian state does not recognize the marriages of Baha'i couples, and thus, for instance, they are not able to rent hotels or own property. Until 1960, Egyptian Baha'is could make their way through this personal status maze by claiming to be Muslim, Christian or Jewish. Yet even then they were prevented from publicly practicing their faith, a serious restriction on religious freedom.

How does this discrimination manifest itself in public policy? Egyptian identity cards include a line for one's religious faith, and needless to say, listing oneself as Baha'i could lead to detrimental consequences of the sort discussed above. Yet the Baha'i community scored a great victory in March of 2009, when it was ruled that Baha'is could leave this line blank to avoid a host of discriminatory housing, employment and personal status issues. The state maintained that since all other citizens were required to list a religion, the Baha'is should be forced to do so as well. When a lower court ruled in favour of the Baha'is in 2006, state attorneys immediately appealed. In an unusal display of parliamentary cooperation between the NDP and the 88 Muslim Brotherhood MPs, it was argued that the rules should not be changed for Baha'is. Religious Endowments Minister Mahmoud Zakzouk dismissed Baha'ism to the *Daily News Egypt* as 'not a revealed religion' and thus not entitled to protection under the laws of Egypt.[19] At least one MP argued in the subsequent parliamentary debate that Baha'is should be executed as apostates. But in March of 2009, an administrative court sent down a ruling supporting the right of Baha'is to leave their religious affiliation blank on their national ID cards. The first recipient of this right declared it 'a victory for the citizen and the civilization of Egypt'.[20] Of course, this was more of a step in the right direction rather than a case that would ameliorate the problems of Baha'is, since in fact a blank religious affiliation is now presumed to signify Baha'i.

During this skirmish, Baha'i SMN activists, particularly bloggers, played a critical role in uniting the community around the demand for an end to religious discrimination. Among the many goals of this movement was precisely, as argued above, to humanize the Baha'is and to provide them with 'an authentic space for human existence'. As one prominent Baha'i blogger argued about his work:

And since then, I didn't want it to be a blog about the Baha'i Faith, I wanted it to be a blog about a Baha'i person, what does it mean to be a Baha'i in Egypt. I tried so much to keep it personal, I tried to comment on the news from my point of view, not just report the news, and not to go into issues of the Faith itself, it was not my intention to you spread the religion or tell people about the Baha'i faith, just about me and setting the facts straight and answering any misinformation in the media.[21]

His words are a familiar articulation of the *raison d'être* of blogging – to change public distortions and misapprehensions about some particular group, and to offer readers a glimpse into their interiority. Just as Muslim Brothers are exhausted with popular depictions of members as fanatical Spartans who never go to the movies or read books, Baha'i bloggers were sickened by popular depictions of the group as heretical or foreign. Samir Shady, the influential administrator of Egyptian Baha'i, argued:

From the beginning of the blog, I was determined not to write anything far from the basic goal: to present my personal thoughts, as an Egyptian Baha'i...I focused on correcting mistaken thinking seen on blogs and the traditional media.[22]

Shady set about commenting frequently on public affairs, and particularly on the pronouncements of mainstream Muslim religious figures like the Sheikh of Al-Azhar. Shady's posts frequently earned dozens of comments, such as when he lambasted an interview given by the Sheikh to journalists with *Al-Masry Al-Youm* in 2008.[23] Similarly, Wijhat Nazhar Ukhra (Another Viewpoint), a Baha'i-focused blog, used its first entry to claim that it would offer 'another viewpoint to what is published in the Arab media and the Western media'.[24]

Other Baha'i blogs also seemed to have some influence, whether they were composed locally or from abroad. The English-language blog Baha'i Faith in Egypt also rarely attracts comments but still forms part of the community of Baha'i bloggers. It is Egyptian Baha' that seemed to form the hub of the Baha'i digital network.

Baha'i blogs are thus not only political platforms, but also critical realms for identity-formation, for appreciating Baha'i history and building linkages with past generations of Bah'ais. Bloggers who are not powerful or elite in real life can thus become leading members of a smaller, tightly-knit community. They have almost become guardians of Baha'ai history, at least since the National Spiritual Assembly was abolished in 1960, and the official narrators of the Baha'i place in the Egyptian national fabric. One blogger claimed that because of the dearth of knowledge about Baha'ism in communities of younger members, 'stories told to me by adults since I was young' were all he had to reinforce his identity.[26] To articulate their claims against a largely hostile, or at best indifferent Egyptian society, these blogs and the individuals who curate Baha'i history had become of critical importance.

It was no accident that Baha'i blogging took off at precisely the moment that the community engaged the state in a battle over national ID cards. Baha'i Faith in Egypt in fact used its second post to articulate the importance of this battle in the larger context of Baha'i issues. As the author argued,

> Because of this recently instituted computerized national ID system in Egypt, followers of the Baha'i Faith are deprived of their basic human rights, including admission to universities, obtaining birth and death certificates, marriage certificates, driver's licenses, purchasing property, obtaining public health care, employment, obtaining social services, pension and inheritance, travel documents, etc. . . .[27]

Even these relatively well-read bloggers, however, would not have been able to accomplish much without being able to transmit their claims to larger communities – to increase the carrying capacity of the Eygptian public sphere by, as Maratea argues, introducing new claims-makers by way of high-profile events. The burning of Baha'i homes in April 2009 appear to focus this kind of attention on the Baha'i community and offered a rare opportunity for activists to press the issue in the public sphere.

Power Law Dynamics and Baha'i Blogging

As argued in Chapter 2, there are a relatively small number of Baha'i bloggers with any kind of readership, and of course, a concomitant group of power bloggers who support the cause of religious freedom for Baha'is even though they themselves are not Baha'i. Those Baha'i bloggers included Living in Egypt Without ID, Egyptian Baha'i, Wijhat Nazhar Ukhra, the Baha'i blog ring, and more. Their work allows us to build theory about the role of SMNs for marginalized groups in Egypt and places like it.

In Chapter 3, I argued that the small elite of Egyptian power bloggers has a disproportionate influence in Egyptian politics due to their access to traditional journalist elites. While Baha'i bloggers cannot in any way claim this level of influence, either in Egypt or abroad, they did seem to have an impact through attaining buy-in from Egyptian power bloggers and independent journalists. Perhaps the most prominent of these supporters was Nora Younis, who has of course appeared in previous chapters as a champion of various causes in the Egyptian public sphere. In a turn of events that only served to underscore the importance of power bloggers to the cause of marginalized groups, Younis was given the prestigious Human Rights Award by Human Rights First in 2008. The organization mentioned her work on behalf of the Baha'is in its description of Younis and her endeavors. Younis was also praised by the Baha'i blogging community for her work in bringing attention to issues faced by the community.[28] Traditional journalists have also been quick to recognize the contribution of power bloggers like Younis to the cause of Bahai rights. *Al-Masry Al-Youm's* Deputy Editor Ehab El-Zalaky argued to me:

> there is no coverage or negative coverage for this case in the traditional media...some independent TV stations, but no one knows exactly what this thing is about, no one knows exactly what the Baha'i people are, some Baha'i blogs appeared on the Internet, wrote about their religion their faith and their right to choose their religion, this is the first time you can find this kind of expression of views in the Egyptian media at all, and on the other hand, many many of the bloggers are making a campaign to support the Baha'i demands, and they have designed logos to put on the blogs and they are in some cases they are attending some proceedings...like publishing a photographs of the stands

to support the Bahaiis and was led by the bloggers, and was led by a very famous blogger Nora Younis...[29]

It should be noted that Younis and El-Zalaky know one another, and of course El-Zelaky's *Al-Masry Al-Youm* was the only Egyptian paper to send a correspondent to the United States. The purpose of that trip was for the reporter to speak with American Baha'is who were lobbying on behalf of Baha'i rights vis-à-vis the identity cards issue.[30]

It was not just Nora Younis, but nearly the entire core of Egyptian power bloggers who joined the cause of Baha'i religious freedom and who wrote on their behalf. Everyone from Mahmoud Salem (a.k.a The Sandmonkey) to Manal and Alaa and Amr Gharbeia wrote pieces advocating for Baha'i rights. Salem used his prominent platform on December 17, 2006 to tell the tale of one Baha'i man's lonely struggle to get his wife buried. Salem opined, 'Stories like this one are not the exception when it comes to what the Baha'is go through on day to day basis, and things will only get worse for them as time goes by.'[31] Manal and Alaa used their page to distribute a link to the protest on behalf of Baha'is, an image of which appears below.[32] In 2008, they wrote a post called 'Yes, they will f—k your sister' connecting a court setback for the Baha'is with the detention and sentencing of the blogger Kareem Amr and a more generalized deterioration of civil rights in Egypt at the time.[33] (Alaa would later modify his position by asking angrily, 'Why defend the minorities if we can't defend the majority?'[34]) Amr Gharbeia asked readers, 'What should we do after the court prevented the Baha'is from providing their religion on ID cards?'[35] The Arabist, Issandr El-Amrani, posted on December 17, 2006: 'It's sad to see such a confluence of bigotry and Gestapo mentality: the Sheikhs cling onto some abstract idea of what's a religion or not, while the security types are too attached to their system and too obsessed with religion to change the system.'[36] Hossam El-Hamalawy, who would later play such a critical role in the labour uprising, also posted numerous articles and thoughts critical of Baha'i persecution. Prior to a critical court decision in December 2006, El-Hamalawy posted a call to action for all bloggers, which transformed digital dissent from the digital to the concrete.

Digital dissent became concretized for the power bloggers when El-Hamalawy, along with Younis and another blogger named Ibn Abdel-Aziz, showed up at the court and conducted a silent protest after the expected ruling against the Baha'is. This silent protest was a kind of preview of the 'silent stands' conducted by We Are All Khaled Said in the summer of 2010, and provides further evidence of the direct line that can be drawn between blogger-activists of the 2004–2008 period and the Egyptian revolutionaries. Abdel-Aziz used his post that day to challenge a number of factual points in *Al-Masry Al-Youm*'s article about the ruling and the protest.[37] Abdel-Aziz claimed that *Al-Masry Al-Youm* said that the protestors were Baha'is themselves and specifically named Younis as such, in an attempt to obscure the cooperation between Baha'i human rights activists and the non-Baha'i power blogging community.[38] Both El-Hamalawy and Abdel-Aziz mocked the presence of counter-protestors, who they presumed were Islamists, who met the court ruling with undisguised glee. Similarly to how Younis would castigate her fellow Egyptians after the Sudanese refugees incident (which would take place shortly after this court case), the power bloggers took a dim view of the behaviour of the crowd. El-Hamalawy provided an unforgettable description of one woman's execrable reaction to the ruling:

> Another veiled woman, joined in the chanting. 'God's religion is Islam! Bahaai's are infidels! They are infidels! Allahu Akbar!' The woman then knelt and kissed the floor. She then stood up, and continued her hysterical outcry outside the court room in the corridor. 'Bahaai's are the cause of problems in Iraq! They also destroyed Lebanon!!' she kept on screaming. I had no clue what the heck she was talking about, and did not know if I should laugh or cry. It was pure bigotry. 'They are germs in our society!'[39]

These power-bloggers, while they surely did not represent mainstream Egyptian opinion about the Baha'i faith, served as critical nodes in a network of dissent that allowed the voices of Baha'is to be heard, and attempted to correct media distortions (even in supposedly independent

Figure 5.1 Nora Younis and another blogger hold enlarged copies of a Baha'i ID card in protest against an Administrative Court ruling upholding the government's right to deny cards to Baha'is who refuse to select Islam, Christianity or Judaism as their religion. December 16, 2006.[43]

publications like *Al-Masry Al-Youm*). It was not just local audiences that were reached by this explosive combination of Baha'i blogging and power-blogging protest. Foreign reporters also spent a great deal of time on the issue of the Baha'is, especially as their court case wound its way through the system. *The Guardian*'s Brian Whitaker wrote of the ultimate ruling that it was 'a small but important step toward freedom of belief and equal rights'.[40] Liam Stack, at the time a reporter for the *Christian Science Monitor*, penned an article called 'Egyptians win right to drop religion from ID cards'.[41] Even Michael Slackman of the *New York Times* argued that the case represented 'hints of pluralism' in Egypt.[42] The case of the Baha'is and their ID cards thus represents preliminary evidence that even marginalized groups can have their voices heard and affect public policy through blogging and other forms of SMN activism.

Of course the grotesque reactions of people inside and outside of the courtroom prove that this campaign has not yet earned the status of

شهادة ميلاد بهائى بشرطه

Figure 5.2 An Egyptian national ID card with a 'blank' for religion. Courtesy of
Egyptian Baha'i.

an 'authentic space of human existence' provided by the existence of a
literary or political public sphere. Baha'is, because of their small numbers and marginal position, were easily 'othered' by predominant discourses in a political system that offered them no stable access to the
public sphere. Prominent Muslim figures have alleged that Baha'ism
is a 'Zionist movement aiming to spread corruption and immorality'.[44]
It was (and is) a common tactic of marginalization to accuse groups or
individuals of association with the hated Zionists, not just in Egypt
but elsewhere in the Middle East, including Iran. Baha'is are, though,
defended not just on blogs, but often in traditional media as well.
Ahmed Abd El-Maki argued in the pages of *Al-Masry Al-Youm* that
to discriminate against Baha'is is 'an assault on the Constitution and
an attack on Egypt's reputation'.[45]

Through the efforts of Baha'i bloggers, power-bloggers and independent media, the cause of Baha'i religious freedom has gone from

a fringe position to a topic of frequent public debate. The table below tracks the number of news stories about Baha'i religious freedom that appeared in the Egyptian print media between 2005 and 2009. In some ways, it has been a long and important journey.

News Stories About Baha'i Religious Freedom
2005: 7
2006: 87
2007: 45
2008: 84
2009*: 233

SMNs and the Muslim Brotherhood

As one of the most popular political and social organizations in Egypt, the Muslim Brotherhood occupies a radically different position in Egyptian public life than the Baha'is. However, the decades-long political persecution of the Muslim Brothers is quite well-documented, punctuated by a pattern of repression followed by periodic re-integration into public life that has been repeated several times even before the coup that brought the Free Officers to power in 1952. The pattern has been repeated so many times, in such a similar fashion, that the Brothers cannot be conceptualized as part of normal political life in the country; rather, the group has occupied a precarious perch in both civil society and the public sphere, operating on the margins, its leadership hounded into submission, and its young members expecting to serve prison time at some point. In Lust-Okar's 'divided structure' of political contestation,[46] the Brotherhood has found itself both on the inside and outside, but more often the latter. This repression has taken place in spite of widespread scholarly agreement that both the leadership and membership of the Muslim Brotherhood adheres to democratic values and expresses a commitment to the norms of electoral participation.[47]

---

* As of October 23, 2009.

Lust-Okar provides one possible explanation for the Brotherhood's moderation, and the moderation of more radical groups in general. Her theory extends the typical typology of inclusion/exclusion to encompass relations between opposition groups in authoritarian societies. Societies in which all opposition groups are either excluded or included in the political system are termed 'unified' structures of contestation, whereas regimes which include some (typically moderate) opposition forces and exclude other (typically more radical) groups feature 'divided structures of contestation'.[48] The included groups therefore have incentives to preserve their own prerogatives and perquisites within the system. (In important ways this formulation seems quite similar to Brownlee's argument that dominant parties unite fractious oppositions and create a cohesive 'in group' that can withstand outside challenges.)[49] In situations of prolonged economic crisis, included moderates will side with the regime against excluded radicals, and neither opposition group will be able to press its demands with the state. With some variations depending on the situation, this is how the Mubarak regime has been able to exclude the Brotherhood so successfully – by including other opposition groups in the formal political system, and by refusing to distinguish, rhetorically, between the Brotherhood and the more violent, anti-establishment groups like the Islamic Group.

The Brotherhood has surely sensed that it is a group on the outside looking in, despite its popularity, and that to win inclusion in the system it would have to moderate its platform and core beliefs, granting leadership to reformist moderates like Khairat el-Shater. This is the advice the group has been getting from Western scholars and strategists for years, and it is behind the group's willingness, even eagerness to meet with anyone visiting the country – scholars, journalists, graduate students, undergraduates. This strategy, however successful it has been in convincing scholars that the group's behavior has been altered, has not achieved a change in the long-term stance of the regime vis-à-vis the organization; this suggests that the regime was never interested in the ideological makeup of the Brotherhood per se, but rather has always seen it as its most threatening rival for executive power. The regime, therefore, adapted to seek ways to exclude the Brotherhood no matter what ideological stance it took – just as moderate secular groups like Ghad Party were persecuted even though, or perhaps because, they were clearly committed to the rules of electoral democracy.

As part of its campaign of normalization both inside and outside of Egypt, the Muslim Brotherhood, an organization with a well-developed grassroots presence, also features a diverse network of social media sites, including comprehensive Web sites in English and Arabic, Ikwhanweb[3] and Ikhwanonline.[4] While the Brotherhood was a late entrant into the medium of blogging, which was dominated in the early days by secular bloggers writing in English, the organization's bloggers soon became influential both inside and outside the organization,[50] with the young, networked blogging corps having a substantial effect on internal debates in the organization. As Lynch argues, 'In each of the major political controversies surrounding the Brotherhood in recent years, the bloggers have taken an active role'.[51] Lynch argues that the young Brothers were particularly influential in the debate surrounding the release of the Muslim Brotherhood's party platform in the fall of 2007. This platform was released in the context of renewed confrontation between the regime and the organization, as the Muslim Brotherhood appeared to be making great efforts towards becoming a normalized political party.[52] However, to the disappointment of the organization's Cairo-based youth (as opposed to the more conservative youth elsewhere), the draft party platform contained a number of provisions that set off alarm bells for democratic observers. Notably, the platform called for the implementation of Islamic law, prohibited women and Copts from assuming the presidency, and refused to contemplate a separation between a Muslim Brotherhood political party and the organization itself.[53] The element of the platform that was most at odds with the spirit of democratic practice was the idea that senior scholars in the organization might have the power to veto legislation that was deemed to be at odds with Islamic law. Taken together, these elements pointed to a Muslim Brotherhood in turmoil, which refused to take the necessary steps to mollify observers within the regime or potential external patrons. The document appeared to please precisely no one, particularly the young bloggers, who attacked it and debated with one another about the direction the organization should take. However, Lynch notes that even in this internal debate, it is not at all clear that the young bloggers were the key factor,[54] inasmuch as the platform itself was not received well by more important and powerful forces in Egyptian society and international observers.

The bloggers, which are tolerated and even encouraged by the senior leadership, do not appear to take direct orders from the organization. Mohamed Habib was circumspect on this point in an interview, refusing to say whether the organization's bloggers were or were not under control:

> Of course bloggers have a role, first they convey the ideas and actions of the brotherhood to others, which gives us a better image, second they analyze anything bad said against the brotherhood, and they say it from their own point of view and in their own way.[55]

Or as one young Muslim Brotherhood activist told me, 'The bloggers can't be brought under control.'[56] However, despite this enthusiasm, it isn't clear that the more liberal bloggers in the Brotherhood are positioned to take control of the organization. The leadership structure of the organization remains opaque. Bloggers finding their voices within the organization may turn out to be an important element of internal reform, but this impact has yet to be demonstrated. More important still are the organization's two substantive websites, which provide commentary, news articles, and hyper-media content for interested observers. The English-language website is a particularly important resource for international observers, and the organization goes to great lengths to develop journalists for these sites as well as to provide its editors with the resources to maintain them. It is also worth noting that a number of bloggers affiliated with the Brotherhood also double as journalists for the site. As Ikhwan web editor Khaled Hamza says, 'Around 10 bloggers work with us, such as Abdel Rahman Monsour ... they are much more flexible than other journalists.'[57] Even these activities, however, are unsafe for members of the organization. Hamza was sent to prison in 2008 for nearly two months[58] for his stewardship

of the site, and the site's offices have been repeatedly raided by security forces. However, there is evidence that other electronic activities
undertaken by members of the organization have had a more concrete
impact.

One of the most important roles of blogs, the websites and other
SMNs, according to the practitioners themselves, is to reach international audiences with news of oppression against the Muslim
Brotherhood. While domestic press outlets now routinely write about
the state's treatment of the Brotherhood and its leaders, it can still
be difficult to change deeply-entrenched beliefs about the goals and
intentions of the group. As Abdul-Rahman Monsour argues, 'The
government in Egypt doesn't want any government in Europe, western
or anything to know what's going on in Egypt, and we ... explain what
we are doing in Egypt.'[59]

Muslim Brothers, Power Bloggers, and Social Networks

Importantly, the most prominent Brotherhood bloggers and SMN activists are either current or former journalists themselves, giving them
critical social network connections into the world of elite Egyptian journalism. One of the most notable of these journalists is Abdel Monam
Mahmoud, who has been profiled a number of times. Mahmoud began
his blog in 2006, and called it Ana Ikhwan, which translates as 'I am
a Muslim Brother'. Monam told me that he began his blog because
he wanted people to understand more about ordinary members of the
Muslim Brotherhood – that they weren't book-banning, movie-hating
fanatics, but largely ordinary people who went to the cinema, worked
normal jobs, and had the same dreams, fears, and hopes as other
Egyptians.[60] His rationale for beginning a blog was remarkably similar
to Samir Shady's reasons for blogging about Baha'is: at heart, theirs is a
project of political and social normalization, and of counteracting what
they see as popular stereotypes about their respective groups.

The Brotherhood bloggers have drawn a great deal of attention, but
SMN activists have also played an important role in transmitting information about the trials of Muslim Brotherhood leaders in 2007–2008.

Family members began blogs dedicated to their imprisoned loved ones, which became sites of contestation and dissent, as well as online platforms to coordinate action for release. One particular clearinghouse of information was the blog Ensaa!, which translates as 'Forget!'. Ensaa! published accounts of all sessions of the military tribunals by various authors including Abdel Monam Mahmoud and other activists. These pages-long diaries included blow-by-blow accounts of the day's events, as well as analysis and commentary. The blog itself typically featured text accounts and occasionally embedded photographs, as well as sidebars reproducing popular slogans and frames[61] and the main Ikhwan site, both of which published accounts of the trial by Ahmed Abdel Fatteh and others. Fatteh described how he was able to gain access to the trials, even though journalists were banned from entering:

> In the military court, only one journalist can enter, that journalist is me. And I enter like I am one of the family of these people and if they knew I was a journalist I would be under arrest.[62]

Fatteh claims that journalists from international news organizations frequently relied on his accounts of the trials for their reporting. As he told me, 'all the journalists in every newspaper take from us to publish, because you don't have any . . . not newspapers only, like Reuters, BBC, etc., they call me after the session.'[63] International news coverage of the trials appeared sympathetic to the imprisoned leaders of the group; while news reports often hedged about the goals of the organization, they seemed to be careful to note the extra-constitutionality of the trials themselves, and to seek out family members and others for comment.[64] Even briefer items tended to note that observers believed the trials to be unfair.[65] Fatteh's presence inside the courtroom surely had something to do with the positive coverage, and at the least prevented the regime from running the trials without any journalists having first-hand access. International reporters have continued, since the trials, to publish sympathetic articles about the Brotherhood, and to note repression of its activists and even bloggers — in fact the arrest of bloggers gets greater press attention than other forms of arrest, even when the bloggers appear to have been arrested for reasons other than their electronic activism. This was the case in April 2009, when the blogger Abdel Rahman Fares was arrested for distributing materials in support of the April 6 General Strike.[66]

In 2007, the government commenced trials for 40 prominent members of the Brotherhood on charges of corruption. The trials took place in military courts, part of the state of emergency that has remained in force in Egypt since the assassination of Sadat in 1981. While the state has certainly faced threats from terrorism, particularly during the bloody confrontations between the state and armed Islamists in the 1990s, it is clear that the use of the law and the relegation of Muslim Brotherhood trials to military courts is for 'political as opposed to security reasons'.[67] Members of the Brotherhood themselves believe they were targeted at this time because high-ranking officials were beginning to sound more plausible to Western states – with the organization rhetorically emphasizing its commitment to democracy. As Zahra el-Shater told a reporter in 2008, 'My father was taken because he was moderate and liked to open dialogue with Western people, with American people.'[68]

Previous to 2010, the government's strategy rested on convincing the international community that the consequences of handing power over to the Brotherhood could be dire.[69] This became particularly true in the aftermath of 9/11, and even more so after the election of Hamas in Palestine, when the Bush Administration appeared to substantially back away from its democracy-promotion activities due to fears that the scenario could be repeated in Egypt. As one of the lynchpins of the geopolitical status quo between the Arab world and Israel, Egypt has been under very little pressure from the US and its allies to give the Muslim Brotherhood a bigger political role in the region. The government also appeared threatened by the strong showing of the Brotherhood in the 2005 parliamentary elections and the well-regarded performance of Brotherhood MPs in parliament, who became well-known for their stand against corruption and human rights violations within Egypt.[70] While the group's stance on the Israeli-Palestinian conflict (which calls for the abrogation of the 1978 Camp David accord between Egypt and Israel) would likely still prevent the group from being embraced by the international community, the regime was unwilling to take that chance, especially since the reformist leadership, including el-Shater himself, had made statements in the past indicating a more accommodating stance toward the Israeli-Palestinian conflict. If the Brotherhood were to adopt a more moderate tone on the Israeli-Palestinian conflict, it would have removed the Mubarak regime's rationale for continued repression, at least as far as Washington was concerned. A change in administrations in Washington D.C. in 2008 did little to change the calculation that the status quo is more important than risking a transference of power to the Muslim Brotherhood. This dynamic of fear surrounding the Brotherhood continued through the Egyptian revolution of 2011 and afterwards, as fears of participation were transformed into fears of the group dominating a newly-democratized Egypt.

Ultimately, the efforts of activists and bloggers were not enough to offset the regime's goal of punishing the Muslim Brotherhood in advance of elections, and of re-establishing hegemony over the group in the wake of its strong 2005 parliamentary showing. While 15 of the 40 defendants in the leadership trials were acquitted, many more received significant prison time, including seven years for Khairat el-Shater, the group's deputy chairman, five years for five defendants, and three years in prison for 13 others. Others were sentenced in absentia.[71] Despite some mild protests from the Bush Administration, relations with the United States were never at stake over these trials. Had they been, as Brownlee and others argue, it is possible that the regime might have been more careful to conceal the extra-constitutional element of the trials.[72] Even in defeat, however, SMNs transmitted frames of dissent and served as outlets for dissatisfaction with the heavy sentences given to the group's leadership.

The Muslim Brotherhood's English-language site, as noted earlier, is of particular importance to international audiences. As Khaled Hamza put it in an interview, 'Interaction from inside Egypt is very small, but we had a lot interaction from American readers and western websites like CNN and BBC and Washington Post.'[73] The site is probably the best existing resource for reporters not based directly in Cairo, or for reporters in Cairo with limited Arabic capabilities. It also appears that Brotherhood SMN activists have had a great deal of influence on the writing of international human rights reports detailing regime violations of rights, particularly those suffered by members of the Brotherhood. As Abdel Rahman Monsour (who would later found We Are All Khaled Said) told me, 'The torture issue, you would find out that the reports that came up on Ikhwanweb were used by international organizations like Amnesty and Human Rights Watch ... to come up with reports talking about human rights in Egypt.'[74] The state took particular notice of this, seeking to prevent the transmission of human rights violations to international actors by using both traditional brute-force repression (Monsour himself was arrested for recording the activities of security forces in his hometown)[75] and more sophisticated measures, like tracking mobile users through their cell phones. As al-Shammi argued, the mobile phone and its information-transmission capability is 'kind of their own nightmare'.[76] Or as Mohamed Habib put it:

> It definitely makes it harder for the state to impose a blockade on us...Of course, they try to confine them and to prevent them from communicating with others and to reach the world, and we use these technologies to prevent this and to help the group reach the world and to reach the media.[77]

Electronic activists also play a role in humanizing members of the Brotherhood, allowing access to their interiority, in the terms of Habermas. Social media websites like Facebook are one locale for this kind of activity. The imprisoned Brotherhood leader Khairat el-Shater maintains a Facebook page with 655 'fans' (individuals who identify as followers of el-Shater by clicking a link on Facebook).[78] The page includes information about el-Shater and a link to his website, maintained by his son Saad el-Shater. The younger el-Shater posted frequent pieces of poetry, reminiscences of his father, and calls to action on the site.[79] In so doing, for the readers, el-Shater became neither the caricature presented by the state media nor the revered leader of the organization, but rather an ordinary man and father being subjected to extraordinary repression for his political and social beliefs. Still, el-Shater's plight never garnered as much attention in the elite Egyptian blogosphere as did the jailings of other Muslim Brothers.

Figure 5.3 Early photo of Khairat el-Shater posted by his son on the latter's birthday.[80]

In other cases, SMNs helped create focal points and frame align-ments for agitating around imprisoned Brotherhood leaders or activ-ists. When Khaled Hamza, the editor of Ikhwanweb, was arrested in 2008, bloggers came to his defense across the political spectrum, including the radical socialist El-Hamalawy. Bloggers posted pictures of Khaled Hamza accompanied by text calling for his release in posts and sidebars (see figure 5.4 below).

These focal points effectively solved the coordination problem inher-ent in trying to arrive at agreed-upon frames without leadership. They also posted information and accounts of his arrest. Nearly all of the A-list bloggers – Demagh, The Arabist, 3Arabawy, Egypt Watchman (who played a critical role in the Al-Qursaya case) and others – posted calls for Hamza's release and reposted one of the above pic-tures (depending on primary language). These posts served to unite the Egyptian blogosphere around the essential injustice of Hamza's arrest. As Snow et. al., would argue, this is a process of frame align-ment, wherein discrete actors with diffuse interests unite around a common cause.[82]

Figure 5.4 Electronic banners calling for the release of Ikhwan web editor Khaled
Hamza. The text reads "Freedom for Khaled Hamza."[81]

Hamza's arrest subsequently became the arrest of not just another
Brotherhood leader, but of someone who the community of bloggers
explicitly identified with, and his freedom was linked to the general
practices of Egyptian authoritarianism, or as El-Hamalawy frequently
puts it, 'Mubarak's Gulag'.[83] But before we imbue the technologies
themselves with this frame-making power, we should return to an
understanding and appreciation of the importance of social networks.
Hamza was, on El-Hamalawy's admission, a 'friend'.[84] He is personally
friendly with the Cairo journalist elite, since many of Hamza's writers were young, college-educated, and traveled between the Muslim
Brotherhood world and the world of other media outlets. Hamza's case
and the agitation around it seems remarkably similar to the campaign
to free Abdel Monam Mahmoud of Ana Ikhwan, who was jailed either
for blogging or for his political activities. As The Sandmonkey revealed
in an otherwise acerbic post, Mahmoud was friends with the power
bloggers, and not surprisingly, his arrest launched the 'Free Monam'
movement, replete with a website, elite blog support, and international
coverage.[85] The campaign reached the Global Voices platform, and

was cross-posted on the Free Kareem site, dedicated to the imprisoned secular blogger Kareem Amer. Unfortunately, the Free Monem site is no longer operational and all that remains are the links and banners on other sites. What is clear, though, is that the social network connections of the arrested matter in determining whether a campaign for their freedom takes place – particular attention seems to be paid, both in the Egyptian blogosphere and internationally, to journalists and bloggers, whereas ordinary members of the Muslim Brotherhood receive much less attention for their plight, in spite of electronic presences such as el-Shater's family website. The point is that social network connections appear to play a determinative role in coverage by elite bloggers – in other words networks don't just change the diffusion dynamics of information, but help determine which information travels along those networks to begin with.

Of course, it is difficult to look at the question of the Brotherhood from today's vantage point – as of this writing, their new political party had just won a sweeping victory in Egypt's parliamentary elections – and argue that the Brotherhood was a marginalized group. But the treatment of the Brotherhood, and the group's position in Egyptian society, has undergone a radical transformation since the January 2011 revolution. We should not forget that during the long years of Mubarak's tyranny, the group was effectively shut out of public debate, its politicians harassed and imprisoned and its leadership constantly surveilled and circumscribed. During the past decade, it was SMN activists who helped keep the group's sense of identity alive and, crucially, helped change public and international perceptions of the Brotherhood. One could argue that it was that process of humanization that allowed the Brotherhood to escape its caricature as the vehicle of joyless fundamentalists.

Conclusions

The network power of SMNs explains nearly every instance of public policy impact examined in this chapter. These spaces are also, clearly, important arenas of discursive contestation and identity-building, and are seen by their participants as such, even when this kind of writing fails to create a broader and tangible policy impact (such as the web-page for Khairat el-Shater). As has been argued in past chapters, the impact of online writing cannot be understood outside the context of social connectedness in the activist and independent media communities. Connectors or network hubs are far more likely to have their arguments heard, and to organize successful campaigns around particular issues in authoritarian systems like Egypt. Journalists read the power bloggers and used them to generate story ideas. In many cases, these journalists and bloggers were the same people, complicating our understanding of who is a digital activist and who is a journalist. But in any case, their preferences and network connections were critical in building solidarity for Baha'i personal status rights and against military trials for members of the Muslim Brotherhood.

The chapter also reinforces the ideas of Watts and Shirky – that the Internet (and thus digital activism more generally) is governed by power laws that make it easier for some individuals to be heard, and makes it vastly more complicated for non-connected individuals to use these technologies effectively. This is not to say that such use is impossible. As we will see in Chapter 6, it is still possible for new entrants without an established social media presence – like We Are All Khaled Said's Wael Ghonim – to have an impact. But even then these new entrants often require the assistance of connected individuals. Knowing that certain nodes in the information network are more critical than others can help us understand why and under what circumstances digital activists are likely to be successful in their efforts to promote political or social change. Individuals in marginalized publics certainly understand the importance of Egypt's power blogging community. The Wijhat Nazhar Ukhra blog argued: 'I believe that simply calling for this support was an important event in the crystallization of the role played by Egyptian bloggers in the electronic expression of opinions.'[86]

Finally, there is data in this chapter to support the idea that it was a small number of issues and activists which catalysed the January 2011 uprising that swept away the regime of Hosni Mubarak. For both Baha'is and Muslim Brothers, the issues that resonated most were about personal freedoms and human rights issues. Whether you are a liberal, a Salafi or a rights activist, most Egyptians would agree that people should not be thrown into prison indefinitely, or sent to the torture gulag without recourse to a civilian attorney. Baha'i personal status rights, of course, are not something that the entire Islamist community agrees on, but their cause was part of a broader campaign against the arbitrary nature of the Mubarak state, and its inability to protect the rights of Egypt's citizens or even to ensure their basic human dignity. This agreement would prove crucial during the Egyptian revolution that began on January 25, 2011. That consensus – against succession to the presidency by Gamal Mubarak, against torture and arbitrary detention, against the state of emergency – would unite disparate groups of Egyptians long enough to depose the regime. While neither Baha'i nor Muslim Brotherhood digital activists took leading roles in this campaign, both groups contributed to a climate of confrontation with the regime, and taught activists that the state could be challenged on certain issues. And if the state could be challenged about ID cards for Baha'is or detention of Muslim Brothers, why couldn't the regime be challenged more comprehensively? Indeed, following the Tunisian revolution, this is precisely the question activists began asking themselves. The answer to that question was unexpected, and transformed Egyptian politics forever. It is to this series of events that the book now turns.

CHAPTER 6

WE ARE ALL REVOLUTIONARIES NOW: SOCIAL MEDIA NETWORKS AND THE EGYPTIAN REVOLUTION OF 2011

'We created the crisis.'

(Amr Gharbeia)[1]

Introduction

This book has theorized that Social Media Networks change power dynamics in authoritarian regimes primarily through three mechanisms. First, by sharing private information about preferences and commitments, SMNs can alter the individual calculus of revolt, mitigating the 'rebel's dilemma' by assuring individuals that their efforts will not be solitary, and by convincing risk-averse fence-sitters that their contributions to collective action will be less likely to result in injury, death or imprisonment. These 'informational cascades' can lead to sudden and unexpected shifts in behaviour inside authoritarian states. Second, SMNs, through network ties between digital activists and independent media practitioners, can alter discourses around authoritarian practices, spark scandals that rock authoritarian politics, and raise awareness of dissent around particular, widely-shared grievances. Finally, SMNs also serve a more concrete utilitarian function for the organization and coordination of protest itself, lowering costs for group-formation and group-joining to nearly nothing, offering protestors a wide array of tools (from SMS to Twitter) to engage in real-time planning and adjustment, and allowing protestors to reach international audiences with news of revolts even in the event of national media blackouts orchestrated by authoritarian regimes. As this theory was developed in conjunction with an in-depth case study of authoritarian Egypt, it seems fitting that these dynamics did in fact come into play in the winter of 2011. From the standpoint of observing the aftermath of the 2011 Arab Spring, with a landscape that now features at least three new proto-democratic regimes (in Tunisia, Egypt and Libya) and several others tottering on the brink of collapse (including Syria), it should be clear that SMNs were not the only factor at play here. It is in Egypt, though, where the dynamics described in earlier chapters had their clearest influence.

The Calm Before the Storm

In spite of the convergence of traditional media practitioners, organized labour, and SMN activists between 2004 and 2010, Egypt did not appear to be moving towards greater openness and democracy, but rather in the opposite direction. In fact, in the winter of 2010, the Egyptian political opposition, to a casual observer, would probably have seemed quite dead. Despite years of work and organizing, public protestors were rarely able to muster more than a few hundred people for a rally or demonstration. In November and December of 2010, the Mubarak regime set about the political extermination of its parliamentary opposition – it openly rigged the first round of the elections, leading the Muslim Brotherhood and other prominent opposition groups and parties to pull out of the second round. The regime, which had claimed for nearly three decades to be overseeing a long and arduous process of democratization and reform, could no longer hide behind even that fragile rhetorical cloak. The National Democratic Party won nearly all of the seats in the People's Assembly, a shocking departure from the 2005 elections, when the Brotherhood won 88 seats and began to behave like an actual opposition party. With the opposition routed from parliament, the stage was set either for Mubarak himself to run for another term in November 2011, or for power to be transferred quietly to his son Gamal. The Emergency Law, still in force, looked as firmly entrenched as ever, and critics who had dismissed the greater freedoms and opportunities of 2004–2005 as nothing but a chimera, a trick designed to let off some steam before a renewed authoritarian closure, appeared to be proven right. Even the novelist Alaa El-Aswany, who wrote the incendiary *Yacoubian Building*, published a tract in 2010 whose title asked: *Why Don't Egyptians Revolt?* A cynic could hardly be blamed for responding, 'Because they have no hope of succeeding.' There appeared to be a nearly universal understanding that the ability to rise up and depose an authoritarian ruler was simply not part of the Egyptian national character.[2] The Egyptian regime of December 2010 was perched at the height of its terrible powers, its internal security services said to employ as many as 1.5 million agents of state repression who had seemingly succeeded in crushing the Egyptian people's spirit. Shortly after the elections, a deranged shark marauded in the Red Sea, killing several people, terrifying tourists, and distracting Egyptians from the dispiriting reality of their own stagnant politics.

And then, seemingly overnight, Egyptian politics suddenly exploded, along with the expectations and assumptions of a generation of scholars and observers. As with many of the crises of the past decade, the instigators of the events of January 2011 were digital activists, trained in the battles of 2004–2010, featuring some new players but still fundamentally composed of the same network of dissidents that fought the state on harassment, torture and minority rights. Shortly after a shocking revolution swept the Tunisian dictator Zine El-Abadine Ben Ali from power, these digital activists chose January 25 – Police Day in Egypt – for a national protest. Major political forces, including ElBaradei's National Association for Change, many of the opposition parties, and the April 6 Youth Movement endorsed the protests and urged members to participate. Even activists themselves did not have the highest hopes for this day. As the activist Ahmed Saleh says about January 25, 'The day came and I was actually very worried, I didn't think we would have a revolution.'[3] But 18 days later, with tens of thousands of Egyptians camped out in what became known as 'The Republic of Tahrir' and the army essentially watching from the sidelines, Hosni Mubarak resigned in disgrace, unleashing a raucous celebration that lasted all night in Cairo and other cities across Egypt. How could this have happened? How could a ragtag band of activists and tech geeks have brought down the *rayyes* himself – in power for nearly 30 years? And what did it mean?

Khaled Said and the Social Media Convergence

To properly answer those questions, we must return again to the power of SMNs and the networked revolt. In the summer of 2010, a Facebook group emerged that both brilliantly 'leveraged the affordances' (as Yochai Benkler would put it)[4] of social media and built on the dedicated work of anti-torture activists like Wael Abbass, Noha Atef, and Mohammed Mareee. It was fitting that an act of lawless brutality brought this group into existence, and that the out-of-control vindictiveness of El-Adly's torture gulag ultimately brought about its own demise. It is also unsurprising that this group was created by a veteran digital activst. The group was called 'We Are All Khaled Said', and it was created by the Cairo-based activist and journalist Abdel Rahman Monsour, who worked for the Muslim Brotherhood's website when I interviewed him in 2008. We Are All Khaled Said represented another step in the evolution of digital activism in Egypt – from lonely bloggers in 2003–2004 to huge networks adeptly creating resonant frames and calls to action in 2011.

Khaled Said was a businessman in Alexandria, who allegedly posted a video to his blog depicting Alexandria police dividing the spoils of a drug bust amongst themselves. The video itself shows what looks like suspicious behaviour but is hardly conclusive. It is not clear whether Said recorded it himself, or was merely the messenger – if anything, posting it to his blog was by now a routine act of sousveillance – still brave, of course, but not extraordinary, considering what was appearing on the pages of Torture in Egypt and Piggipedia every day. Still, this was to be the last video that Khaled Said would post, and the last blog entry that he would write, though hardly the last to be written under his name. Shortly after this video was posted, police abducted him from an Internet café in Alexandria, beat him savagely in front of witnesses, and then drove off with him. His body was returned to his family several days later, and along with his lifeless corpse, the police deposited the kind of up-is-down tall tale that was truly one of the grotesque hallmarks of modern Arab authoritarianism. According to the police, Said was not killed for posting a video – rather he was a drug dealer who, despondent over his arrest, had committed suicide in police custody by swallowing a bag of marijuana. This patently preposterous story, obscenely unbelievable even had there been no countervailing evidence, was refuted with one look at the photos of Said's body, released by his family. In that infamous photo, Said's jaw is quite obviously broken, his disfigured face hardly recognizable in comparison to the photos of the handsome young man he had been before he disappeared into the torture gulag. The case immediately sparked an outcry, and Monsour's group began operating its Facebook page a few days after Said's story became public. From the beginning, We Are All Khaled Said struck a nerve with Egyptians, in the same way that the Emad El-Kabir case did. Said was not a radical Islamist accused of plotting to blow up tourists in the Khan El-Khalili, but rather an ordinary young Egyptian, whose obvious murder and cover-up prompted many Egyptians to ask themselves: 'If it can happen to Khaled Said, what's to stop it from happening to me?' Monsour was soon joined by the Dubai-based Google executive Wael Ghonim, who brought his marketing savvy to the operation. Monsour began his military service shortly before the Egyptian revolution began, and thus has been unavailable for interviews, but Ghonim has discussed his group's creation:

> A page was created, an anonymous administrator was basically inviting people to join this page. And there was no plan. We didn't know what are we gonna do... It was an amazing story how everyone started to feel the ownership. Everyone was an owner in this page. People started contributing ideas. In fact, one of the most ridiculous ideas was, hey let's have a silent stand, let's get people to go in the street, face the sea, their back to the street, dressed in black standing up silently for one hour, doing nothing and then just leaving, going back home... People are making

fun of the idea, but when actually people went to the street, the first time it was thousands of people in Alexandria. It felt like, it was amazing, it was great because it connected people from the virtual world, bringing them to the real world... There was no leader, the leader was everyone.[5]

We Are All Khaled Said soon staged its first demonstrations, demanding the arrest of the officers responsible for Said's beating and death – and shockingly, this actually took place. But the group was always about more than just seeking justice for Khaled Said – it was about an effort to end the practice of torture for all Egyptians. Thus the group's activities and protests were sometimes deliberately mournful, as in the 'silent stands' mentioned by Ghonim above. Other political forces in Egypt, including the April 6 Youth Movement and the Egyptian Movement For Change (Kefaya), were quick to recognize the symbolic potential of this nascent movement, and these three groups coordinated together almost from the beginning. They organized a June 13

Figure 6.1 Silent Stand in Alexandria[7]

demonstration in front of the Interior Ministry, which was dispersed by force by riot police and resulted in dozens of arrests. As has been the case with many cases of official malfeasance, these protests were initially covered only by independent press outlets like *Al-Dustur* and *Al-Masry Al-Youm*, and were completely ignored by the official press organs *Al-Ahram* and *Al-Gomhoriya*.[6] Notable actions included the July 23 'silent stand' referenced above by Ghonim, in which protesters stood silently facing the sea in Alexandria.

Repeating its past practice of occasionally yielding to bottom-up mobilization, the regime, out of embarrassment or fear, took two of the officers responsible for Said's death into custody to await trial. That trial began swiftly in July, and pro-Said protestors were often met by demonstrators taking the side of the officers (even though these protestors were almost certainly paid agents of the regime) outside the court in Alexandria.[8] Bloggers reported that the signs hoisted by pro-regime demonstrators bore more than a passing resemblance to placards for the ruling National Democratic Party.[9] Mubarak's regime did not appear to interfere directly in the proceedings of the trial, but defense counsel for the accused officers insisted upon their difficult-to-believe version of events, citing an autopsy which confirmed that Said had swallowed a narcotic. Meanwhile, prosecution attorneys called eyewitnesses to the stand who testified that police had savagely and publicly beaten Said, and that they had 'broken his teeth' before whisking him away.[10] The case was postponed in December 2010 and did not resume until after the events of the Egyptian uprising which began on January 25, 2011. It was postponed yet again in the summer of 2011 for a fresh autopsy, in the midst of ongoing ferment in Tahrir Square.

The campaign for Khaled Said could never have been successful without earlier anti-torture efforts by activists like Wael Abbas and Noha Atef. Their work to document and contest the Egyptian 'torture gulag' created the normative environment in which a group like We Are All Khaled Said could successfully capture the public imagination and challenge state authority. The group did not appear out of nowhere like some talismanic *deus ex machina*, and only by understanding the power of Egypt's digital elite to drive discourse and coverage of torture can we understand how We Are All Khaled Said was ultimately so successful. The group was operating in both a critically changed discursive environment – one in which criticism of the regime's torture policy's had become routine – and in an organizing environment that boasted more than seven million Egyptian Facebook users, an exponential increase since the April 6 Youth Movement began its work in 2008. Furthermore, as noted earlier, opposition to torture is an issue that enjoys widespread consensus in Egyptian politics and society, crossing lines between secularists and Islamists, as well as divisions between pro-Western and anti-Western foreign policy elites. It was thus nearly the perfect expression of mature digital activism in the Egyptian polity. Finally, the group was created by a veteran digital activist, Abdel Rahman Monsour, with extensive contacts in both the digital activist and journalist communities. Monsour was able to leverage his connections with this elite.

Vote-rigging and the Spark of the Revolt

In the fall of 2010, with the We Are All Khaled Said campaign in full gear, the regime executed its long-held plan to obliterate the organized opposition from parliament. The regime proceeded with this plan in spite of heightened attention to the elections, including monitoring from the Ushahidi crisis mapping platform. Crisis mapping involves the creation, using specialized software, of a GIS live map displaying the location of the activities in question. Crisis maps were pioneered with a service called Ushahidi in Kenya during the 2007–2008 elections crisis, in which citizens would report abuses or atrocities taking place all over the country; those reports were then collated in a live map. Activist and organizer Bassem Fathy argues that 'Geotagging the [election] violations was the last step before the revolution.'[11] Indeed many of the same individuals and groups involved in digital activism since 2004 were involved in the election mapping scheme, including April 6 co-founder Esraa Abdel Fatteh. The Egyptian version was dubbed U-Shahid, and volunteer monitors filed 2,700 reports with the site during the elections themselves.[12] Volunteers filed reports about everything from companies illegally shipping workers into polling places to vote to 'deliberate power cuts to prevent people from voting'.[13]

Reporters even relayed the precise price of vote-buying at various hours of the day. The result of U-Shahid was a devastating indictment of the electoral process, one that made it clear to observers just how crooked the elections really were.

When the dust had settled on December 5 after the second round, NDP politicians held 93.3 per cent of the seats, and tolerated opposition parties held only 3 per cent.[14] This represented a major reversal in regime policy from that which had prevailed throughout the decade, particularly in the abortive 2005 elections that saw greater openness and participation in response to a number of factors, including US pressure and increased ferment at the grassroots level. The regime was clearly willing to gamble that it could outflank its opposition one more time, to ensure the continuation of the Mubarak family's authority. This delusion lasted less than two months before the events of January 25, 2011 would overtake the election-rigging.

The rigging of the elections proved to be the catalyst for yet another digital innovation, operated through SMNs, that helped upend the Egyptian government. This innovation was called RNN News Network – RNN being an acronym for *Raqib* (Monitor), *Sower* (Record), *Dowin* (Write). As co-founder Abdullah Al-Fakharany tells it, 'We started during the last parliamentary elections. We were just a group of youth, we cared about Egypt.' Al-Fakharany's innovation was not to use Facebook and Twitter to disseminate information about corruption, but rather to create an entire text-only, volunteer news network around the model of 140 characters. Al-Fakharany makes it clear just how intimately the activists understood the properties of the networks they sought to take advantage of:

> We brought cameras inside the rooms [where voting was happening], and everyone who videoed something, vote-rigging, bring it to us and we'll publish it everywhere. And because we are active on Facebook, I have 1,000 friends, so we created a small circle of 20,000.[15]

The multiplier effect of Facebook's network connections immediately created a large audience for RNN's news, albeit a network whose members had no idea that they were about to participate in an innovative news experiment. RNN was the first to report that Zine el-Abadine Ben Ali was headed to Saudi Arabia after fleeing Tunisia (Al-Fakharany claims he had a friend in Jeddah who knew someone important was coming to the airport). While RNN was very much an activist news network – their correspondents were by no means neutral when it came to making or evaluating claims of corruption at the highest levels of Egyptian government – the network still instituted a three-tiered policy of evaluating the trustworthiness of the information they gathered from their dozens of correspondents all over Egypt – 'Not Confirmed' stories were based on information received by RNN's hotline. 'Partially Confirmed' stories were those which received numerous hotline calls detailing fundamentally the same thing. And stories were 'Confirmed' when an RNN correspondent checked in with the information. RNN became, effectively, an institutionalized form of sousveillance, in which non-professional journalists came to perform the watchdog function over the state – the kind of function that traditional media practitioners were unwilling or unable to undertake themselves. RNN can thus be conceptualized as the mature expression of a culture of sousveillance, first developed by practitioners like Wael Abbas and Noha Atef, who broke through red lines about torture and malfeasance. By the time RNN released videos of corruption taking place at Egyptian polling places in November and December of 2011, networked Egyptians had grown accustomed to seeing grainy video footage of state agents committing fraud, accepting bribes, dividing drug busts, beating suspects and torturing. If the first reaction of an Egyptian to a YouTube video depicting such things in 2005 might have been 'What on earth is this?' then the first reaction of Egyptians to such footage today is most likely to be: 'Where did this abuse take place and who is responsible?'

RNN also explicitly conceptualized itself as an activist news network – in other words there was no pretense to impartiality. From the beginning, Al-Fakharany and his colleagues conceptualized RNN as the media arm of a potential uprising. As he tells it,

> We started to focus on motivating people to do something, to never be silenced, to take their rights. We are mainly news but we send a message through the news, by sharing opinion,

by focusing on a speech by activists. In that way you don't say it clearly, but you can send your message in the middle of the news. We have the same idea as the activists, that we want to end the corruption.[16]

It is notable that none of the RNN founders were from among Egypt's power-blogging core, making it clear that new entrants to the digital elite are possible if the value they add is clear and distinct enough. While it has become increasingly difficult for new bloggers to start writing and to get major traffic, the new affordances of the social networking and micro-blogging sites means that it is still possible to go from completely unknown to having hundreds of thousands of followers overnight, as was the case with both RNN and We Are All Khaled Said. While the latter featured a battle-tested veteran of the digital protest movement, the former did not, meaning we should be careful about making sweeping assertions about who does and does not get heard in cyberspace. While Hindman may be correct that it is difficult for new writers to be heard, and that cyberspace tends to be dominated by a small number of outlets,[17] we require deeper theorizing about precisely how new organizations and new individuals acquire status, fame and trust through online social networks.

In between the rigging of the December elections, the founding of RNN and the events of January 25 was the Tunisian revolution. While SMNs played a substantial role in spreading news and information about the revolt (contributing to cascade dynamics), they do not appear to have been foundational in causing the uprising itself – i.e. the date of the protests was not circulated in advance online, as it was in Egypt. The Tunisian revolution was spontaneous and unexpected, the result of a confluence of unlikely events that produced an even unlikelier critical juncture in one of the world's most repressive police states. In Tunisia digital activists played a leading role in publicizing the protests which were sweeping the country, but they did not catalyse or organize them. This is in large part a function of the Tunisian regime's long and determined effort to muzzle digital activism through censorship, rather than repression as in Egypt. It is telling that most of Tunisia's most widely-known digital activists, including Sami Ben Gharbeia, the creator of the group blog Nawaat, were in exile. In Egypt, where mature Social Media Networks were in place to capitalize on this moment of opportunity, and where digital activists were hiding in plain sight of the regime, the story was quite different.

Khaled Said, Frame-Alignment and the Leaderless Revolt

When the time came to capitalize on the Tunisian revolution, Egypt's digital elite debated the various options before them. Activists argue that they always conceptualized 2011 as an important year, since it was likely to be the year of the succession of Mubarak's son Gamal. But the Tunisian revolution presented a unique opportunity to the activists – the Tunisians had proven that even the most ruthless of the Arab dictators could be taken down with sustained, widespread and peaceful direct action. The departure of Ben Ali erased any of the lingering doubt left by the quelling of the Green Revolution in Iran, proving that revolutionaries at least stood a chance against the forces of repression. The Tunisians also provided critical information to Egyptians about street tactics during prolonged confrontations with security services. Long-time activist and blogger Amr Gharbeia, who now works for the Egyptian Initiative for Personal Rights, was there the night that January 25 was chosen as the date. 'It was Abdel Rahman Monsour's idea,' he insisted.[18]

The process of choosing that date can be traced on the group's Arabic page, Kulna Khaled Said, back to December 30, when an administrator identified January 25 as Police Day and wondered sarcastically if the group could help in its 'special way'. The post ended with '*ay rayikum?*' (What's your opinion?). The post received 121 comments and 471 'Likes', which underlines just how widespread engagement was on the page in Egypt. For the following two weeks, the group was engaged in activities revolving around the horrific bombing of an Alexandria church, presumably by Islamic militants. The bombing, which killed dozens of innocent people, further underlined for many Egyptians how the state was more interested in corruption than in protecting citizens from attack. But the group returned to thinking about an Egyptian revolt by January 15. The administrator wrote, 'Today is January 15. January 25 is Police Day, an official holiday. If 100,000 of us go out in Cairo, no one can stand in our way. Can we do it?'[19] After debating on the page whether to move the protests up to January 21, the group began producing slogans for the 25 itself. On January 15, the administrator posted a plea for everyone to write and post pictures of the slogan '*Ha'anzil youm 25 yanayir*' (I will go out on January 25).[20] Later that day the administrator posted a 'letter to the people of Egypt', on how to make January 25 the 'spark of change'. From then on, the group's wall became a clearinghouse of information, frame-building and debate in the days leading up to the revolution. The wall itself serves as an archive of the kind of frame-alignment and focal point creation discussed in Chapter 2. Those frames were produced with minimal interference from administrators. As Bassem Fathy told me, in spite of the presence of administrators on these sites, decisions were taken democratically. 'There is a big myth that there was somebody behind the revolution.'[21]

From Protest to Direct Action

The critical transition in the January 25 uprising was the move from protest – by now a routine occurrence on the streets of Cairo and other cities – to direct action. Hands argues: 'The difference between mass protest and direct action is not always clear, but it can be usefully compared to that between dissent and resistance'.[22] The former involves the public expression of grievances, whereas the latter involves 'some form of intervention or disruption'. While there is no clear evidence that the January 25 organizers envisioned their protests leading to the end of the Mubarak regime, there is circumstantial evidence that they foresaw a more serious confrontation than those staged either by the April 6 Youth Movement over the past several years, or by Kefaya since 2004. Shortly after the uprising began, strategy documents were leaked to the international media, which included, among other things, tactical advice on how to weather a tear-gas assault, how to defend against and beat back the ubiquitous riot police, as well as agreed-upon frames and slogans, including 'The people and the army are one hand'. It was clear that the organizers anticipated, or at least hoped for, some kind of prolonged street confrontation with agents of the state and that they prepared their members for this confrontation, and not simply for a one-off march, demonstration or sit-in. One of the goals of the protests, as delineated in this document, was 'to take over important government buildings'.[23] Thus it becomes clear that while there was no clear internal or horizontal hierarchy between the digital groups who arranged this protest, someone was clearly responsible for deciding upon the goals of this action. The protests may have been 'leaderless' in a broad sense, but both the April 6 Youth Movement and the We Are All Khaled Said group had long-serving leaderships who were responsible for the activities of these organizations.

January 25 dawned, and little activity was seen. Protest organizers feared the worst; that popular stereotypes of Egyptians as quiescent and willing to submit to authority would be confirmed once again. But as the day progressed, the protests picked up. Organizers changed routes and destinations at the last moment to avoid security services, who were already aware of the group's plans. However, around noon Cairo time, several large marches developed simultaneously all over Cairo, and began converging on Tahrir Square downtown. Protesters on Ramses Street, outside Moustapha Mahmoud Mosque in Mohandiseen (which had been the site of the horrific slaughter of Sudanese refugees by the regime discussed in Chapter 3) and elsewhere broke through police cordons downtown – the regime anticipated the investiture of Tahrir Square with great significance, but their preparations proved to be both inept and inadequate. Protesters armed with sophisticated riot advice broke through police lines, and police and security forces proved unwilling or unable to deploy the necessary level of violence against them. It is not yet clear the degree to which social media assisted the protesters at this stage, but the regime appears to have switched off mobile networks downtown very early on. The move toward Tahrir was successful in a very short period of time, and just before 4 p.m. Cairo time, the English language page announced: 'Confirmed: Tahrir Square is now COMPLETELY ours.'[24] While security cleared the square that evening, protesters succeeded in taking it back the following day. [25] If there had been any doubt that this was going to be bigger than a standard protest in Egypt, surely they were erased by midday on the 25th. The regime was likely caught off guard by this shift in the protesters' tactics, despite the ousting of Ben Ali's regime in Tunisia a few weeks earlier. Mubarak had survived for nearly three decades, through protests, a major Islamist insurgency during the 1990s, and a renewed civil society and labour movement throughout the first decade of the new century. It is unsurprising that they believed this would be just another bump on the road to continued authoritarianism.

During the protests themselves, the We Are All Khaled Said pages (English and Arabic) on Facebook remained a clearinghouse for information, exhortations, cautions and advice. On January 29, after some called for violence against Gamal Mubarak (Hosni Mubarak's eldest son and heir apparent), a post read: 'Regarding the Gamal Mubarak Protest idea: There is no other option other than a peaceful protest. Hurting him or even getting out of line, not only it is wrong & illegal but it will also cause us MUCH harm.'[26] The regime decided, belatedly, to shut down the country's major Internet service providers on January 28, hoping that by doing so they could isolate Egyptians from one another and, amid uncertainty, convince fence-sitters to return home and accept the regime's meager concessions. The We Are All Khaled Said page carried this urgent status on January 27: 'BREAKING NEWS: URGENT – Internet has been completely switched off in Egypt by the Egyptian government 10 minutes after AP published this video of the killing of an Egyptian protester by Egyptian police sniper [sic].'[27] In other instances, the group's updates repeated wild rumors and could be accused of fanning the flames of public fear. On January 27, the status read: 'I am not exaggerating: A massacre in Egypt is about to take place if the world doesn't interfere.'[28] Those same updates provided clear evidence that the protesters expected and had prepared for an interruption in both cell phone service and Internet connectivity. In the early evening on the first day of the protests, the group's status read: 'Mobile phone network has now been cut off in Tahrir area. No cell phone network all over Tahrir, Central Cairo area. We temp lost connection with people there. Message to

Egyptian Police: Don't worry, we have prepared other methods for it.'[29] Where this last point was concerned, it was clear that the organizers were not bluffing. The page also served as a coordination mechanism (along with Twitter, of course) for those seeking to bring supplies to Tahrir and other squares. On February 3, for instance, the administrator posted a plea to those interested in bringing food and water to the square to contact the person responsible for logistics. 'He is inside the square, and responsible for the entrances.'[30] Kulna Khaled Said, the Arabic version, also provided readers with workarounds for the Internet blackout. 'For the people asking how I connect to the Internet – I connected with dialup at 07777000 or 07777770. The line is slow and doesn't always work.'[31] Such pieces of advice were repeated not only on Facebook but also on the blogs and Twitter feed of elite power bloggers like Alaa Abdel Fatteh.[32]

Twitter, of course, also played a vital role in the early days of the protest. The service's 'hashtag' function made it easy for organizers and participants to share information with users they did not know personally, and to coordinate tactics and logistics. The planning largely took place on Facebook and offline, but the #jan25 hashtag enabled ordinary Egyptians to participate in a conversation about the upcoming protests. Simply by typing in the hashtag #jan25, anyone in the world could follow what was effectively a live stream of events and reports, unfolding in real time. As Idle and Nunns note, 'Many Tweeters considered themselves "citizen journalists" and made it their mission to get the word out with (usually) accurate bites of information and a flow of videos and pictures.'[33] And even when the Internet was shut off, activists and protesters could post to Twitter (and listen to messages) via a service called Speak-2-Tweet, whereby users dial landlines outside of Egypt.[34]

The decision to shutter the Internet had little affect on the trajectory of the protests, which by this point were quite large and likely out of reach of any attempt to interfere with the technology that had instigated them. Activists also claim that without the Internet everyone was forced to leave home and see what was happening in the streets – thus inadvertently growing the protests. Had the regime shut down the Internet on January 22, it might have been a different story.

But by allowing the activists to proceed with their plans, the regime took a calculated risk that the demonstration would fizzle out, as the April 6, 2009 follow-up strike and many similar planned protests had in the past. The cascade happened not during the call to protest but during the days that followed, when Egyptians saw their fellow citizens on the streets and concluded that it was safe to join them. In a society in which arrest, abuse, detention and torture were meted out to the poor and disenfranchised as a matter of routine, the psychological barriers to joining the (primarily) young, wealthy technological elite on the streets of Cairo were high. But as a We Are All Khaled Said status update read, 'An activists [sic] just said that many poor people never dreamt they can be equal to a policeman. When they saw others standing up to police, they just joined in instantly.'[35] What happened between the shutdown of the Internet and the resignation of Mubarak has much less to do with digital activism than it does with the dignity and persistence of the Egyptian people.

The Internet shutdown was also futile because Al-Jazeera continued its live coverage of the events in Egypt throughout the crisis. Even when many Internet users were unable to access mobile networks, they were able to follow along via the site's live feeds on its Arabic and English web pages. Al-Jazeera broadcasted material directly from citizen journalists, including YouTube videos taken by ordinary Egyptians. They did so in spite of the fact that, especially after 'The Day of the Camels',[36] journalists were increasingly targeted by pro-regime forces for detention and harassment.[37] In addition activists were able to 'piggyback' on the connection of the wireless provider Noor, which because of its extensive usage by business interests, foreign companies, and hotels, was allowed to remain on during most of the blackout.[38]

Organizing the Ground Revolt

The revolt of January 25 has often been described as 'leaderless', but interviews with the activists themselves belie this claim and give support to the theory that 'power bloggers' and other digital elites – whose influence was created and sustained by power laws – were the most important actors in plotting and executing the protests. Far from simply choosing the date, taking to the streets, and hoping for the best, the activists relied on a series of innovative tactics that ultimately helped bring millions of people into the streets. Ahmed Saleh, a founding member of the April 6 Youth Movement, described these maneouvres to me. First, concerned about the number of protesters who might show up, Saleh and some friends traveled to different neighbourhoods in Cairo posing as journalists, and asked people for their opinions of the upcoming protests.[39] Saleh contends that the overwhelming response was negative – people were afraid of reprisals, or they were afraid of failure, or they claimed they couldn't leave their jobs long enough to take part in the protests. But he said that again and again he heard the same refrain when he asked what it would take to get people into the streets. As Saleh tells it, his last question was always:

> 'Would you ever do it?' And the answer was yes, but, I heard it from everybody. The answer was, when everybody else goes out first I'll go. When it is a big day, I'll show you what I'm going to do, nothing will stop me. If it is a real thing, I'll be out there.[40]

Saleh argues that even with the power of SMNs, they did not have the power to put as many people on the streets as it would take to convince these ordinary Egyptians to take part in the protests. So organizers decided to undertake tactical maneouvres on the day of the protests to make the crowds appear larger than they actually were. Though he did not use the words, Saleh's tactics clearly indicate an understanding of cascade dynamics and the necessity of influencing an individual's revolutionary threshold – the idea that an individual's willingness to participate in risky protest activity depends intimately on their understanding of the intentions and behavior of their fellow citizens.

Now, Social Media Networks by their very nature mitigate this problem by providing private information to their networks about the preferences of friends and acquaintances. The Egypt of January 2011 was a vastly more linked-in and dense digital network than even the Egypt of April 2008, and as we know from Reed's Law, the denser a network, the greater its utility. There were nearly ten times as many Facebook users in Egypt in January 2011 as there were in April 2008.

Even conceding the reality that many people who sign up for a protest or join a group are engaging in 'slacktivism', the dramatic increase in the potential number of recruits means that a far larger number were likely to show up on that day, even without taking into account a large increase in the general willingness to protest. And building that network took little conscious action on the part of organizers – rather, as the tools developed and became easier to use, and as Internet use in Egypt continued its methodical growth, the activist network grew accordingly and organically. As Amr Gharbeia notes:

> The blogs required a bit more technical skill, writing skill to be in the community. Now that the social tools have developed enough, the floodgates have opened, people can share, tag things and the network just doubled, tripled in size.[41]

Concurrent with the continued rise in the use of social media was the ongoing and exponential increase in the number of mobile phone users in Egypt. Not only were there many more mobile phone users in Egypt in January 2011 than there were in April 2008, but the devices themselves had continued to advance in sophistication and utility. Of course, the most advanced mobile devices still remain out of the financial reach of most Egyptians. As Jon Agar notes, 'the mobile phone is by far the most expensive object ever to be routinely carried on the person'.[42] But these devices certainly had penetrated Egypt's digital elite. Several digital events appear to have played substantial roles in the development of the protests themselves. The first was the circulation of the call to protest on the We Are All Khaled Said Facebook page. By this time the page had hundreds of thousands of followers, and any démarche from the administrators would reach those followers instantaneously. Even if only a small percentage of the group's members committed to participate, if even 20 per cent followed through, it would be among the largest demonstrations in recent Egyptian history. A young organizer for the April 6 Youth Movement named Asma'a Mahfouz also appears to have influenced large numbers of Egyptians with a video she posted to her Facebook page and which also circulated through email networks in the country in the days before the protest. In the video, Mahfouz addresses the watcher directly, and talks about how she and several female friends went into the streets to protest on January 22, and were not joined by any of their fellow Egyptians and were roughed up by police. She appealed to male honour, arguing that it was the obligation of Egyptian men to protect female protesters who would be risking their honour in the streets on the 25. And she told viewers that if they stayed home, 'you deserve everything that will happen to you'.[43] Together with calls to demonstrate on the main April 6 website, the We Are All Khaled Said page, and the separate page set up for the demonstrations, the protests by January 25 had broad coverage and buy-in in the Egyptian digital community, ensuring effectively that everyone who could be reached by digital means would be reached, and that tens of thousands had already committed themselves to participating in the most serious challenge to regime authority since the 'dirty war' against the Islamists in the early-to-mid 1990s.

But in Egypt, which remains a country where Internet penetration is relatively low, even if everyone who committed to the protest on Facebook actually showed up, it still would not have been enough to fill Cairo's streets. And that forced the organizers to attempt other tactics. As Saleh tells it,

> There is a way to do this, the idea is, imagine a small room. How many people can you fit in a small room? A small room, a small number, it would be crowded. The room cannot take more, so you would assume there is a lot of people.[44]

The decision was thus taken to begin gathering people in the maze-like and narrow streets of Cairo's 'informal areas' – streets that in many cases are too narrow to fit cars and developed in an unplanned process over the past 30 years.[45] By first gathering people in these back streets, far from Tahrir, Saleh hoped with the illusion of density to sway individuals whose thresholds are higher. By the time the march reached Tahrir Square, the organizers hoped, such illusions would no longer be necessary – buoyed by the sight of their fellow Egyptians taking to the streets, even fence-sitters would descend from their homes, offices and shops to take part in the protest. Organizers also believed that security forces would have to stretch themselves too thin to break up these protests while they were developing in the neighbourhoods, and would be forced to retreat and defend positions in more open areas. They hoped to have the numbers and determination to break through whatever cordons were set up by the security forces by the time they reached such a confrontation.

According to other organizers, such plans were certainly not left to chance. Abdullah Halmy, a member of the Union of Revolutionary Youth and a founder of the Reform and Development Party, claimed that organizers went so far as to time how long it would take to march from various points in the city to the big downtown sites.[46] Far from being totally spontaneous, the protests were in fact intricately plotted by the young organizers, who knew full well the kind of security response they were likely to face from Mubarak's forces, and who also knew that some would not come home alive. As Halmy argued, 'The particular thing we understood is that freedom costs blood; if we want freedom we must be ready to give blood.'[47]

International observers were largely pessimistic about the chances of success for the young organizers. After all, in many ways the activists had been down this road before with only limited success. Global newspapers were filled with articulations of why Tunisia was a unique case, and how Egypt's mighty security forces would quell any potential rebellion. Perhaps most importantly, analysts dutifully came forward to worry about what might happen if Arabs were actually allowed to govern themselves, with particular concern expressed about the future of Arab-Israeli relations in a region governed democratically. Robert D. Kaplan, in a *New York Times* op-ed, succinctly captured this reactionary trend when he noted, 'It was not democrats, but Arab autocrats, Anwar Sadat of Egypt and King Hussein of Jordan, who made peace with Israel.'[48] The message of such intermediaries was unmistakable – global elites were at best ambivalent about empowering Arabs at the expense of their rulers. Thus a number of forces appeared arrayed, perhaps impenetrably, against the activists – on the one hand there were the 1.5 million people employed by Egyptian security forces; on the other there were the forces of the global status quo, purchased with billions in American aid and guaranteed by the army's multifarious economic interests, all dependent on Egypt remaining 'stable'. One can hardly blame them for such an assessment, since even after hundreds of protests and strikes over the past six years, the regime remained frustratingly intact.

The protesters would defy these expectations though. Through a loosely-knit and collaboratively produced leadership structure, their committees maintained control of Tahrir Square, even after a brutal assault by thugs associated with the Mubarak regime on February 2 that killed a number of protesters and injured as many as 1,500 in what became known as 'The Day of the Camels'. Because the regime flipped the Internet 'kill switch' three days into the revolt,[49] text-messaging, Twitter and Facebook became much less important for the day-to-day organizing of street action. Unfortunately for the regime, by the time this decision was taken, it was far too late to influence events. If anything, activists claim that the absence of information online led individuals out into the streets to check on what was happening – thus unintentionally making the revolution even bigger. Still, even with easy access to the Internet turned off, Egyptians found creative ways to get the word out. Some dialed landlines and manually updated their Twitter accounts with help from friends outside the country. Others managed to use the Internet at some of Cairo's posh hotels, which as noted earlier, used Noor and remained on nearly without interruption during the revolt.

All of Egypt's mature Social Media Networks played an important role in disseminating information during the revolution, even if the actual coordination of the protests was taking place elsewhere. The thousands-strong Twitter community was vital in coordinating the supply of food, water and other necessities to protest areas. The dynamic within this community was captured almost immediately after the revolution with the publication of *Tweets From Tahrir*,[50] and certainly Twitter took on all the trappings of a community during this time period. Twitter's hashtag function is absolutely critical in this regard. As noted earlier, both the English-language and Arabic-language We Are All Khaled Said pages continued publishing throughout the crisis, providing crucial information to both domestic and international audiences about how events were unfolding. And many of Egypt's leading power bloggers, including Hossam El-Hamalawy and Wael Abbas, continued to post updates throughout the 18 days of the revolution. Perhaps even more critically, citizen journalists, including some from the RNN network, recorded and disseminated some of the most iconic videos from the revolution. One video from January 28 depicts a pitched battle between security forces and protestors on the 'Asr El-Nile bridge. Green trucks from CSF are dispatched to unleash water cannons on the crowd, including during one of the mass prayers which occurred routinely during the revolution. The protest is pushed back temporarily. However, the crowd regains the upper hand, pushing the security forces backwards over the bridge in a moment of triumph – you can even hear the applause at the end from onlookers, after it becomes clear that the revolutionaries have taken the bridge.[51] Such videos gained widespread international attention, and helped spark international demonstrations in front of Egyptian consulates and embassies. Unlike during past confrontations between the state and protesters, the regime was wholly unable to control the information narrative, as posited in Chapter 3.

The General Strike Breaks the Regime

Despite the insinuations of regime elites that the protesters were agents of the West, few believed anything that was being said by Mubarak, his agents, or the state press. If Egyptians wanted the truth, they had merely to tune into Al-Jazeera, whose broadcasts from the revolution were almost non-stop, or to Twitter and Facebook, where activists provided up-to-date accounts of the action on the ground. The revolt proved finally that the power of the Egyptian state to control the narrative during moments of crisis had completely vanished.

However, even with the 'Republic of Tahrir' erected, defended, and increasingly lionized, Mubarak would not budge. It would take even more radical events, largely outside of Cairo, to convince the armed forces to stage their coup against Mubarak. Amr Gharbeia notes, 'Tahrir itself- the 15-day sit in-was the crisis that in the last three days created a general strike, public transit, the railways, the 8, 9 and

10 of February. And those three days convinced the military to stage a coup against Mubarak.'[52] The inability of even widespread and sustained protest to shift power within authoritarian regimes is a distinct echo of the failure of the Iranian Green Movement to dislodge Ahmedinejad and his allies from power in 2009 (see Chapter 7 for further details), and is consistent with the theory presented in Chapter 2. Again, SMNs can help create critical junctures and crises, bring people into the streets and inform local and international audiences about what's happening, but they cannot in and of themselves bring down authoritarian regimes. Of course, internal regime power dynamics can themselves be changed by putting hundreds of thousands of people in the streets, creating economic havoc and causing international benefactors like the US to back away from supporting a regime. However, similar mobilizations took place in Syria and the Obama Administration similarly called for Assad to step down, and yet Assad persists (as of this writing) while Mubarak is gone. The trajectories of the crises created by SMNs remain very difficult to predict.

Mubarak repeatedly attempted to diffuse the crisis with concessions that seemed inadequate to the protestors. On January 29, he announced a Cabinet reshuffle, which was greeted by disbelieving crowds that only grew larger. With Tahrir Square reaching a density of 250,000 people by February 1, Mubarak announced that he would not run for re-election but would serve out the remainder of his term. He also announced that his son Gamal would not run for president. As the Twitter user @ashrafkahlilv noted on Twitter, 'Mubarak's speech immediately rejected'.[53] So this concession too did nothing to satisfy the demands of the protestors.[54] On February 8, the dynamic in Egypt shifted considerably. A number of new unions announced their independence from the ETUF and issued calls for Mubarak's resignation. On February 9, public transportation workers in Cairo announced an open-ended strike and issued demands including the end of Mubarak's regime.[55] Even the actors' syndicate got in on the action, announcing their support for the revolution on February 10 and marching from their headquarters to the Republic of Tahrir that afternoon.[56]

These strikes together amounted to an almost unprecedented paralysis of the country, putting the army's considerable economic assets in increasingly greater peril. With factories shuttered, transit grinding to a halt, and tourists watching from abroad on Al-Jazeera instead of throwing money around Upper Egypt, Egypt was teetering on the brink of a full-scale economic meltdown. And while the inside story of the army's decision to abandon Mubarak has yet to be told, it is clear that the final straw was certainly Mubarak's inability to diffuse the crisis in a way that would not threaten the country's already-fragile economy. As rumors began to leak on February 10 that Mubarak would resign, hundreds of thousands thronged in Tahrir Square to listen to Mubarak's speech live. They waited and waited, and then Mubarak gave another long, rambling, self-indulgent speech in which he refused to resign, reiterating the concessions he had already made. Immediately a defiant roar rose from the crowd, as protesters promised to step up their work on Friday and force Mubarak's departure. That need never materialized, however. At just after 4 p.m. GMT on the 11, Vice-President Omar Suleiman made a terse announcement that Hosni Mubarak had resigned the presidency, and that the armed forces would be assuming power. A different kind of roar erupted this time, one of elation and public joy – the *rayyes* was gone. The people had gotten what they wanted: the fall of the regime, or at least its figurehead. Analysts began to fret almost immediately about who or what would replace Mubarak's authority, but for Egyptians, a day of unparalleled celebration was unleashed.

Social Media Networks Beyond the Revolution

But the revolution had unleashed more than joy – during the heady days of Tahrir, multiple youth groups had sprung up claiming to represent the young revolutionaries. First there was the *I'tilaf Shabab al-Thawra*, the Coalition of the Youth of the Revolution. The largest and most cohesive of the youth groups produced by January 25, the Coalition had competition from the Union of Revolutionary Youth and myriad others. All such groups, of course, made SMNs a central feature of their organizing and public presence, with the Coalition maintaining the largest and most organized Facebook page. It was the Coalition that came to speak for Egypt's youth, in spite of multiple splinterings and internal disagreements about policy. And it was this group that continued to play a leading role in organizing the ongoing protests that gripped Egypt long after Mubarak had departed from the scene. As most expected, clashes between protesters and Mubarak were replaced by battles between protesters and the SCAF – the Supreme Council of the Armed Forces (or as one journalist liked to call it, The Supreme Council of Aging Fools).[57] As winter turned to spring and then summer, activists increasingly regarded their revolution as unfinished and, using their well-established online networks, organized for ongoing protests, marches and civil disobedience to resist various decisions by the SCAF. However, they had difficulty making the transition from dissidents to ordinary political organizers. As Bassem Fathy argues:

> We feel like we have been imprisoned in the cyber world, and we are very skilled in using the internet tools, making videos, at the same time we don't have the skill of reaching out to people directly, to make public conferences, canvassing, I'm afraid that we still have the mindset of dissidents, those who are still in opposition.[58]

The first and most unsuccessful of these campaigns revolved around the SCAF's decision to proceed with a constitutional referendum, confirming changes to several articles of the Egyptian constitution that infringed most egregiously on peaceful assembly, free and fair elections, and due process. Once the constitution was amended, fresh parliamentary elections would be held six months later, and the new legislative assembly would be tasked with writing a new constitution altogether. While this process sounded transparent and open in theory, activists considered it a kind of coup d'état against the forces of the revolution. They argued that those likely to benefit from quick parliamentary elections would be the most organized forces – the Muslim Brotherhood, and cast-offs from the NDP (it was not clear at that point what exactly would happen to former members of the ruling party) – and that those forces would then collaborate to produce a regressive constitution that might imperil the gains of the revolution. The SCAF's hasty execution did nothing to inspire confidence in their ultimate motivation for holding the referendum so soon after the revolution, and with so little preparation, particularly for a country where truly free elections had never been held. Who would supervise these elections? Would external poll monitors be brought in? As became typical with the SCAF, decisions were rarely justified or defended, but merely announced, often on their Facebook page.

For ordinary Egyptians who didn't necessarily jump onto Twitter every day, this was a difficult sell. After all, didn't Egyptians just revolt precisely so that they might be allowed to vote in free and fair elections to determine their own future? Why were the activists now denouncing the process that would lead, through a free and fair referendum, to free and fair elections? Who exactly would write this constitution that was to come prior to the elections, and how democratic would that be? While the 'no' campaign may have had a certain internal coherence, it never appealed to poor and marginalized Egyptians, many of whom had begun to want the activists out of the square (and out of the way) so that the country might resume normal economic life, particularly in terms of getting the tourists back into the country. There is nothing quite like the threat of large-scale unrest to deter package tourists from drifting down the Nile on their way to Luxor. And March was typically the high season for Egyptian tourism.

When March 19 finally came, despite the best efforts of the 'Constitution First' movement led by the activists, the changes to the constitution were approved by an overwhelming 77 per cent. Had the activists' moment passed so quickly, already eclipsed by the very forces that international observers most feared? To their credit, the activists quickly rebounded from this very public defeat, regrouping around a set of unrealized demands from the revolution itself. First, the SCAF had never actually lifted the 'state of emergency' law, one of the key demands of those who led the January 25 Revolution. With the emergency law still in place, civilians were still being tried in military courts. Second, the SCAF had so far done nothing, besides putting Habib El-Adly in prison, to meet demands for the reform of the Interior Ministry and Egypt's vast security apparatus. Finally, to appeal to the great mass of Egyptians who did not care one way or the other about the constitution, activists demanded a raise in the minimum wage, and justice for the 'martyrs of the revolution' (shuhada' al-thowra).

On July 8, the activists launched an open-ended sit-in in Tahrir Square, promising not to leave the square until their demands were met. July 8 is square in the middle of Egypt's unforgiving summer months, and it quickly became clear that the heat, rather than the regime's security forces, would be the primary enemy of the sit-in. Activists Tweeted desperate calls for more water in the square, while the regime seemed content to let the activists burn off their own energy in Tahrir Square. The Brotherhood and even some Salafi forces showed up for the first day of the protests, but they soon melted away, leaving only the digital activists and their strange bedfellows in the form of the families of poor and forgotten martyrs of the revolution. The atmosphere of the square during this time period returned to the carnivalesque – juice sellers, hawkers of revolutionary merchandise and new political groups thronged the square. Activists began to hold Tweet Nadwas – live discussions of sensitive and pressing political topics, with a projector in the background showing a live feed of all the Tweets on the subject, organized by the hashtag #tweetnadwa. While there were rarely more than a few thousand demonstrators at any given time, the crowds picked up at night, and the crowd on Friday July 16 was quite large, numbering tens of thousands. Despite grumbling from local business owners about how the activists were destroying their businesses, the regime appeared to take the potential of the demonstrations quite seriously. On July 13, Prime Minister Essam Sharaf announced the firing of hundreds of police officers, and the reassignment of still more, as part of an effort to begin the restructuring of the Ministry of the Interior. This move did not dislodge the protestors from the square either. As Amr Gharbeia told me on the evening of the 13, for the protestors 'If it's not structural, it doesn't matter.'[59]

With Ramadan looming, most of the activists (literally) folded up their tents and went home at the end of July. However as with most issues, the community was hardly united across all factions, and some groups chose to remain in the square. Sensing an opportunity to cleanse the square of lingering activists, the SCAF sent in forces (including tanks) to the square on August 1, effectively ending what remained of the sit-in.[60] Still, even if one concedes that the victories achieved over the summer were piecemeal, it remains a remarkable moment for Egypt. In a country where any protest at all was entirely illegal until very recently, you had citizens taking to the streets to press their demands through what was, at the time, the only mode available to them – protest politics. Despite oppressive heat, the scorn of much of the elite political and journalist classes, and divisions across the many activist and youth factions, they maintained a presence in Tahrir long enough, and with enough density, to force the regime to back off and to wring some concessions out of the SCAF (it was by this time widely assumed that Sharaf himself had little actual power, however much he might sympathize with the demands of the protestors).

This is not to say that the SMN activists have successfully broken Egypt of its many bad authoritarian habits. The emergency law which had governed Egypt since 1981 was still in effect and the regime had rounded up nearly 1,600 civilians and tried them in military courts since March. But to sit on a curb in Tahrir Square in mid-July 2011, and to simply observe what was happening, was to understand the enormity of the changes wrought by the revolutionaries in January and February. Egyptians who just a year earlier would never have dared to pitch a tent in Tahrir Square, let alone sit underneath banners calling for Hosni Mubarak's trial and execution, did so openly, without apology and apparently without any real fear. Young people who could barely keep a tiny movement like the April 6 Youth Movement together had happened upon a system of what Shirky calls 'collaborative production'[61] that almost magically created security and structure inside and outside the square. To get into Tahrir you had to get past a phalanx of plainclothes (but entirely pleasant) young men, who would pat you down and check your ID before sending you onwards into the square. In other words, the entire authoritarian system of surveillance, information control and fear had been brought down in a matter of months, replaced, at least in Tahrir, with an egalitarian, communal ethic that prized cooperation, non-violence and persistence as the values that could successfully confront and bring down the 'rumuz al-nitham' (the remnants of the regime). Outside the square, elements of that system remained in control, but something had undeniably changed. At one end of the square, many of the digital activists whose exploits were detailed in previous chapters gathered for a Tweet Nadwa – individuals and organizations whose often lonely and unappreciated confrontation with authoritarianism had paved the way for the now-celebrated activists of We Are All Khaled Said and the 25 January. Many of the activists who appeared to be in charge of Tahrir Square were the very same power bloggers whose efforts beginning in the early 2000s helped pave the way for a revolution. They looked stressed from the ongoing battle with the regime, but also imbued with a renewed confidence. And who could blame them? It is rare to see so just and yet so unlikely a dream come true as this. There was special irony in the fact that it was the digital activists – not the Brotherhood – who sparked the crisis that ultimately brought Mubarak down. The regime had focused almost exclusively on disrupting political Islam, and clearly had not regarded the digital activists and their SMNs as a threat to its existence; whereas, at least since the assassination of Sadat, they had regarded the Brotherhood and its offshoots as the most serious rival to the regime.

Of course, there would be further struggles and violence to come in the months ahead, including setbacks for freedom of expression. Coptic Christian protestors were brutally and openly attacked by the military on October 9, as they proceeded to Maspero to demonstrate in front of state TV, and 26 were killed. Alaa Abdel Fattah, who has done so much to advance the cause of freedom of expression as one of the leading lights of the blogger-activist community, was arrested on October 26 on preposterous charges of inciting violence during the military attack on Coptic Christian protestors on October 9.[62] Fresh violence erupted ten days before parliamentary elections were to begin on November 28, killing dozens of protestors and adding to the continued tense atmosphere in the country. Activists maintained their presence in Tahrir through this writing and organized huge demonstrations on the anniversary of the revolution that were attended by all elements of Egyptian political society, some demanding the prosecution of Mubarak, the reform of the Ministry of Interior, and the end of military trials for civilians, and others (notably the Salafis and the Muslim Brotherhood) celebrating the revolution and its gains. The parliamentary elections that began on November 28 appear to have resulted in the dominance of the Muslim Brotherhood's Freedom and Justice Party and a better-than-anticipated showing for the Salafi's Nour Party. As many predicted from the beginning, these activists were not going to inherit the revolution they helped author – at least not yet. But there can be no doubt that the digital activists who organized the January 25 revolts succeeded in increasing the sum total of human freedom in the world, through a combination of audacity, courage, cleverness and fortitute.

Conclusions

The findings of this study of the Egyptian revolution suggest the following conclusions. First, the protests were conceptualized and executed by veteran digital activists, using the networked tools of Social Media Networks. The We Are All Khaled Said movement was built upon a foundation of digital activism and an evolving human rights consensus that brought all of Egypt's leading political and social groups together. Digital activists were able to create the frames and calls to action that led other Egyptians into the streets. That digital organizing was married to a sophisticated ground operation which corrected the flaws of past mobilizations by a) taking advantage of a critical juncture rather than failing to manufacture one and b) preparing strategies to mobilize Egyptians without access to the Internet as well as fence-sitters. The resulting informational cascade brought millions into the streets and, when it triggered a labour strike, finally convinced regime elites to undertake a realignment of power. If this wasn't a 'social media revolution', then there is no such thing. A social media revolution does not have to be a revolution with no other causes or contributing variables – to say that digital media were critical catalysts is not to say that there were no other causes. As Lesch argues, those causes included economic stagnation, ongoing corruption, labour mobilization and the whole panapoly of protest movements that emerged with and after Kefaya.[63] Only by understanding the history of digital activism in Egypt – including the processes by which elite bloggers attained their status as arbiters of public discourse, and the movement of digital activism away from blogs and toward Facebook and Twitter – can we understand how digital activists were able to successfully execute the protests on January 25.

Theorists of social media are often caricatured as arguing that the technologies themselves will somehow magically ignite revolutions in authoritarian countries. It should be clear from the narrative presented here that no such argument is being made about Egypt. Clearly the moment that led Mubarak off the stage was created not just by the properties of digital media technologies, but also by grassroots organizing and protest, by years of frustration on the part of ordinary Egyptians, by the efforts of organized labour, by coordination with independent media elites, and finally by a split within the ruling regime that led Mubarak to lose whatever support he had left inside the military apparatus. The regime itself contributed much to its own demise, principally by remaining uninterested in the plight of its destitute majority, investing its billions in failed development schemes, rapaciously privatizing the public sector and allowing its security forces free rein to detain, torture and murder with almost total impunity. In other words, a more competent, less repressive authoritarian regime may very well have survived the successive mobilizations of organized labour and digital activists.

Egypt's digital activists were perfectly aware of their own limitations in relation to the broader society of which they were a part. The theory presented in this book seeks to explain the influence of these digital activists in a context of low Internet connectivity and authoritarianism. Through the networks they built with independent media practitioners and with organized labour, activists were able to overcome their own marginal position in Egyptian society to spark an unlikely confrontation with an entrenched authoritarian regime. The link structure of the Internet helped create and maintain a cadre of elite bloggers whose importance far exceeded the limited reach of the Internet in Egypt. These elite bloggers, who burnished their credentials with hard work and activism throughout the decade of the 2000s, were granted generally less attention during and after the revolution because of the presence of We Are All Khaled Said and April 6, but they were just as important in the overall picture. The evolution of digital activism in Egypt simply brought new actors and groups into the ecosphere of protest. But without the work of pioneering bloggers, the events of January 2011 would never have been possible. To grant Social Media Networks some of the credit for this confrontation is not to imbue them with predictable causality under all circumstances, but rather to appreciate the very real and stable advantages they gave to activists in Egypt and countries like it. One of the lessons of this study is that we should not take a technologically deterministic approach to understanding the use of SMNs, in Egypt or anywhere else. Outcomes still depend on political, social, economic, and even natural forces, which can't be predicted in advance, and which we will almost certainly struggle to understand if and when they are unleashed.

This book began with a story about a Facebook group, and asked how that group might impact politics in Egypt. I believe the answers have been provided here. Even in 2010, we knew that the Mohamed ElBaradei Facebook group could do many things – alert individuals to the preferences of their friends and acquaintances, build shared meaning about ElBaradei's presidential candidacy, even disseminate calls to action and facilitate debate. However, we also knew that levels of commitment to this group were likely to be quite low, and that without organizing on the ground by committed individuals with ties into the non-networked mass of poorer Egyptians, it was unlikely to play a direct role in any succession crisis. We simply could not predict the long-term consequences of this kind of networked, public dissent. These media – particularly those written and analyzed in Arabic – give us an important glimpse into the everyday workings of Egyptian society, and give their users the means of expression and organization which they have long been denied. Even a savvier regime than Egypt cannot fully shut down this discourse, nor can it predict the consequences of its flowering. In short, there can be no revolutions without revolutionaries. But neither can there be authoritarianism with no means to control information. In Egypt, the regime of Hosni Mubarak fell pray to a fatal combination of networked activism and popular dissatisfaction, an outcome that surely terrified the world's remaining authoritarian rulers. For the digital activists who orchestrated those protests, it was an unparalleled triumph. Their lonely and dangerous organizing throughout the 2000s was often mocked as ineffectual elitism, even though it frequently earned them detentions or beatings at the hands of the police. But after the revolution, whatever its ultimate course, this small group of courageous individuals could finally say that they had changed Egypt, and by extension, the world.

CHAPTER 7

CASCADES, COLOURS, AND CONTINGENCIES: SOCIAL MEDIA NETWORKS AND AUTHORITARIANISM IN GLOBAL PERSPECTIVE

Introduction

Thus far this book has theorized and confirmed limited but substantive changes in Egyptian politics as a result of Social Media Networks, and examined the way that those networks (and those changes) contributed to the massive mobilization in January 2011 that led to the downfall of Hosni Mubarak's regime. Chapter 2 established the mechanisms by which Social Media Networks reduce the amount of private information about the preferences and behaviour of other individuals in extended social networks in authoritarian environments, thereby triggering informational cascades that meet individuals' revolutionary thresholds. Chapter 3 argued that Social Media Networks, with the aid of independent journalists and global rights activists, created informational cascades that led to media events inside Egypt, restructuring discourses on sexual harassment, torture, and refugees. Chapter 4 demonstrated the utility of Social Media Networks for short-term collaboration, cooperation and coordination under conditions of severe repression, but also explained why large-scale mobilization required either an external shock or ties to popular grassroots organizing, even in the event of informational cascades. Chapter 5 demonstrated the discursive potentialities of Social Media Networks for groups without stable access to the public sphere in authoritarian societies. Chapter 6 extended these insights to provide a historically-grounded and theoretically informed account of the Egyptian revolution. In Chapter 7, I seek to apply the theories outlined in the preceding chapters to the broader universe of authoritarian societies, engaging the very limited literature on the subject, and offering some preliminary expectations.

From the preceding study, we can surmise that the most pertinent variables when gauging the impact of Social Media Networks appear to be as follows:

1) the capacity and will of repressive forces;
2) the presence or absence of independent media practitioners in the authoritarian public sphere who can transmit the claims of elite bloggers and SMN activists (i.e. the open or closed nature of mediaspheres);
3) the mobilizing capacity of SMN activists;
4) the relative level of connectivity to the Internet in a given society.

For our purposes, I will define 'high connectivity' as 25 per cent or more of the population having access to the Internet – anything below that will be defined 'low connectivity'. For definitional purposes, open mediaspheres are ranked as 'free' by Freedom House, contested mediaspheres are 'partly free' and closed mediaspheres are 'not free'. Highly repressive security apparatuses are 'not free' in the Freedom House rankings, while moderately repressive regimes are 'partly free' and non-repressive apparatuses are 'free'.[1] Pertinent rankings for the project are presented in the table below.

This chapter will use the measures compiled by Freedom House to categorize states according to media and political freedom. And to best test this confluence of variables, I will apply the theory to the following out-of-Egypt cases: the mobilization against the 2009 presidential election results in Iran; the change of government in Ukraine in 2004; the mobilization around contested election results in Kenya in 2008 and the so-called 2009 'Twitter Revolution' in Moldova. These cases were selected for the following reasons: first, they include two cases in which

	Egypt 2008/2010	Ukraine 2004	Moldova 2009	Iran 2009	Kenya 2007
Political Freedom	6/6 (Not Free)	4 (Partly Free)	4 (Partly Free)	6 (Not Free)	4 (Partly Free)
Media Freedom	59/60 (Partly Free)	68 (Not Free)	66 (Not Free)	85 (Not Free)	60 (Partly Free)
Internet Access*	15.4% /22.1%	<5%	19.7%	48.5 %	8.5%

Figure 7.1 Relevant rankings, Freedom House. Internet access figures from Internet World Stats

mobilization succeeded in changing governments, and two in which those efforts failed. These cases have been extensively detailed through case studies by journalists and area specialists and offer rich data in the form of first- and second-hand accounts of the events in question.

This chapter should also provide a framework for evaluating competing theories of the durability of authoritarianism. Lust-Okar argues that divided structures of contestation (SoC), whereby certain groups are included in, and certain groups excluded from the political sphere, provide a more stable means to withstand economic crises. As she argues, 'where incumbent elites have fostered a division between legal moderates and illegal radicals, moderates become less likely to mobilize the masses and demand reforms as the crises continue'.[2] While Lust-Okar's theory was geared toward economic crises, there is no reason it cannot be evaluated against the political crises to be explored in this chapter. Brownlee, meanwhile, argues that the presence of a robust ruling party serves as a channel to satisfy elite demands and leads to regime stability during crisis situations, challenging the idea that 'strong opposition movements can simply push elites out of power'.[3] These two theories overlap partially, but not fully. Both theories anticipated Egypt being perhaps the most durable authoritarian regime under consideration here (indeed these theories were drawn at

	Divided Structure of Contestation	Unified Structure of Contestation
Robust Ruling Party	Egypt	Moldova
No Ruling Party	Iran	Ukraine, Kenya

Figure 7.2 Party and contestation arrangements in the cases.

least partially from case studies of Egypt). They would also anticipate Ukraine, and Kenya, neither of which had robust institutional ruling parties, as the most susceptible to unrest. However, Lust-Okar would likely argue that Iran's divided structure of contestation would successfully pit Iran's included and excluded elites against one another, whereas Brownlee explicitly expected Iran to be susceptible to elite divisions during moments of crisis. This chapter will seek to provide evidence for and against these competing theories.

The theory advanced by this project posits the idea that SMNs are most useful for short-run coordination and communication during times of strife. It also argues that such moments are most likely to arise in competitive authoritarian regimes, centered around elections. This can be formulated in hypothesis form as:

H1: Social Media Networks can trigger informational cascades even in the tightly-controlled media environments of authoritarian regimes

They are able to do so because, as Mary Joyce argues, 'the networked nature of the digital world allows for people to communicate and take action outside of – and sometimes in opposition to – traditional hierarchical power structures',[4] or as Castells would put it, to wield 'counter-power'. My theory indicates that the networked structure of SMNs – whether on Facebook or on cell phones – vastly increased the speed of diffusing information, particularly across social clusters, and also decreases the costs of creating and sharing that information. SMNs shrink the already-small worlds of human social networks, and reduce the barriers erected by authoritarian regimes to open information sharing. They can trigger informational cascades, as outlined in Chapter 2 and tested in Chapters 3, 4, 5 and 6. Those informational cascades can take many forms – in Egypt on April 6, 2008 and again on January 25, 2011, it meant the swift diffusion of information about and support for a sympathy strike on Facebook, and then subsequently through the public sphere. This chapter will evaluate the ability of SMNs to trigger informational cascades in other settings – primarily during the course of power struggles following contested elections in competitive authoritarian regimes. I also argue that the technologies by themselves will be unable to ensure the desired change in power, or to affect serious change in the face of sustained institutional resistance to activist demands. In other words, SMNs are likely to generate substantial press coverage, and to facilitate protest and organization. Such linkages are likely to be not just between individual activists within authoritarian regimes but also between activists and international journalists and elites. This generates the second hypothesis:

H2: Competitive authoritarian regimes with contested mediaspheres are more likely to be the sites of SMN-mediated activism.

Where individual moments of mobilization go from there, however, depends on domestic press environments and elite commitments to repression. Chapter 3 argued that it was the presence of an independent mediasphere in Egypt that made it possible for online informational cascades to generate press coverage and contestation in the real world. Therefore I argue here that countries with independent media outlets are more likely to be the sites of informational cascades triggered by SMNs. This leads to the third hypothesis:

H3: SMN usage will have little effect on the ultimate outcomes of struggles in authoritarian countries

If the expectations of this hypothesis are correct and SMNs have little to no effect at all, we should expect SMNs to play marginal roles in the unfolding of events in competitive authoritarian regimes. In the cases that follow, I will seek to disentangle the role attributed by popular press outlets to the technologies from their actual effects on the ground in authoritarian regimes. Overall these hypotheses are designed to lead to better understandings of when and where Social Media Networks are likely to generate successful activism, and to challenge technological deterministic understandings of new media activism which assume positive outcomes for digital activism. They will also shed light on ongoing debates in the study of authoritarian durability.

H4: SMN activism is likely to generate greater repression.

In a quantitative analysis, Whitten-Woodring argues that by providing sources of information to regime elites, independent media outlets can actually lead to greater levels of repression.[5] If this is true, it must also be true that increased use of SMNs for organizing and protest might lead directly to repression. Therefore, I posit a trade-off between the openness of SMNs and regimes' ability to use the information that's easily attainable from those SMNs for repressive purposes. We should thus expect repression to increase in tandem with the success or perceived success of the activists themselves. The null hypothesis would be that levels of repression are constant.

SMNs and the 'Green Revolution' in Iran

On June 12, 2009, the Islamic Republic of Iran held elections for the presidency, which turned into what Abbas Milani calls 'an electoral coup'.[6] Iran, an authoritarian regime which is considered 'unfree' according to the Freedom House political and media variables identified above, holds regular, competitive elections for the presidency. The Supreme Leader and the Guardian Council, an unelected body of religious leaders, nevertheless possess what amounts to veto power over the candidacies of individuals, severely curtailing freedom of competition for the executive. The elections themselves ultimately come down to different candidates approved by the Guardian Council competing for control over an unusually weak presidency. Nevertheless, Iranian elections are spirited

CASCADES, COLOURS, AND CONTINGENCIES 185

affairs that engender heavy turnout by regional and global standards, and which take on many of the trappings of fully democratic executive elections. In past elections, reformist candidates have been unexpectedly elected, ushering in periods of hope for greater reform. However, because the Iranian president possesses quite limited power in the context of the regime itself,[7] those hopes have been frequently dashed, particularly with the election of Mohamed Khatami in 1997. Khatami was seen as a reformist, someone with whom the international community and particularly the United States might work.[8] While some détente occurred during the Clinton Administration, it is widely felt within Iran that overtures made towards the United States after 9/11 were rebuffed by the Bush Administration. The election of Mahmoud Ahmedinejad in 2004 was seen as both a rebuke to the reformers and a repudiation of the Bush Administration's continued refusal to engage even reformist elements in Iran in dialogue. In 2009 the sitting president, Mahmoud Ahmedinejad, battled challenger Mir Hussein Mousavi in what observers expected would be a close election that nevertheless favoured the incumbent. On election day, it became clear that the result was bound to be contested, as allegations of fraud preceded the announcement of election results that showed Ahmedinejad an overwhelming victor. Almost immediately, forces of the opposition began to organize protests and send reports out of the country via blogs, videos, and Twitter.

The scenes of protest, violence, and chaos inside Iran captivated global audiences for weeks. Theatrical elements like the chanting of *Allahu Akbar* from rooftops (the same cry that was heard after the 1979 revolution)[9] only served to make the events more dramatic to international audiences, where sympathies were almost entirely with the protestors. Millions of protestors took to the streets to demand new elections in the kind of informational cascade theorized in Chapter 2 and in accordance with the first hypothesis presented above. The two defeated candidates, Mousavi and Mehdi Karroubi, led the movement, which was dubbed the 'Green Revolution' since many protestors wore or carried signs, garments or banners in that particular colour. The United States government, while refusing to intervene in the situation, condemned the Iranian regime's crackdown on the protestors. 70 individuals were killed in the ferment following the events, according to movement leaders, but the protestors were unable to repeat the election. Supreme Leader Ali Khameini certified the election in August, and Ahmedinejad assumed office for another term. However, while protests tapered off, they continued to flare sporadically during the months following the election, as the protest movement, once awakened, seemingly would not die. With explicitly anti-regime protests banned, the movement according to the BBC has '…adopted the tactic of using the relative safety of officially-sanctioned demonstrations on important days in the religious and political calendar to come out in big numbers and turn the official rallies into a show of force of its own, with an entirely different and opposing set of slogans.'[10] Protestors commandeered Quds Day – typically a demonstration of solidarity with the Palestinians – for their own ends. Typical of this tactic were the protests that occurred on the day of Ayatollah Ali Hossein Montazeri's funeral.[11] Montazeri had been known as a critic of the Iranian regime. This most recent flare-up took place in December 2011.

What has been the contribution of SMNs like Twitter to these events? As the Egyptian activist Ahmed Abdel Fatteh writes, one of Twitter's great advantages is the multiple channels of access it offers to its updates. Because you can receive Twitter updates on your cell phone, and make Twitter updates through mobile telephony as well as the Internet, regimes must eradicate multiple channels of communication at the same time to put a stop to updates that take place via Twitter.[12] The Iranian regime even threatened Twitter users with prison if they used the site to disseminate information about the uprising; however, users continued to rather unapologetically use the site for this very purpose. One further advantage for Twitter users is the ability to update the site through mobile telephones and to hide the user's phone number.[13] Given the sheer number of individuals posting Twitter updates at any given time, the regime's task effectively became impossible – it simply could not carry out the delicate task of maintaining order while simultaneously repressing individual Twitter users who numbered in the tens of thousands. This is how and why Iranian Twitter users became the primary source for on-the-ground updates during the events following the elections. But the multiplicity of access points to the service is not the only reason it was so useful during the Iran events – more useful than other tools like blogs and Facebook.

Another substantial factor for Twitter is the service's filtering and crowd-sourcing potential, achieved through what are known as 'hashtags'. By placing the symbol "#" before a subject tag, users can aggregate posts around a particular subject area, and thus spread information out of network. So for instance the tag '#greenrevolution' can be used to aggregate posts by users on that subject – even users who do not know one another and are not connected as 'friends' as you must be for similar action on Facebook.[14] The particular hashtag adopted by the Green Revolutionaries was '#gr88'.[15] Hashtags eliminate the need for interested observers or participants to spend time and energy collating information.

The international press certainly noticed the prominence of Twitter during the post-election tumult. Year-end press round-ups inevitably mentioned the Iranian election protests and Twitter's role therein as one of the defining events of 2009. One paper even called 2009 'The Year of Twitter'.[16] With their own journalists barred from the country, news organizations relied on the Twitter reporters and their interlocutors for information. This is in spite of the fact that it was unclear how much Twitter was being used by Farsi-language activists, since Twitter did not support Farsi at the time.[17] Some reports even included a reference to the case of the imprisoned American journalist who Tweeted his way out of prison, mentioned earlier. During the initial stages of the aborted revolution, CNN's correspondent Octavia Nasr was reading the Twitter posts of Iranians live on the air.[18] In addition to Twitter, individuals seeking information about the day's events turned to Facebook, where groups sprouted and where Mousavi's 'fan' page soon had more than 50,000 members.[19] International tech elites, some of them located as far away as California, helped collaborate with Iranians to provide proxy servers, which avoid the regime's blocking of certain websites and ISPs.[20] As Jonathan Zittrain told the *New York Times*, 'The qualities that make Twitter seem inane and half-baked are what make it so powerful.'[21] Zittrain is referring to the very short messages that Twitter allows users to send, which made it easy to dismiss from the start as a boutique service that allows people to broadcast mundane updates about their daily activities.

The accelerant for all the press coverage of Iranian Twitter users, however, was not the Iranians but rather their supporters in the elite global mediasphere, particularly the British-born American blogger Andrew Sullivan.[22] Sullivan's blog became a 'one-stop shop' for all updates out of the Iranian Twitter universe, and gave support to media claims that Twitter was responsible for the protests themselves, or at least a critical component of them.[23] Sullivan used his very well-trafficked English-language blog to post update after update from Iran, many simply cut-and-pasted or translated directly from the source material. Of particular importance were the bilingual bloggers and Tweeters, who could act as mediators between the Farsi-language mediasphere and the English-speaking Western world eager to consume bytes of information about what was happening in the streets of Tehran. In many cases, these intermediaries were Iranian political exiles in the ever-growing diaspora who engaged in 'flooding the country's throttled Internet and heavily controlled airwaves with news, videos and insight.'[24] One Washington-based Iranian exile, using YouTube, claims that more than 500,000 Iranians had seen the daily videos he posted to the video-sharing website.[25] The Iranian case appears to corroborate findings in Chapters 3–6 about the importance of elite bloggers (domestic and foreign), particularly well-connected, multilingual local bloggers.

Ultimately, however, the mobilizations against the elections were unsuccessful in forcing the regime to relinquish power, and as of January 2011, the situation appears to be more dire than ever. International journalists and observers belatedly took note of the inability of the tools themselves to affect actual change on the ground. Mozorov has dismissed ineffective Facebook and Twitter campaigns as 'slacktivism'. He defines slacktivism as when 'our digital effort make us feel very useful and important but have zero social impact. When the marginal cost of joining yet another Facebook group are low, we click "yes" without even blinking, but the truth is that it may distract us from helping the same cause in more productive ways.'[26] As the *Daily Telegraph*'s Will Heaven noted in an acerbic December op-ed, 'There has been no revolution in Iran'.[27] Heaven went so far as to argue that the government's sophisticated cyber-security techniques were greater than the activists' ability to resist or evade them, and that the Internet might be a boon to the regime's repressive efforts as much as it is an aid to the activists. As if to underscore this concern, Twitter was hacked in December by a group that may be affiliated with the regime. And there is no question that the government used Twitter to monitor the activities of protestors.[28] Indeed as time wore on, and more and more members of the opposition were arrested, some for their activities online, it looked like the usefulness of Twitter had run up against the trade-off between openness and repression to which SMNs are subject in such environments. With no independent media to speak of in Iran (which receives the lowest Freedom House ranking for press freedom),[29] no one in the country was able to contest this crackdown.

To explain the subsequent events, we must rely on the more familiar theories and explanations from comparative democratization. With the executive unified and with 'softliners' unable to exert control over the armed forces, the Green Revolution has so far petered out, far short of its goal of a new election. This conclusion to the summer's events had nothing to do with the mobilizational capabilities of the technologies themselves and everything to do with larger institutional arrangements in Iranian politics and society beyond the control of SMN activists or even Mousavi himself. Milani, for instance, situates the ongoing protests within splits internal to the regime.[30] Boroumand, on the other hand, locates the success of the protests in organization undertaken by civil society groups over a period of years.[31] While the US took a number of steps to informally side itself with the opposition, Mousavi's history also suggests that the US foreign policy elite was not convinced that his government would be substantively all that different from the one that currently rules. But even had the US been convinced that Mousavi would have represented a break with the Iranian status quo, it is unclear if anything concrete could have been done to support the opposition. The regime's dedicated security forces – particularly the Revolutionary Guards – seemed unwilling to defect to the opposition. Absent such a defection, the means of violence remain in the state's hands, no matter the volume of Twitter posts at home and admiring blog posts from all quarters of the international elite.

Tent Cities, Elections, and the Orange Revolution in Ukraine

In the winter of 2004, shortly after the bitterly-contested US elections narrowly won by George W. Bush, the world was transfixed by what appeared to be a similarly bitter and narrowly-won contest in Ukraine. The election, which broke down along ethnic lines as well as political ones, featured Party of Regions candidate Viktor Yanukovych – the successor to post-communist dictator Leonard Kuchma and the favorite of both Russia and the ethnically Russian Eastern Ukraine – in a very close election against the opposition candidate, the independent Victor Yuschenko. Yuschenko was aligned with the US and the EU, and favored NATO membership for Ukraine, while Yanukovych was supported by Russia and favored a more eastern orientation.[32] Ukraine at the time was considered 'partly free' by Freedom House.[33] The period following independence from the USSR was marked by continued autocracy under Kuchma, as well as intense economic dislocation during the transition to a more market-oriented economy. By 2005 the economy, measured by GDP, was still far below the level of 1989, creating widespread dissatisfaction with the government, and resentment against economic elites.[34]

In addition to its bitter ethnic features and high-stakes democratization implications, the election featured a sinister plot against Yuschenko that seemed straight out of a Hollywood thriller. Only months before the election, Yuschenko fell gravely ill after a dinner, and it was later determined that he had been poisoned, probably by forces of the regime.[35] Yuschenko, who had been a handsome, dashing young reformer, was transformed seemingly overnight into a brittle older man, and it was said that he was in so much pain that he traveled during the campaign with a spinal painkiller IV. Of course, there are still dissenting voices who suggest that Yuschenko was not poisoned, and that it was part of a stunt by opposition forces. The truth of the matter is difficult to determine, but there is no doubt that the poisoning allegations added an element of theatricality to the proceedings, and generated widespread sympathy for Yuschenko. On election day, official returns gave Yanukovych a narrow, 54 to 46 per cent victory, which was immediately charged as suspect by neutral observers. Opposition forces rallied and set up camp in downtown Kiev, in Independence Square. And there they stayed, in the unforgiving Ukraine winter weather, for 11 days and nights, the crowd growing to as many as 500,000, camped out in tents, surrounded by the uneasy security forces of the regime. They demanded not an immediate revolution, but merely a repeat of the election, since by that time the actual results were greatly in doubt. Still, it was clear that simply giving the election to either candidate at this point would have caused a massive crisis of leadership legitimacy, since both camps would have regarded the election as stolen.

A re-vote was eventually granted, and Yuschenko emerged victorious. Observers dubbed the events in the Ukraine the 'Orange Revolution', and the tactics of the Ukraine protestors would be mimicked and adopted in places as far away as Lebanon and Iran – the coordinated colour campaign, the non-violent street protests, and the demands for new votes after crooked elections. (These tactics, and the scholarship they have inspired, are far from uncontroversial. As David Lane argues, 'The literature on these phenomena, however, is often journalistic in approach, partisan in orientation and normative rather than objective in content'.)[36] Bunce and Wolchik call this 'the electoral model', which they define as 'a distinctive and unprecedented set of activities that are consciously designed to maximize the prospects for an opposition victory at the polls. . .'.[37]

What was the role of SMNs in the election contest? Michael McFaul's oft-cited argument that the Orange Revolution 'may have been the first in history to be organized mostly online'[38] is bold but so far largely unsubstantiated in precisely the same way that Iran's 'Twitter Revolution' is a finding in search of empirics. Goldstein argues that Ukraine, while a competitive authoritarian regime, nevertheless featured a mainstream media environment that was almost entirely controlled, directly or indirectly by the regime.[39] One prominent method of control was self-censorship, punctuated by occasional acts of violence by the regime against the opposition. A climate of fear was reinforced by the 2000 murder of Georgiy Gongadze, an opposition journalist who used the Internet as a platform for dissent. Gongadze's murder, almost certainly at the hands of Kuchma allies, sent an unmistakable signal to opposition journalists that pursuing the truth could put their lives in danger. However, it also spurred such journalists to continue using the Internet as a site of dissent, and in the years between Gongadze's murder and the 2004 elections such online news sites (as opposed to blogs in other locales) grew in importance, despite the tiny number of Ukrainians using the Internet at this time.[40]

Goldstein uses the Katz and Lazerfield Two-Step Flow model of information – in which the mass media influences a select few opinion leaders, who then influence their friends – to come to essentially the same conclusion that this book arrived at in Chapter 3: bloggers and online journalists can still have immense importance in a society even if very small numbers of people are online. This is due to the influence of 'Online Political Citizens', people who consume blogs and online information sources and then disseminate that information to mass publics. In Egypt this happened through the independent media, whereas in the Ukraine the argument is that it happened through existing social networks. Observers of the Ukraine revolution also believe that the existence of independent media outlets played an important role in the events, with McFaul going so far as to generalize the existence of independent media as a direct causal contributor to all of the so-called 'colour revolutions'.[41]

Goldstein also argues that the protest group Pora made particularly good use of the Internet before, during and after the elections. In particular, the well-developed network of text-messages was activated early in the crisis and played a significant role in organizing and coordinating the tent cities which played such a vital role in bringing international attention to the plight of the Ukrainian protestors.[42] Sites like the online opposition site Pravda[43] provided real-time updates as protestors across Ukraine (including groups outside of the capital city of Kiev) set up their own tent cities and joined the growing protest movement. This is similar to the role played by the We Are All Khaled Said network in Egypt before and during the uprising. Goldstein ends his research note with a question: 'are these tools inherently conducive to the expansion of civic engagement and democratization, or will authoritarian governments adapt the technology to their own advantage?'[44] The answer to this question, explored more fully in the conclusion to this chapter, argues that the efficacy of SMN activism depends deeply on institutional features of existing authoritarian regimes.

The technologies themselves cannot explain the defection of the Ukrainian security services, nor the refusal of the Kuchma government to unleash violence on the protestors. The regime could conceivably have chosen to break up the protests before they reached the level of hundreds of thousands. It was the diffusion dynamics of SMNs (which helped generate the initial gatherings), together with the fateful decision to allow the protestors to camp out in Independence Square, gathering momentum and international press attention, that probably doomed the regime's attempts to rig the election. This lends substantial support to my first hypothesis, as well as to the second. It may also have been Western support for the favoured opposition which tipped the scales against the regime, providing support for my third hypothesis (that outcomes are independent of mobilizations themselves). The apparent lack of repression of activists, though, appears to contradict the fourth hypothesis – that levels of repression will increase with greater use of SMNs.

The Twitter Revolution in Moldova

In April 2009, the Communist Party of Moldova (PCRM) appeared to sweep parliamentary elections. Moldova was one of a handful of remaining post-Soviet states that were still ruled by the vestiges of the *ancien régime* – vestiges which had actually returned to power via what were considered free elections in 2001. But since that time, Moldova's democratic situation has deteriorated.[45] This backsliding, which accelerated after 2001, took place despite sustained democracy-building efforts by European organizations.[46] Similar to many post-Soviet states, Moldova is divided by a rivalry between a Russian-speaking minority (in this case concentrated in the breakaway province of Transnistria) and an indigenous majority. This conflict has been so potentially destabilizing that the EU has not promoted membership for Moldova. There seems to be a consensus that offering incentives for EU membership positively affects the level of political and civil rights in Eastern Europe.[47] This conflict has manifested itself in electoral politics via the support by ethnic Russians for the PCRM and by younger Moldovans (ethnically Romanian) who support opposition parties. In practice, this split is almost identical to the split between European-oriented Western Ukraine, and Russian-oriented Eastern Ukraine. In the April 2009 parliamentary elections, a coalition of opposition parties also claimed victory and accused the communists of rigging the elections by fabricating votes by people who had left the country (impoverished Moldova has a very high rate of emigration, particularly to EU-member and neighbour Romania). The opposition parties differed on many issues, including the relationship of Moldova to Romania (some parties like the Liberal Democratic Party (PLDM) want to reunite with Romania) but they all shared a fundamentally pro-EU outlook that clashed severely with the eastwards orientation of the PCRM.[48]

The capital of Chişinău was soon gripped by the kinds of organized people-power demonstrations that took down regimes in Ukraine and Georgia. Natalie, the woman credited with organizing the protests, claims not to have had any idea that her call to demonstrate would resonate with so many people. As she told *The Guardian*, 'we expected at the most a couple of hundred friends, friends of friends, and colleagues.... When we went to the square, there were 20,000 people waiting there. It was unbelievable.'[49] Such a swelling from initial low expectations to sudden mass protest can only be characterized as an informational cascade. The low barriers to the transmission of information on SMNs meant that Natalie's message reached a huge number of people instantaneously. Aware of their friends' preferences and intentions (the revelation of private information), individuals were therefore more likely to act on their desire to contest the fraudulent elections. In other words, the diffusion of this information increased expectations of turnout to protest, thereby meeting the revolutionary thresholds of individual protestors.

While the official media cloaked the events in a shroud of silence, word spread, both within Moldova and outside the country, via the now-familiar pathways of Twitter, YouTube, and text messaging. Observers estimate that as many as 30,000 people descended on the capital's center to express their dissatisfaction with the results. As in Georgia, however, the demonstrations were not entirely peaceful, as demonstrators stormed and then burned down the parliament building. Still, a report from the OSCE (the Organization for Security and Cooperation in Europe) argued that the April parliamentary elections had been fair, while members of the opposition denounced Russian influence in the OSCE.[50] In any case, the communists remained in power and commenced a massive crackdown on the opposition. Activists and journalists were arrested. The regime tightened control over the media, expelled foreign journalists, and blocked access to Romanian media sources.[51] However with only 60 of the 101 seats in parliament, the communists were unable to secure the election of a new president as per Moldovan law.

The opposition managed to block the election of a new communist president, an impasse which continued for months as then-President Vladimir Voronin continued to rule. Because of that, new elections were scheduled for later in the summer, and in fact did take place. However the street presence of the opposition gradually waned, as the EU appeared to throw its support behind the legitimacy of the elections. The crucial fulcrum shifted then from the activists in the streets to the opposition members in parliament, whose demands for a new election had to be met. In the meantime, however, the putative organizer of the flash mob that led to the burning of the parliament building went into hiding. Natalie Morar, who had been thrown out of Russia for making print allegations about the murder of a prominent Russian central bank leader, apparently also feared retribution from Russia, which sided with the regime.[52] While she later returned from hiding, a cloud of legal uncertainty remained over her head.

Security forces appeared quite ineffectual overall, however. The ruling party held fast at first but over the course of the summer, as global attention was fixated on Iran, it eventually relented and agreed to new elections. While still winning a plurality of votes, the Communists were unable to maintain their grip on power, as a coalition of opposition parties cobbled together enough victories to unseat them. While the 'Twitter Revolution' in Moldova hasn't received nearly the level of attention as similar events (perhaps because Moldova is an impoverished country of five million people that is both strategically and culturally marginal), the events of 2009 are no less instructive about the effects of SMNs on political outcomes. The regime's initially successful attempt to retain power appears to corroborate hypothesis 3 presented above; that informational cascades triggered by SMNs are not predictive of outcomes.

Indeed, the Moldova case highlights the enduring importance of authoritarian institutions. While the state, on paper, still possessed the capability to deploy violence against its own citizens, it lacked the will to do so, at least in the long run. Clearly SMN activists in Moldova were no more clever or brave than their counterparts in Iran – their success was not due to short-run contingencies or unique strategies like the burning of government buildings. As Schell argues, power comes not when violence is deployed, but rather when individuals act together in concert.[53] The case thus confirms the importance of SMNs for reducing the costs associated with the collective action problem.

Conversely, the success of non-violent action depends not on the characteristics of the actors but rather on the unwillingness or inability of the state to defeat them violently in the streets. While the state employed moderate violence (including a handful of fatal casualties), it was certainly capable of greater harm. After the events, the Moldovan president, Vladimir Voronin, expelled the leader of the National Democratic Institute, a Washington-based NGO that was involved in many of the other 'colour revolutions'.[54] However, the degree to which the NDI was actually involved in the Moldovan unrest is difficult to determine. If anything, in this geostrategic backwater, the state could conceivably have cracked down violently with little to no consequences from the international community. Certainly, even in the context of wrangling with Russia (which may have influenced the case of Georgia and certainly had influence in Ukraine), Moldova was of far less consequence than Ukraine. Therefore international variables alone cannot explain the outcome here. In fact, because the 'revolution' appeared to fail at the outset, observers appear to have drawn all the wrong conclusions from the events. Writing in July 2009, just months after the initial unrest, Mungiu-Pippidi and Munteanu drew the unsurprising conclusion that 'The Moldovan case underlines the lesson that democratization cannot make progress in strongly unfavorable external environments'.[55] Because Russia was so invested in the success of the Communists, this line of thinking goes, activists were powerless to affect a non-violent transfer of power to the opposition

However, if the PCRM remained in control of events and the security services, why were new elections ordered? Why submit to opposition demands for new elections when they could easily have simply foisted a new Communist president on the opposition by fiat? This is a question that Mungiu-Pippidi and Munteanu left unanswered. Clearly, though, there are steps that even parties and factions allied with Russia are unwilling to take in the light of international attention. In fact, subsequent events demonstrate that oppositions can in fact make headway in spite of 'strongly unfavourable external environments'. Those events also underscore the reality that, in such situations, SMNs can influence the coordination and execution of protest and can reach outside observers and media organizations with their work, but cannot fundamentally control the shape of subsequent decision-making processes. Those decisions depend on, among many other things, contingent decisions of relevant actors, which can be explained within the elite decision-making models of Schmitter and O'Donnell, and Przeworski.[56] Again, as with Iran, the attribution of the revolution to Twitter alone can lead to dangerous misunderstandings of the actual capabilities of these technologies. What, for instance, would have happened if Yanukovych had won his run-off with Yuschenko? Would the Orange Revolutionaries have put another 500,000 people in the streets until they obtained the desired result? Don't both cases, in fact, demonstrate the same outcome? Perhaps the Russians, nervous about the thousands of Moldovans in the streets, about the potential involvement of Romania and the EU in its Transnistria problem, submitted to new elections, figuring that as long as they controlled the breakaway province, their interests in Moldova were more or less assured. In other words, let us not reify our understandings and preconceptions about the geopolitics of these transitions – three of which now, the Ukraine, Georgia, and Moldova, have taken place despite strong and vocal Russian criticism.

Violence and Narrative-Control in the Kenya Election Crisis

To disentangle some of these factors highlighted by events in post-Soviet countries, it would be useful to step out-of-area to Africa, where a violent electoral crisis gripped Kenya and where SMNs played a role, both positive and negative, in the subsequent events. In stark contrast to the crises described above, the Kenya crisis led to widespread violence and suffering, with more than 1,000 people killed and hundreds of thousands turned into IDPs.[57] The situation was all the more alarming and dismaying given Kenya's international reputation as one of the more successful postcolonial states in Africa.[58] This reputation existed in spite of great corruption within Kenya, where the president is granted immense, super-presidential privileges, and in which legislators have enormous salaries that dwarf the average per capita income, sparking outrage.[59] The disputed election was grafted onto a longstanding ethnic rivalry between the Kikuyu, who had been privileged during and after the period of British colonialism, and other groups.

On December 27, 2007, the incumbent government of Mwai Kibaki won what appeared to be a narrow victory over the opposition, led by Raila Odinga. Kibaki's victory was certified quickly by Kenya's electoral commission.[60] Particularly problematic was the apparent last-minute swing in the election totals, which took days. As of December 29, Odinga and his allies were cruising toward a huge victory, with an 18 per cent lead halfway through the count.[61] Kibaki was supported by the Kikuyu, and his disputed victory ignited the tragic violence that followed the elections. It was largely Kikuyu residents who were expelled from their homes in the Rift Valley (where the violence was centralized). The valley is one of Kenya's most troublesome areas – a Presidential Task Force recommended, in 2004, the formation of a Truth, Justice and Reconciliation panel to help resolve the region's longstanding grievances, but the body was never formed[62] Luos were also victims of violence in different parts of the country.[63] SMS messaging was used to spread messages of hatred and violence, much as radio was used in the Rwandan genocide to mobilize.[64] However, government officials were persuaded to keep the mobile network running, in the hopes that messages of peace sent by the provider Safaricom might counteract the more predatory messages being spread by would-be *genocidaires*.

The opposition and its supporters also organized huge street protests, which were brutally suppressed by the government, which had adopted a 'zero tolerance' policy.[65] Clashes between police and protestors frequently turned deadly as members of the opposition and – in a move familiar from other cases – the government harassed foreign journalists, particularly those following Odinga.[66] Non-partisan observers, including Kenyan civil society groups, Transparency International and American diplomats declared the elections fraudulent. Ultimately the government refused to step down, and in fact the human rights situation for members of the opposition continued to be quite fragile, with human rights activists under protection and several killings suspected of being perpetrated by the state itself.[67]

Goldstein and Rotich note the effectiveness of blogs for countering official narratives in Kenya.[68] While the official state media peddled the government's line, bloggers – and their connections abroad and in the Kenyan diaspora – helped decouple the horrific violence taking place in the Rift Valley from what they saw as the unanswered question of election-rigging. As in other cases, perhaps the most important use of the technology was information dissemination. As the state media tried to downplay the violence, citizen journalists wielding cell phone cameras posted videos and first-hand accounts of what was actually happening in the streets. Again it was cell phones rather than the Internet per se that had the greatest impact, since at the time only 3.2 per cent of Kenyans had Internet access.[69] SMS messages transmitted from ordinary Kenyans were posted on prominent Kenyan websites, as well as international forums like the BBC's Have Your Say.[70] This information exchange boomeranged back into the Kenyan press environment, leading one prominent Kenyan blogger to state: 'I'm getting more news from BBC than from anywhere else right now.'[71] And the prominence of English-language bloggers like Kenya Pundit[72] highlights the importance, noted in Chapter 3, of these bilingual bridge bloggers who are able to translate events in far-flung places for global audiences, giving them enormous power over the shape of the debates that take place in the international public sphere. This is particularly true when the state temporarily turns off the information spigot. On the other hand, it is also instructive, and should serve as a further note of caution, that the state was successfully able to disable the SMS network when it so desired. The state also maintained the capacity to track individuals sending text messages, and threatened to prosecute anyone caught sending inflammatory messages to others.

The Kenya case further underlines the reality that the effects of SMN activism are contingent. In some circumstances, SMNs can help topple unsteady regimes (Ukraine, Moldova) and in others they can put together the organizing that threatens more entrenched authoritarian

regimes (Iran). And in still others, they can both instigate and mitigate violence, as well as document abuses and organize demonstrations
against crooked election results.

Causal Implications

The case material presented above appears to lend at least qualified
support to the four hypotheses outlined at the beginning of the chapter. First, the cases lend further support, on top of the evidence from
Egypt, to the hypothesis that Social Media Networks can trigger informational cascades in authoritarian countries. Cascades appear to be the
mechanism for each of the cases discussed above. In each instance, as
in Egypt, we see the properties of Social Media Networks being leveraged for their utility in coordinating protest, driving coverage of those
protests locally and globally.

The cases under examination here would seem to challenge both
institutional theories presented earlier. Brownlee's expectations that
the Iranian regime would be vulnerable to elite divisions have not been
borne out by the 2009–2010 electoral crisis. Indeed, while the regime
has witnessed substantial intra-elite division, it has tenaciously clung
to power for reasons that are not yet clear to observers. And Lust-Okar's
expectation that regimes with unified structures of contestation are most
vulnerable during prolonged crises does not seem supported by the case
of Kenya, which allowed all groups to participate and yet also weath-
ered its electoral crisis, nor of Egypt, whose divided structure of contestation collapsed under prolonged attack in January-February of 2011.
The collapse of the Moldovan regime and its ruling communist
party also appears to challenge Brownlee, whereas the survival of the
Egyptian regime and the collapse of the Ukrainian regime appear to
lend support to both Brownlee and Lust-Okar's theories. Overall, the
set of outcomes here leads me to conclude that neither the presence of
political parties nor the prevailing structure of contestation are determinative of outcomes during electoral crises in authoritarian regimes.
It seems clear that there are other variables that would help explain
these divergent trajectories.

Second, mobilizations triggered by Social Media Networks appear to
have no determinative relationship to the success or failure of activism

in a given authoritarian context. The divergent outcomes of SMN-driven activism in Kenya, Ukraine, Moldova and Iran demonstrate that scholars and observers cannot simply assume the democratizing impact of SMNs. Indeed, in Kenya, the technologies were put to much more nefarious uses, whereas in Iran SMNs were turned on their users quite effectively. The success of Ukrainian, Moldovan and ultimately Egyptian SMN activists should be studied further for better understanding of the dynamics which allowed these groups to succeed.

The third hypothesis, that independent media are critical variables for the transmission of claims made through SMNs, is more challenging. I conclude that while independent media systems make it possible for SMNs to transmit claims during ordinary political times, those independent media outlets are not necessary variables during the kinds of crises discussed here, where tactical tools like Twitter and text-messaging can circumvent media blackouts and facilitate informational cascades. This is especially clear following the events in Tunisia, which filtered and censored its Internet heavily and where there was no independent press or domestic political opposition to speak of. And yet in Tunisia, Facebook and Twitter, while they didn't start the crisis that began with the self-immolation of Mohammed Bouazizi in December 2010, helped accelerate the crisis once it began. In other words, the lack of an established domestic digital activist community[73] did not prevent Tunisians from seizing on the tools of SMNs during the crisis and using them to their great advantage over the regime. When President Ben Ali departed for Saudi Arabia in humiliation, he did so partly because Tunisians were able to communicate with one another, share images and ideas and coordinate on platforms like Twitter and Facebook.

The primary effect of the independent media variable within authoritarian countries is to make newsworthy a whole host of issues and events that would normally be unintelligible or uninteresting to global audiences. In other words, the routinized presence of opposition or independent media practitioners in authoritarian public spheres makes possible daily contestations and dissent, as opposed to the more sensational events – like elections and electoral fraud – that tend to draw the attention of international media. Thus in Egypt, independent press outlets were critical in the dissemination of news stories about sexual harassment, refugees, torture and other issues that are rarely of great interest to global media elites. Rather, they are noteworthy to international NGOs and rights organizations with a vested interest in a certain kind of activism. In Kenya and Ukraine, both partly-free states with partly-free media systems, blogs and new media had for years served as alternative sources of news and information to state-run media agencies and as workarounds to self-censorship.

However, in Moldova, bloggers and Twitter users appeared on the scene as new actors in state politics. Little attention was paid prior to April 2009 to bloggers, Twitter activists or other individuals deploying these tools. This might be because in 2008, Moldova's media system was considered 'not free' by the Freedom House ranking.[74] Just like in Tunisia, though, once the crisis arrived networks of text-messagers, Tweeters and YouTubers were able to circumvent the regime's media blackout and reach critical external audiences (even if those external audiences were not, ultimately, ready to make sacrifices for them). And in Iran, another media environment considered 'not free', the change we see in the SMN age is that the state has been unable to control the information environment during these critical junctures. The state no longer has the capability to close its doors and promote its own alternative (one might say fictional) account of what actually took place in its streets. With citizens aware at all times of the protests, accessing international media outlets via proxy servers and sending information to international journalists, authoritarian regimes – even in the most closed societies which have gone to great length to control the Internet – have been unable to control emerging media narratives around discrete events in the political system.

Conclusions

These conclusions appear to be further reinforced by the broad scope of the Arab Spring which began in Tunisia in December 2010 and is still ongoing as of this writing. Mobilization in Tunisia – which strictly censored the Internet prior to December 2010 – was triggered not by a call to action circulated on Social Media Networks, but rather by the actions of a despondent fruit seller who immolated himself. In Syria, where firm architectures of filtering and control were in place, unexpected protests swept the country starting in March 2011. Digital organizers appeared to play a role in circulating calls to protest, but did not generate the crisis itself. And in Bahrain, where digital organizing and dissent has a longer history, the mobilization was crushed by a determined regime with the cooperation of the Saudi military forces. What is the meaning of these different trajectories? As Srinivasan and Fish argue, 'A successful revolutionary movement that uses technology may be successful despite the technology. And an unsuccessful movement may be squelched despite the overall positive contributions of the technology in that movement.'[75] We can thus conclude that Social Media Networks are neither necessary nor sufficient to explain mobilizing outcomes. This does not make them meaningless – under the right circumstances, as in Egypt, they can instigate a regime-level crisis that results in a transfer of power. In others, such as Bahrain, even successful mobilizations can result in a failure to dislodge authoritarian elites. However, we should be careful not to confuse outcomes with revolutionary success. The 'outcome' of digital organizing through Social Media Networks is mobilization. Once mobilized, protestors may find themselves aligned against immovable authoritarian structures, impervious to even the most ingenious digital protest.

Authoritarian regimes have devised many clever and innovative strategies for combating online dissent, from co-optation in Russia to paid subterfuge in China and finally to old-fashioned killing in Syria and Iran. But we should not confuse these short-term setbacks and authoritarian victories with the bigger picture – with an open Internet and an evolving toolkit of circumvention devices, digital activism remains the only real choice for many activists toiling under tyranny and hoping to build long-term movements to challenge authoritarianism. From Russia to Tunisia, the networked revolt has become the de facto choice of publics fed up with authoritarian excess and seeking to capture the spirit of Tahrir at home and internationally. Companies that supply authoritarian regimes with surveillance and blocking software should be called to the carpet in the global public sphere, as campaigns like Access Now add to the pressure on Internet-filterers and their apologists. No one can say that these campaigns will be successful in places like Syria, where authoritarian rulers maintain an edge in arms and resources, but digital tools are still one of the primary weapons of the weak even where service is cut off and disrupted, websites filtered and attacked and activists murdered in the streets. Without the open Internet, we would not know what was happening in the streets of Homs, Damascus and Manama, and the documentation of these brave activists will continue to provide an unfolding record of the cruelty and savagery of their tormentors.

The results of free elections in Egypt and Tunisia, which led to the election of political Islamists, may lead policy-makers to tamp down on their efforts to promote digital freedom and activism, simply because these revolutions brought groups to power whose interests clash with London and Washington. In the long run, however, the activists took a crowbar and wrenched open the door to democracy in this region, and their efforts should be applauded and appreciated. Policy-makers, academics and international organizations should always side with freedom against tyranny, and furthermore, understand that digital tools will be one of the primary paths of resistance to any renewed authoritarian politics in Egypt, Tunisia and elsewhere. The tsunami of dignity and courage unleashed by April 6, We Are All Khaled Said, and Tunisia bloggers like the administrators of Nawaat cannot be reversed permanently, and in fact, activists all over the region now know that the formula for success includes a role for digital platforms like Facebook and Twitter. We must not confuse short-term policy disagreements with the long-term benefits of global democratic politics. Digital activism is the only way forward.

In January 2011 Egyptians inspired the whole world, from the Occupy Wall Street protestors to the Wisconsin occupations, and reminded us of the power that ordinary individuals can harness through the ordinary digital tools they carry around in their pockets. Yes, there will always be corporate and authoritarian threats to those tools, and no, they will not always or even usually succeed. But the networked revolt is here to stay, as are the activists of the digital world. This remains true even as Egypt's newest military government arbitrarily imprisons both Islamists and activists. They remain defiant, and they still express that defiance through social media. Don't be surprised if in a decade or two, they do indeed belatedly inherit the beautiful revolution they authored.

NOTES

Chapter 1 Social Media and Authoritarian Politics in Egypt

1. 'Waiting For Baradei' *Al-Masry Al-Youm* English, February 19, 2010.
2. http://www.facebook.com/Elbarad3i
3. Dunn, Michael Collins. 'ElBaradei Facebook Group Past 100,000; Either Mubarak, Not So Much'. *The Middle East Journal Editor's Blog.* Accessed March 1, 2010. http://mideasti.blogspot.com/2010/03/elbaradei-facebook-group-past-100000.html
4. Cook, Steven A. 'Is ElBaradei Egypt's Hero?'. *Foreign Affairs.* Accessed March 26, 2010. http://www.foreignaffairs.com/articles/66178/steven-a-cook/is-el-baradei-egypts-hero?page=show
5. ElBaradei's group did circulate calls to protest, and some of its members were leading organizers in the ad hoc Coalition of the Youth of the Revolution, formed during the revolt itself. As of October 1, 2011, the 'ElBaradei for the Presidency of Egypt 2011' Facebook group had over 250,000 'likes'.
6. http://www.facebook.com/elshaheeed.co.uk (English), https://www.facebook.com/ElShaheeed (Arabic)
7. Joyce, Mary ed. *Digital Activism Decoded: The New Mechanics of Change.* New York, NY: International Debate Education Association, 2010. pp. vii, ix.
8. See Carothers, Thomas. 'The End of the Transition Paradigm.' *Journal of Democracy* 13:1 (2002): 5–20; Kassem, Maye. *Egyptian Politics: The Dynamics of Authoritarian Rule*, Boulder, CO: Lynne Rienner Publishers, 2004; Lust-Okar, Ellen. *Structuring Conflict in the Arab World: Incumbents, Opponents and Institutions.* Cambridge, England: Cambridge University Press, 2007; Brownlee, Jason, *Authoritarianism in an Age of Democratization*, New York, NY: Cambridge University Press, 2007; Bellin, Eva. 'Coercive Institutions and Coercive Leaders'

in Posusney, Marsha Pripstein and Michele Penner Angrist, eds., *Authoritarianism in the Middle East: Regimes and Resistance*. Boulder, CO: Lynne Rienner Publishers, 2005, pp. 21–38. 2005; Cook, Steven. *Ruling But Not Governing: The Military and Political Development in Egypt, Turkey and Algeria*. Baltimore, MD: The John's Hopkins University Press, 2007; Heydemann, Steve. 'Upgrading Authoritarianism in the Arab World.' The Saban Center For Middle East Policy at the Brookings Institution. Analysis Paper Number 13 (October 2007).

9. See Brownlee: *Authoritarianism in an Age of Democratization*.

10. See Lust-Okar: *Structuring Conflict in the Arab World*.

11. Lust-Okar: *Structuring Conflict in the Arab World*, pp. 147–148

12. See Kassem: *Egyptian Politics*.

13. See Bellin: 'Coercive Institutions and Coercive Leaders'.

14. See Heydemann: 'Upgrading Authoritarianism in the Arab World', p. 7

15. See El-Ghobashy, Mona. 'Constitutional Convention in Contemporary Egypt.' *American Behavioral Scientist* 51 (July 2008); and Rutherford, Bruce K. *Egypt After Mubarak: Liberalism, Islam and Democracy in the Arab World*. Princeton, NJ: Princeton University Press, 2008.

16. See Hanna, Michael Wahid. 'The Son Also Rises: Egypt's Looming Succession Struggle.' *World Policy Journal*, 2009, vol. 26, issue 3; and Cook, Steven A. 'Adrift on the Nile'. *Foreign Affairs*, March/April 2009.

17. El-Ghobashy, Mona. 'Constitutionalist Contention in Egypt'. *American Behavioural Scientist* 51 (2008): 1–21.

18. El-Mahdi, Rabab. 'The democracy movement: cycles of protest' in El-Mahdi, Rabab and Philip Marfleet eds., *Egypt: The Moment of Change*. London, UK: Zed Books, Ltd., 2009.

19. Beinin, Joel. 'Worker's struggles under "socialism" and neoliberalism' in El-Mahdi, Rabab and Philip Marfleet eds., *Egypt: The Moment of Change*. London, UK: Zed Books, Ltd., 2009.

20. Bradley, John R. *Inside Egypt: The Land of the Pharoahs on the Brink of a Revolution*. London, UK: Palgrave MacMillan, 2009.

21. http://baheyya.blogspot.com/

22. Baheyya. 'Four Myths About Protest.' *Baheyya: Eygpt Analysis and Whimsy*. May 16, 2008. http://baheyya.blogspot.com/2008/05/four-myths-about-protest.html. Accessed December 10, 2008.

23. Shorbagy, Manar. 'The Egyptian Movement For Change – Kefaya: Redefining Politics in Egypt.' *Public Culture* 19/1 (2007): 175–196 (175).

24. Baheyya: 'Four Myths About Protest.'

25. El Amrani, Issandr. 'Kifaya and the Politics of the Impossible.' Znet. January 4, 2006. http://www.zcommunications.org/kifaya-and-the-politics-of-the-impossible-by-issandr-el-amrani. Accessed April 14, 2008.

26. Interview with Issandr El-Amrani, Cairo, Egypt. February 16, 2008.

27. Shorbagy: 'The Egyptian Movement For Change', p. 190.

28. El-Mahdi, Rabab. 'Enough! Egypt's Quest For Democracy.' *Comparative Political Studies* 42 (2009): 1011–1039. p. 1035.

29. Snider, Erin A. and Faris, David M. 'The Arab Spring: U.S. Democracy Promotion in Egypt.' *Middle East Policy* Vol. 28, No. 3 (Fall 2011): 49–61.

30. This is not to suggest that there were not other newspapers prior to *Al-Masry Al-Youm* which carried criticism of the regime, but these papers were linked to certain political parties and did not enjoy the kind of readership and respect eventually garnered by *Al-Masry Al-Youm*.

31. Starkey, Paul. 'Modern Egyptian culture in the Arab world' in Daly, M. W., ed., *The Cambridge History of Egypt, Volume 2: Modern Egypt, from 1517 to the end of the twentieth century*. Cambridge, U.K.: Cambridge University Press, 1998, p. 413.

32. Vitalis, Robert. 'American Ambassador in Technicolour and Cinemascope: Hollywood and Revolution on the Nile' in Armbrust, Walter, ed., *Mass Mediations: New Approaches to Popular Culture in the Middle East and Beyond*. Berkeley: University of California Press, 2000, pp. 278–9.

33. Lerner, Daniel. *The Passing of Traditional Society: Modernizing the Middle East*. New York, NY: The Free Press, 1958, p. 251.

34. Jankowski, James. *Egypt: A Short History*. Oxford, U.K.: Oneworld Publications, 2000, p. 139.

35. Lerner: *The Passing of Traditional Society*, p. 254.

36. Lerner: *The Passing of Traditional Society*, pp. 255–258.

37. Lerner: *The Passing of Traditional Society*, pp. 54.

38. Rheingold, Howard. *Smart Mobs: The Next Social Revolution*. New York, NY: Basic Books, 2002.

39. Shirky, Clay. *Here Comes Everybody: The Power of Organizing Without Organizations*. New York, NY: Penguin Press, 2008, p. 153.

40. Karpf, David. 'Understanding Blogspace.' *Journal of Information Technology and Politics*. Volume 5, Issue 4 (December 2008): 369–395.

41. Bimber, Bruce, Flanagin, Andrew J., and Stohl, Cynthia. 'Reconceptualizing Collective Action in the Contemporary Media Environment.' *Communication Theory* 15:4 (November 2005): 365–388.

42. Castells, Manuel. 'Communication, Power and Counter-Power in the Network Society.' *International Journal of Comunication* 1 (2007): 238–266; Diamond, Larry. 'Liberation Technology.' *Journal of Democracy* 21/3 (July 2010): 69–83

43. See Mozorov, Evgeny. 'The Internet: A Room of Our Own? *Dissent* 56/3 (Summer 2009): 80–86; Deibert, Ronald J., Palfrey, John G. and Rohozinski, Rafal (eds). *Access Denied: The Practice and Policy of Global Internet*

Filtering. Cambridge, MA: MIT Press, 2008; Zittrain, Jonathan. *The Future of the Internet – And How to Stop It.* New Haven, CT: Yale University Press, 2008; Kalathil, Shanthi and Taylor C. Boas. *Open Networks, Closed Regimes: The Impact of the Internet on Authoritarian Rule.* Washington, DC: Carnegie Endowment for International Peace, 2003.

44. Faris, Robert, and Etling, Bruce. 'Madison and the Smart Mob: The Promise and Limitations of the Internet for Democracy.' *The Fletcher Forum of World Affairs* 32 (2008): 65–85.

45. Mozorov. 'The Internet: A Room of Our Own?'

46. Morozov, Evgeny. *The Net Delusion: The Dark Side of Internet Freedom.* New York, NY: Public Affairs, 2011.

47. Lynch, Marc. 'Young Brothers in Cyberspace.' Middle East Report 245 (Winter 2007). http://www.merip.org/mer/mer245/mer245.html, pp. 50–51.

48. Hofheinz, Albrecht. 'The Internet in the Arab World: Playground for Political Liberalization.' *Internationale Politik und Gesselschaft* (March 2005): 78–96 (78).

49. Anderson, Jon W. 'The Internet and Islam's New Interpreters' in Jon W. Anderson and Dale F. Eickelman eds., *New Media in the Muslim World: The Emerging Public Sphere.* Bloomington, IN: Indiana University Press, 2003, p. 50.

50. A blog is a agent-created website in which authors post entries in a journal-like format that are displayed with the most recent entry first. Blogs can be maintained by individuals, groups of individuals, or even corporations, governments, and political campaigns (author's definition).

51. Dreyfus, Hubert L. *On the Internet.* London: Routledge, 2001, p. 8.

52. Bucar, Elizabeth M. and Fazaeli, Roja. 'Free Speech in Weblogistan? The Offline Consequences of Online Communication.' *International Journal of Middle East Studies* 40 (2009): 403–419 (414).

53. Best, Michael L. and Wade, Keegan W. 'The Internet and Democracy.' *Bulletin of Science, Technology and Society* 29/4 (August 2009): 255–271.

54. Meier, Patrick. 'The Impact of the Information Revolution on Protest Frequency in Repressive Contexts.' Paper presented at the 50th International Studies Association Conference in New York City, February 15–17, 2009.

55. Rahimi, Babak. 'Cyberdissent: The Internet in Revolutionary Iran.' *Middle East Review of International Affairs,* 7/3 (September 2003), p. 1.

56. Teitelbaum, Joshua. 'Duelling for *Da'wa*: State vs. Society on the Saudi Internet.' *Middle East Journal* 56/2 (Spring 2002): 222–239 (237).

57. Teitelbaum: 'Duelling for *Da'wa*: State vs. Society on the Saudi Internet.'

58. Wheeler, Deborah L. *The Internet in the Middle East: Global Expectations and Local Imaginations in Kuwait.* Albany, NY: State University Press of New York, 2006, pp. 5, 17.

59. Lynch Marc. *Voices of the New Arab Public: Iraq, Al-Jazeera and Middle East Politics Today*. New York, NY: Columbia University Press, 2006, p. 54.

60. Postman, Neil. *Amusing Ourselves to Death: Public Discourse in the Age of Showbusiness*. New York, NY: Penguin 1985.

61. Boyd, danah m., and Ellison, Nicole B. 'Social Network Sites: Definition, History, Scholarship.' *Journal of Computer-Mediated Communication* 13(1) (2007), article 11.

62. Wheeler, Deborah L. 'Empowering Publics: Information Technology and Democratization in the Arab World: Lessons From Internet Cafes and Beyond.' *Oxford Internet Institute, Research Report* No. 11, July 2006: 2–18. p. 14.

63. Howard, Philip N. *The Digital Origins of Dictatorship and Democracy: Information Technology and Political Islam*. Oxford, UK: Oxford University Press, 2010.

64. Berman, Jerry, and Dierdre K. Mulligan. 'Digital Grass Roots: Issue Advocacy in the Age of the Internet,' In Anderson, David M. and Michael Cornfield eds., *The Civic Web: Online Politics and Democratic Values*. Oxford, UK: Rowman and Littlefield Publishers, Inc., 2003, p. 84.

65. Morozov, Eugene. 'Downside to the "Twitter Revolution".' *Dissent* 56/4 (Fall 2009): 10–14.

66. Boas, Taylor. 'Weaving the Authoritarian Web.' *Current History* 103, no. 677 (December 2004): 438–443.

67. Zittrain, Jonathan. *The Future of the Internet – And How to Stop It*. New Haven, CT: Yale University Press, 2008.

68. Boas: 'Weaving the Authoritarian Web: The Control of Internet Use in Non-Democratic Regimes.'

69. Boas: 'Weaving the Authoritarian Web: The Control of Internet Use in Non-Democratic Regimes.'

70. 'Egypt.' The Open Net Initiative. August 6, 2009. Accessed February 21, 2010 at http://opennet.net/research/profiles/egypt.

71. Kalathil and Boas: *Open Networks, Closed Regimes: The Impact of the Internet on Authoritarian* Rule, p. 122

72. 'Egypt.' The Open Net Initiative.

73. Levinson, Charles. 'Egypt's Growing Blogger Community Pushes Limits of Dissent.' *Christian Science Monitor*, August 24, 2005. Accessed at http://www.csmonitor.com/2005/0824/p07s01-wome.html on September 12, 2006; Shapiro, Samantha. 'Revolution, Facebook-Style.' *New York Times Magazine*, January 22, 2009; Faris, David. 'Revolutions Without Revolutionaries? Network Theory, Facebook and the Egyptian blogosphere.' *Arab Media & Society* Issue 6 (Fall 2008); Faris, David. 'The End of the Beginning: The Failure of April 6th and the Future of Electronic Activism in Egypt.' *Arab Media and Society* Issue 9 (Fall 2009); Faris, David. '(Amplified) Voices for the Voiceless.' *Arab Media and Society* Issue 11 (Summer 2010).

74. Lynch, Marc. 'After Egypt: The Limits and Promise of Online Challenges to the Authoritarian Arab State.' *Perspective on Politics*, Vol. 9, Issue 2 (June 2011).

75. Snider, Erin A. and Faris, David M. 'The Arab Spring: U.S. Democracy Promotion in Egypt.' *Middle East Policy* Vol. 28, No. 3 (Fall 2011): 49–61.

76. Khamis, Sahar, and Vaughn, Katherine. 'Cyberactivism in the Egyptian Revolution: How Civic Engagement and Citizen Journalism Tilted the Balance.' *Arab Media and Society* 13 (Summer 2011).

77. Hirschkind, Charles. 'The Road to Tahrir.' *The Immanent Frame*. Social Science Research Council. February 9, 2011. Accessed on March 30, 2011 at http://blogs.ssrc.org/tif/2011/02/09/the-road-to-tahrir/

78. Wheeler. 'Empowering Publics: Empowering Publics: Information Technology and Democratization in the Arab World: Lessons From Internet Cafes and Beyond.'

79. Wheeler, Deborah L. *The Internet in the Middle East: Global Exectations and Local Imaginations in Kuwait*. Albany, NY: State University Press of New York, 2006. pp. 34–35.

80. Kalathil and Boas: *Open Networks, Closed Regimes: The Impact of the Internet on Authoritarian Rule*, pp. 28–31.

81. MacKinnon, Rebecca. 'Flatter world and thicker walls? Blogs, censorship and civic discourse in China.' *Public Choice* 134 (2008): 31–46.

Chapter 2   A Theory of the Networked Revolt: Social Media Networks, Media Events and Collective Action

1. Kuran, Timur. 'Now Out of Never: The Element of Surprise in the East European Revolution of 1989.' World Politics 44/1 (October 1991): 7–48.

2. Matthew, Richard and Shambaugh, George. 'The Limits of Terrorism: A Network Perspective.' *International Studies Review* 2005 (7), 617–627.

3. Freyberg-Inan, Annette. 'Just how small is this world really?': An application of Network Theory to the Study of Globalization.' *Global Networks*, 6(3) (2006): 221–244.

4. Slaughter, Anne-Marie. 'America's Edge: Power in the Networked Century.' *Foreign Affairs* 88/1 (Jan/Feb 2009).

5. Cederman, Lars-Erik. 'Modeling the Size of Wars: From Billiard Balls to Sandpiles.' *The American Political Science Review* 97/1 (Feb. 2003): 135–150.

6. Elhafnawy, Nader. 'Societal Complexity and Diminishing Returns in Security.' *International Security* Vol. 29, Issue 1 (Summer 2004): 152–174.

7. Ackerman, Gary, James, Molly, and Casey T. Getz. 'The Application of Social Bookmarking Technology to the National Intelligence Domain.' *International Journal of Intelligence and Counterintelligence* 20/7 (2007): 678–698.

8. Pedhazur, Ami, and Perliger, Arie. 'The Changing Nature of Suicide Attacks: A Social Network Perspective.' *Social Forces* 84/4 (June 2006): 1969–1986.

9. Watts, Duncan. *Six Degrees: The Science of a Connected Age.* New York, NY: W.W. Norton and Co., 2003, p. 27.

10. The unfortunate and misleading term 'scale-free' has been applied to networks that exhibit these characteristics. The term is misleading because such networks certainly *do* have a scale, just one that differs from other kinds of networks.

11. Watts: *Six Degrees: The Science of a Connected Age,* p. 107.

12. Barabasi, Albert-Laszlo. *Linked: How Everything is Connected To Everything Else and What It Means For Business, Science, and Everyday Life.* New York, NY: Penguin Books, 2002, p. 86.

13. Image reprinted from http://orionwell.files.wordpress.com/2007/06/random-vs-power-law-distribution-2.jpg.

14. O'Reilly, Tim. 'What is Web 2.0?' September 30, 2005. http://www.oreillynet.com/pub/a/oreilly/tim/news/2005/09/30/what-is-web-20.html?page=2, Accessed February 12, 2008

15. Shirky, Clay. *Here Comes Everybody: The Power of Organizing Without Organizations.* New York, NY: Penguin Press, 2008.

16. The term 'crowdsourcing content' is borrowed from Brian Solis and his graphical illustration of the social media world, 'The Conversation Prism'.

17. Hindman, Matthew. *The Myth of Digital Democracy.* Princeton, NJ: Princeton University Press, 2008; Shirky, Clay. *Here Comes Everybody: The Power of Organizing Without Organizations.* New York, NY: Penguin Press, 2008; Karpf, David. 'Understanding Blogspace.' *Journal of Information Technology & Politics* 5/4 (December 2008): 369–385; Drezner, Daniel and Henry Farrell. 'The Power and Politics of Blogs.' *Public Choice* 134 (January 2008): 15–30.

18. 'Hits' refers to the number of unique visitors to any given web page.

19. Hindman: *The Myth of Digital Democracy.*

20. Castells, Manuel, et al. *Mobile Communication and Society: A Global Perspective.* Cambridge, MA: MIT Press, 2007, p. 209.

21. Drezner and Farrell: 'The Power and Politics of Blogs', p. 20.

22. Shirky: *Here Comes Everybody: The Power of Organizing Without Organizations.*

23. Ajemian, Pete. 'The Islamist opposition online in Egypt and Jordan.' *Arab Media & Society* Issue 7 (January 2008).

24. Maratea, Ray. 'The e-Rise and Fall of Social Problems: The Blogosphere as a Public Arena.' *Social Problems* 55/1 (2008): 139–160 (144).

25. Garrett, R. Kelly. 'Protest in an Information Society: A Review of Literature on Social Movements and New ICT's.' *Information, Communication and Society* 9/2 (2009): 202–224.

26. Woodly, Deva. 'New competencies in democratic communication? Blogs, agenda setting and political participation.' *Public Choice* 134 (January 2008): 109–123 (110).
27. Milner, Helen. 'The Digital Divide: The Role of Political Institutions in Technology Diffusion.' *Comparative Political Studies*, 39/2 (March 2006): 176–199.
28. Fandy, Mamoun. 'CyberResistance: Saudi Opposition Between Globalization and Localization.' *Comparative Studies in Society and History*, 41/1 (January 1999): 124–147; Lynch, Marc. *Voices of the New Arab Public: Iraq, Al-Jazeera and Middle-East Politics Today.* New York, NY: Columbia University Press, 2006; Schliefer, S. Abdallah. 'The Impact of Arab Satellite Television on Prospects for Democracy in the Arab World.' *Transnational Broadcasting Studies* 15 (2006); Sreberny, Annabelle. 'Mediated Culture in the Middle East: Diffusion, Democracy, Difficulties.' *Gazette*, 63/2–3: 101–119, 2001; Rahimi, Babak. 'Cyberdissent: The Internet in Revolutionary Iran.' *Middle East Review of International Affairs*, 7/3 (September 2003); Hofheinz, Albrecht. 'The Internet in the Arab World: Playground for Political Liberalization.' *Internationale Politik und Gesselschaft* (March 2005): 78–96. I want to be clear that I am not attributing to any of these authors *uncritical* claims about the democratizing potential of new media; rather they have all wrestled with the question and argued that there is at least such potential.
29. Somer, Murat. 'Resurgence and Remaking of Identity: Civil Beliefs, Domestic and External Dynamics, and the Turkish Mainstream Discourse on Kurds.' *Comparative Politics* 38/6 (August 2005): 591–622 (606).
30. Somer: 'Resurgence and Remaking of Identity', p. 609.
31. Shirky: *Here Comes Everybody: The Power of Organizing Without Organizations.*
32. Sunstein, Cass. *Infotopia: How Many Minds Produce Knowledge.* New York, NY: Oxford University Press, 2006.
33. Zuckerman, Ethan. 'Success. Success? Success.' ...*My Heart's in Accra.* January 24, 2008. Accessed March 21, 2010 at http://www.ethanzuckerman.com/blog/2008/01/24/success-success-success/
34. Gould, Roger. 'Collective Action and Network Structure.' *American Sociological Review* 58/2 (April 1993): 182–196 (182).
35. Gould: 'Collective Action and Network Structure', p. 182.
36. Kuran, Timur. 'Sparks and Prairie Fires: A Theory of Unanticipated Revolution.' *Public Choice*, Vol. 61, No. 1 (April 1989): 41–74.
37. Kuran, Timur. 'The Inevitability of Future Revolutionary Surprises.' *American Journal of Sociology* 100/6 (May 1995): 1528–51.
38. D'Anieri, Paul. 'Explaining the success and failure of post-communist revolutions.' *Communist and Post-Communist Studies* 39 (2006): 331–350 (334).
39. Berk, Richard A. 'A Gaming Approach to Crowd Behavior.' *American Sociological Review* 39 (June 1972): 335–73 (355).

40. Ibid., p. 363.

41. Ibid., p. 369.

42. Somer: 'Resurgence and Remaking of Identity', p. 593.

43. D'Anieri: 'Explaining the success and failure of post-communist revolutions.', p. 333.

44. Granovetter, Mark. 'Threshold models of collective behavior.' *American Journal of Sociology* 83/6 (May 1978): 1420–1443.

45. Ibid., p. 1422.

46. Barabasi: *Linked: How Everything is Connected To Everything Else and What It Means For Business, Science, and Everyday Life*, p. 131.

47. Granovetter: 'Threshold models of collective behavior.', p. 1436.

48. Ibid., p. 1434.

49. Lessig, Lawrence. *Remix: Making Art and Commerce Thrive in the Hybrid Economy*. New York, NY: Penguin Press, 2008, pp. 153–4.

50. Kuran: 'The Inevitability of Future Revolutionary Surprises', p. 1528.

51. Somer, Murat. 'Cascades of Ethnic Polarization: Lessons from Yugoslavia.' *Annals of the American Academy of Political and Social Science*, Vol. 573 (Jan. 2001): 127–151 (135).

52. Somer: 'Cascades of Ethnic Polarization', p. 142.

53. See for example Kramer, Martin. *Ivory Towers on Sand: The Failure of Middle Eastern Studies in America*. Washington, D.C.: Washington Institute for Near East Affairs, 2001.

54. Lustick, Ian S. and Miodownik, Dan. 'Neighborhoods and Tips: Implications of Spatiality for Political Cascades.' Paper presented at the annual meeting of the American Political Science Association, Washington, DC, September 1, 2005. p. 3.

55. Bikhchandani, Sushi, Hirschleifer, David, and Ivo Welch. 'A Theory of Fads, Fashion, Custom and Cultural Change as Informational Cascades.' *Journal of Political Economy* 100/5 (1992): 991–1026 (994).

56. Ibid., p. 996.

57. Ibid., p. 998.

58. Kuran: 'Sparks and Prairie Fires: A Theory of Unanticipated Revolution', p. 47.

59. Kuran: 'Sparks and Prairie Fires: A Theory of Unanticipated Revolution', p. 17. Somer cautions that under conditions of widespread preference falsification, individuals are unlikely to really believe what they hear in public (Somer: 'Resurgence and Remaking of Identity', p. 608). However, this leaves the problem of how these individuals, even if they sense the hypocrisy of publicly-expressed beliefs, are to ascertain the true level of support for their private positions.

60. Kuran: 'Sparks and Prairie Fires: A Theory of Unanticipated Revolution', p. 18.

61. Ibid., p. 19.

62. Ibid., p. 20. One could add that 'revolutionary thresholds', inasmuch as they exist in the real world, may not be known to the individual in question either.
63. Moore, Will H. 'Rational Rebels: Overcoming the Free-Rider Problem.' *Political Research Quarterly* 48/2 (June 1995): 417–454 (446).
64. Lustick and Miowdownik: 'Neighborhoods and Tips: Implications of Spatiality for Political Cascades', p. 6.
65. Schell, Jonathan. *The Unconquerable World: Power, Non-Violence and the Will of the People*. New York: Henry Holt and Co., 2004.
66. Lustick and Miodownik: 'Neighborhoods and Tips: Implications of Spatiality for Political Cascades'.
67. Somer: 'Resurgence and Remaking of Identity', p. 608.
68. Lustick and Miodownik: 'Neighborhoods and Tips: Implications of Spatiality for Political Cascades', p. 20.
69. Ibid., p. 26.
70. Kuran: 'Sparks and Prairie Fires: A Theory of Unanticipated Revolution', p. 47.
71. Kuran: 'The Inevitability of Future Revolutionary Surprises', pp. 1538–39.
72. Kuran, Timur, and Cass R. Sunstein. 'Availability Cascades and Risk Regulation.' *Stanford Law Review* 54/1 (April 1999): 683–768 (685).
73. Ibid., pp. 691–697.
74. Ibid., p. 690.
75. Ibid., p. 767.
76. Shirky: *Here Comes Everybody: The Power of Organizing Without Organizations*, p. 288.
77. Sunstein, Cass. *Infotopia: How Many Minds Produce Knowledge*. New York, NY: Oxford University Press, 2006, p. 81.
78. Ibid.
79. Ibid., p. 82.
80. Bimber, Bruce, Flanagin, Andrew J., and Stohl, Cynthia. 'Reconceptualizing Collecting Action in the Contemporary Media Environment.' *Communication Theory* 15:4 (November 2005): 365–388.
81. Gould, Roger. 'Collective Action and Network Structure.' *American Sociological Review* 58/2 (April 1993): 182–196 (194).
82. Kuran: 'The Inevitability of Future Revolutionary Surprises', pp. 1538–1541.
83. Barabasi: *Linked: How Everything is Connected To Everything Else and What It Means For Business, Science, and Everyday Life*, p. 36.
84. See Watts: *Six Degrees: The Science of a Connected Age*.
85. Gladwell, Malcolm. *The Tipping Point: How Little Things Can Make a Big Difference*. New York, NY: Back Bay Books, 2002.
86. Watts: *Six Degrees: The Science of a Connected Age*, p. 15.
87. Freyberg-Inan, Annette: 'Just how small is this world really?: An application of Network Theory to the Study of Globalization.'

88. Barabasi: *Linked: How Everything is Connected To Everything Else and What It Means For Business, Science, and Everyday Life*, p. 53.

89. Shirky: *Here Comes Everybody: The Power of Organizing Without Organizations.*

90. Sunstein: *Infotopia: How Many Minds Produce Knowledge.*

91. Ibid.

92. D'Anieri: 'Explaining the success and failure of post-communist revolutions', pp. 347–348.

93. Matthew and Shambaugh: 'The Limits of Terrorism: A Network Perspective', p. 618.

94. Zittrain, Jonathan. *The Future of the Internet – And How to Stop It.* New Haven, CT: Yale University Press, 2008.

95. Calfano, Brian Robert and Emile Sahlieyeh. 'Transmitting Reform? Assessing New Media Influence on Political Rights in the Middle East.' *Critique: Critical Middle Eastern Studies* 17/1 (Spring 2008): 63–77.

Chapter 3 Agenda-Setters: Torture, Rights and Social Media Networks in Egypt

1. Seth Godin in an interview with Kim Zetter of Wired.com, February 2, 2009.

2. From 'Four Myths About Protest' published May 16, 2008, on the blog Baheyya: Egypt Analysis and Whimsy.

3. Woodly 2007, 109

4. See Shapiro, Samantha. 'Revolution, Facebook-Style.' *New York Times Magazine*, January 22, 2009.

5. Drezner, Daniel and Henry Farrell. 'The Power and Politics of Blogs.' *Public Choice* 134 (January 2008): 15–30.

6. Mosahel, Mohamed Abdel Khaliq. '*Los Angeles Times*: Mubarak's Opposition Hums With Disparate Voices.' *Al-Masry Al-Youm*, 29 April 2009.

7. Rutherford, Bruce K. *Egypt After Mubarak: Liberalism, Islam and Democracy in the Arab World.* Princeton, NJ: Princeton University Press, 2008.

8. Kalathil, Shanthi, and Taylor C. Boas. *Open Networks, Closed Regimes: The Impact of the Internet on Authoritarian Rule.* Washington, DC: Carnegie Endowment For International Peace, 2003, p. 122.

9. Eid, Gamal. 'The Internet in the Arab World: A New Space of Repression?' The Arabic Network for Huuman Rights Information, 2004. Accessed on 21 December 2996 at http://www.hrinfo.net/en/reports/net2004/all. shtml#12. Informally, accessing the Internet has become more difficult and more expensive between the summer of 2008 and the summer of 2009. Internet cafes that formerly offered free Internet access had locked down their service through Mobinil, and required registration through a cell phone.

This practice was clearly intended to introduce an element of surveillance to what had been relatively open access practices in Egypt.

10. Wheeler, Deborah L. 'Egypt: Building an Information Society for International Development.' *Review of African Political Economy*, No. 98 (2003): 624–642 (631).

11. http://www.cairolive.com

12. Interview with Tarek Atia, Cairo, Egypt. February 6, 2008.

13. Ibid.

14. Interview with Hossam El-Hamalawy, Cairo, Egypt. May 27, 2009.

15. Ibid.

16. Radsch, Courtney C. 'Core to Commonplace: The evolution of Egypt's blogosphere.' *Arab Media & Society* Issue 6 (Fall 2008).

17. Ibid.

18. http://www.thearabist.net

19. http://www.sandmonkey.org

20. http://www.bigpharaoh.org/

21. Interview with Wael Abbas.

22. Drezner and Farrell: 'The Power and Politics of Blogs.'

23. http://misrdigital.blogspirit.com/

24. http://malek-x.net/

25. http://www.arabawy.org/

26. http://www.norayounis.com/

27. Faris, David. 'Revolutions Without Revolutionaries? Network theory, Facebook and the Egyptian blogosphere.' *Arab Media & Society* Issue 6 (Fall 2008); Shirky, Clay. *Here Comes Everybody: The Power of Organizing Without Organizations*. New York, NY: Penguin Press, 2008.

28. Ajemian, Pete. 'The Islamist opposition online in Egypt and Jordan.' *Arab Media & Society* Issue 7 (January 2008).

29. Interview with Tarek Atia, Cairo, Egypt. February 6, 2008.

30. Maratea, Ray. 'The e-Rise and Fall of Social Problems: The Blogosphere as a Public Arena.' *Social Problems* 55/1 (2008): 139–160 (140).

31. Maratea: 'The e-Rise and Fall of Social Problems', p. 141.

32. Delli Carpini, Michael. 'The Internet and an Informed Citizenry,' with Scott Keeter, in David Anderson and Michael Cornfield, eds. *The Civic Web: Online Politics and Democratic Values*. New York, NY: Rowman and Littlefield, 2002.

33. Pajnik, Mojca. 'Citizenship and Mediated Society.' *Citizenship Studies* 9/4 (September 2005): 349–367.

34. Maratea: 'The e-Rise and Fall of Social Problems', 142.

35. Rugh, William A. 'Do National Political Systems Still Influence Arab Media?' *Arab Media & Society* (May 2007), p. 9.

36. Ibid.
37. Black, Jeffrey. 'Egypt's Press: More free, still fettered.' *Arab Media & Society* (January 2008), p. 11.
38. Salih, Khalid. 'Hurriyat al-Sahafa.' Cairo Center for the Study of Human Rights, 2007, pp. 13–15.
39. Iskander, Adel. 'Problematizing Arab Media in the Post-Taxonomic Era.' *Arab Media & Society* (May 2007).
40. 'Egypt editor sentenced to six months, free on bond.' Reuters, March 26, 2008. Accessed on 8 April 2008 at http://africa.reuters.com/top/news/usn-BAN635621.html.
41. Simon, Mallory. 'Student "Twitters" his way out of Egyptian jail.' *CNN*. April 25, 2008. Accessed on April 26, 2008 at http://articles.cnn.com/2008-04-25/tech/twitter.buck_1_cell-phone-blog-anti-government-protest?_s=PM:TECH.
42. Interview with Ehab El-Zalaky, Cairo Egypt. April 8, 2008.
43. http://egyptianchronicles.blogspot.com/
44. At least in the case of the Sandmonkey, the author eventually came to feel that the security forces did indeed know who he was.
45. Shapiro: 'Revolution, Facebook-Style.'
46. Zuckerman, Ethan. 'The connection between cute cats and web censorship.' *My Heart's in Accra*, July 16, 2007. Accessed on August 22, 2011 at http://www.ethanzuckerman.com/blog/2007/07/16/the-connection-between-cute-cats-and-web-censorship/
47. See for example the comments of Abdullah Schleiffer at the December 17, 2007 *BBC Free To Speak* debate held in Cairo, Egypt.
48. http://www.minazekri.net/
49. Interview with Mina Zakry, Cairo, Egypt. March 27, 2008.
50. Interview with Ahmed Abdel Fattah, Cairo, Egypt. December 10, 2007.
51. Maratea: 'The e-Rise and Fall of Social Problems', p. 156.
52. Interview with Hossam El-Hamalawy, Cairo, Egypt. May 27, 2009.
53. Radsch: 'Core to Commonplace: The evolution of Egypt's blogosphere.'
54. http://globalvoicesonline.org
55. Ibid.
56. Al-Malky, Rania. 'Blogging For Reform: The Case of Egypt.' *Arab Media & Society* 1/1 (Spring 2007): 1–9.
57. See for instance '*al-Dakhiliya ankarat 'adat al-taharrush fi-l-Qahira wa qalat inna kullu shay' tamam ya fandim!*' (The Interior Ministry denied the return of harassment in Cairo and said 'Everything is fine, Effendim!'). Mohamed Khayr, *Al-Dustur Weekly*, November 1, 2006.
58. El-Hamalawy, Hossam. 'Rose Al-Youssef hits new rock bottom', 3arabawy, October 31, 2006. Accessed on March 14, 2009 at http://www.arabawy.org/2006/10/31/rosa-al-youssef-hits-new-rock-bottom/.

59. This aspect of the case remains, unfortunately, very murky.

60. http://woundedgirlfromcairo.blogspot.com/

61. Girl4Cairo. 'LOOK AT ME.' Wounded Girl From Cairo, Thursday, November 9, 2006. Accessed on September 17, 2009 at http://woundedgirlfromcairo.blogspot.com/2006/11/look-at-me.html.

62. Interview with the Sandmonkey, Cairo, Egypt. March 23, 2008.

63. Interview with Wael Abbas, Cairo, Egypt. April 14, 2008.

64. Interview with Ehab El-Zalaky, Cairo, Egypt. April 8, 2008.

65. Research through the Middle East Monitor (formerly Zad) confirms the absence of any coverage of these events.

66. Interview with Ehab El-Zalaky, Cairo, Egypt. April 8, 2008.

67. Egyptian Center for Human Rights. 'The Collective Harassment During the Eid El Fitr Holiday and the Absence of a Law.' Press release, October 8, 2008.

68. Interview with Gamal Eid, Director of the Arab Network for Human Rights Information. Cairo, Egypt, February 26, 2008.

69. Interview with Ehab Zalaky, Cairo, Egypt. April 8, 2008.

70. Nkrumah, Gamal. 'Insecure but incisive.' Al-Ahram Weekly. 24–30 November, 2005.

71. BBC News. 'UN "Shocked" By Violence in Cairo.' December 30, 2005.

72. Interview with Nora Younis, Cairo, Egypt. April 2, 2008.

73. Interview with Ehab Zelaky, Cairo, Egypt. April 8, 2008.

74. Interview with Nora Younis, Cairo Egypt. April 23, 2008.

75. *Ta'dhib fi Masr.* January 2, 2006.

76. Al-A'oumi, Yusef. 'Wazarat al-siyaha: laji'u al-Sudan fi Misr siyah.' *Al-Masry Al-Youm,* January 5, 2006.

77. Research conducted through the *Middle East Monitor* (formerly *Zad*). Comprehensive searches not available prior to 1998.

78. Slackman, Michael. 'Egypt Says It Won't Deport Any of the Jailed Sudanese.' *New York Times,* January 18, 2006. See also Wright, 'Activists Demand Probe in Cairo Killings'. Reuters, January 1, 2006; Ibrahim, Saad Eddin. 'Egypt's Democratic Charade.' *Globe & Mail,* January 17, 2006; BBC News: 'UN "Shocked" By Violence in Cairo.'

79. http://www.demaghmak.com

80. Interview with Wael Abbas, Cairo, Egypt. April 14, 2008.

81. Saleh, Heba. 'Fears for Egypt torture victim.' BBC News, January 16, 2007. Accessed on May 8, 2009 at http://news.bbc.co.uk/1/hi/world/middle_east/6264193.stm.

82. Abdel Fattah, Wael. 'Officer from Qism al-Haram torture video arrested.' *El-Fagr,* November 27, 2006.

83. Al-Sayyid, Emad. 'Al-Masry Al-Youm: Alone in publishing the first picture of the officer in Bulaaq accused of torturing Emad Al-Kabir'. *Al-Masry Al-Youm*, December 29, 2006.

84. Al-Sayyid, Emad. *'El-Fagr batal fadihat al-ta'dhib fi bulaq: al-mabahith sawamatni wa-'arghamatni 'ala takdhib'* (El-Fagr is the hero of the torture scandal in Bulaq: the secret police coerced and forced me into lying).

85. El-Hamalawy, Hossam. 'El-Adly Videogate: Torture Victim Receives 3 Months in Prison for "resisting authorities"!' *Arabawy*, January 9, 2007.

86. Baghdadi, Mohamed. *'Fanta'dhib al-muwatin'* (The art of torturing the citizen). *Al-Masry Al-Youm*, August 7, 2007

87. Shalaby, Ahmed. '16 cases of torture inside police stations in July alone.' *Al-Masry Al-Youm*, August 4, 2007.

88. Al-Dassouki, Farouk. *'Adawat al-ru'b fi aqsam al-shurta'* (Instruments of horror in police stations). *Al-Masry Al-Youm*, August 18, 2007.

89. McDonough, Challis. 'Prison Term for Egyptian Police in Widely-Published Torture Case.' *VOA News*, November 6, 2007.

90. Chapter 4 will explore how this de facto alliance uses SMNs, particularly Twitter, to facilitate on-the-ground organizing.

91. Abdel Halim, Khaled Omar. 'Eyptian Human Rights Organization Calls for Amending the Laws to Conform to International Conventions.' *Al-Masry Al-Youm*, 9 February 2009.

92. Human Rights Watch. 'Egypt: Hold Police Accountable For Torture.' December 12, 2006. Accessed on September 17, 2009 at http://www.hrw.org/en/news/2006/12/22/egypt-hold-police-accountable-torture.

93. http://www.manalaa.net

94. Interview with Noha Atef, Cairo, Egypt. July 7, 2011.

95. http://tortureinegypt.net/

96. Interview with Noha Atef, Cairo, Egypt. July 7, 2011.

97. http://www.arabawy.org/tag/piggipedia/

98. Interview with Mohammed Maree, Cairo, Egypt. July 15, 2011.

99. http://egytimes.org/

100. Interview with Mohammed Maree, Cairo, Egypt. July 15, 2011.

101. BBC World Service. 'An island occupied in Egypt.' Accessed on April 15, 2009 at http://www.bbc.co.uk/worldservice/outlook/2008/01/080121_qursaya_egypt.shtml.

102. 'Cairo farmers fight army for land.' *AFP*, November 11, 2007.

103. Interview with Mina Zakry, Cairo, Egypt. March 24, 2008.

104. Ibid.

105. Sandmonkey. 'Al-Qursaya Island.' Rantings of a Sandmonkey, Tuesday, November 13, 2007. Accessed on 10 February 2009 at http://www.sandmonkey.org/2007/11/13/al-qursaya-island/

106. 'Cairo farmers fight army for land', *AFP*.
107. This version of events was confirmed to me by anonymous sources inside the newspaper.
108. In Arabic: *bi-l-fidyu: iqtiham al-jaysh jazirat al-qursaya*.
109. Egyptian security forces are divided into a dizzying array of different services.
110. Abdel Hamid, Heba and Shaima el-Karnashawi. 'Afrah fil Qursaya b'ad al-Hukm bi Tamkinihim min manazilihim' (Happiness in Qursaya after ruling about expulsion from their homes). *Al-Masry Al-Youm*, November 17, 2008.
111. Fenton, Natalie. 'Mediating hope: New media, politics and resistance.' *International Journal of Cultural Studies* Vol. 11 (2008), p. 233.
112. Al-Hiwari, Ahmed. 'Al-Qursaya: Island of Fear.' Accessed on January 20, 2008 at http://masr.20at.com/newArticle.php?sid=12711.
113. http://www.thearabist.net
114. El-Hamalawy, Hossam. 'Resisting Mubarak's Army.' 3ara bawy, December 4, 2007.
115. Facebook group, 'Save the People of Qursaya', http://www.facebook.com/wall.php?id=19903372840&page=1&hash=8177ac749eb7a592f4d53da247f9c038
116. Singer, Michaela. 'Angry Qursaya Residents Complain at State Council.' *Daily News Egypt*, November 29, 2007.
117. 'Egyptian army weighs in on disputed Nile island.' *Reuters*. December 12, 2007. Accessed on September 19, 2008 at http://www.reuters.com/article/inDepthNews/idUSL0664802420071212?pageNumber=2&virtualBrandChannel=0.
118. Carr, Sarah. 'Threatened Qorsaya Resident: I was born here and I'll die here.' *Daily News Egypt*, December 20, 2007.
119. Monsour, Ibrahim. 'Al-Hukuma ta'tarif bi 'ightiSab jazeerat al-Qursaya' ('Government admits to rape of Al-Qursaya'). *Al-Dustur*, January 4, 2008
120. Research was conducted through keyword searches via the Middle East Monitor (formerly Zad).
121. See for example, the November 7, 2007 story in *Al-Gumhuriya*.
122. Fayza, Hassan. 'The last frontier.' *Al-Ahram Weekly*, 26 July August 1, 2001.
123. Research was conducted through the Middle East Monitor (formerly Zad) at the American University of Cairo. Searches pulled in 111 articles between 2007 and 2009, and only one prior to that period; it was published in 1998 in *Al-Ahrar*, a government daily.
124. Rutherford: *Egypt After Mubarak: Liberalism, Islam and Democracy in the Arab World*.

125. Interview with Amira Howeidy, Cairo, Egypt. April 19, 2008.
126. Howard, Philip N. *The Digital Origins of Dictatorship and Democracy: Information Technology and Political Islam.* Oxford, UK: Oxford University Press, 2010.
127. Calfano, Brian Robert and Emile Sahlieyeh. 'Transmitting Reform? Assessing New Media Influence on Political Rights in the Middle East.' *Critique: Critical Middle Eastern Studies* 17/1 (Spring 2008): 63–77; Hofheinz, Albrecht. 'The Internet in the Arab World: Playground for Political Liberalization.' *Internationale Politik und Gesselschaft* (March 2005): 78–96.
128. Asen, Robert and Brouwer, Daniel C. *Counterpublics and the State.* Albany, New York: State University of New York Press, 2001.
129. Habermas, Jürgen. *The Structural Transformation of the Public Sphere: An Inquiry Into a Category of Bourgeois Society.* Cambridge, MA: MIT Press, 1989.
130. Castells, Manuel. 'Communication, Power and Counter-Power in the Network Society.' *International Journal of Communication* 1 (2008): 238–266.

Chapter 4 New Tools, Old Rules: Social Media Networks and Collective Action in Egypt

1. Lust-Okar, Ellen. *Structuring Conflict in the Arab World: Incumbents, Opponents, and Institutions.* Cambridge, England: Cambridge University Press, 2007.
2. Brownlee, Jason. *Authoritarianism in an Age of Democratization.* New York, NY: Cambridge University Press, 2007, p. 4; Albrecht, Holger. 'How can opposition support authoritarianism? Lessons from Egypt.' *Democratization* 12/3 (June 2005): 378–397 (378); Kassem, Maye. *Egyptian Politics: The Dynamics of Authoritarian Rule.* Boulder, CO: Lynne Rienner Publishers, 2004, p. 188.
3. El-Ghobashy, Mona. 'Constitutional Contention in Egypt.' *American Behavioral Scientist* 51 (2008): 1–21.
4. Al-Khamissi, Khaled. *Taxi.* Translated by Jonathan Wright. Wiltshire, UK: Aflame Books, 2008, pp. 24–25.
5. Lichbach, Mark I. *The Rebel's Dilemma.* Ann Arbour, MI: University of Michigan Press, 1998.
6. Mitchell, Timothy. *Rule of Experts: Egypt, Techno-Politics, Modernity.* Berkeley, CA: University of California Press, 2002, p. 286.
7. Al-Malky, Rania. 'Blogging For Reform. The Case of Egypt.' *Arab Media & Society* 1/1 (Spring 2007): 1–9.
8. Interview with Hossam El-Hamalawy, Cairo Egypt. May 27, 2009.

9. Lynch, Marc. *Voices of the New Arab Public: Iraq, Al-Jazeera and Middle East Politics Today.* New York, NY: Columbia University Press, 2006; Sakr, Naomi. *Satellite Realms: Transnational Television, Globalization and the Middle East.* London, UK: I.B.Tauris and Co., 2002.

10. Interview with Hossam El-Hamalawy, Cairo, Egypt. May 27, 2009.

11. Ibid.

12. Wolff, Sarah. 'Constraints on the promotion of the rule of law in Egypt: insights from the 2005 judges' revolt.' *Democratization* 16/1 (2009): 100–118.

13. Rutherford, Bruce K. *Egypt After Mubarak: Liberalism, Islam, and Democracy in the Arab World.* Princeton, NJ: Princeton University Press, 2008, p. 45.

14. Ibid., p. 54.

15. Ibid., p. 52.

16. Wolff notes that the regime renewed the State of Emergency on April 30 2006, on the dubious pretext that the question would be revisited at another, more amenable time.

17. Wolff, Sarah. 'Constraints on the promotion of the rule of law in Egypt: insights from the 2005 judges' revolt', p. 105.

18. Ibid.

19. El-Amrani, Issandr. 'Black Referendum Day – demo recap.' The Arabist, May 25, 2006. Accessed on June 24, 2008 at http://arabist.net/archives/2006/05/23/black-referendum-day-demo-recap/.

20. Ibid.

21. El-Amrani, Issandr. 'Pro-judges demo pics.' The Arabist, May 18, 2006. Accessed on September 4, 2008 at http://www.arabist.net/blog/2006/5/18/pro-judges-demo-pics.html.

22. El-Ghobashy: 'Constitutionalist Contention in Egypt', p. 9.

23. Ibid.

24. Interview with Issandr El-Amrani, Cairo, Egypt. February 16, 2008.

25. Gharbeia, Amr. '500 Central Security soldiers around the Judges' Club.' Gharbeia.net, October 26, 2006. Author's translation. Accessed on January 22, 2009 at http://gharbeia.net/node/179.

26. Abbas, Wael. 'Today's Activities in Egypt.' Misr Digital, May 25, 2006. Author's translation. Accessed on May 27, 2009 at http://misrdigital.blog-spirit.com/archive/2006/05/index.html.

27. Mana and Alaa's Bit Bucket. '*Muzhahara bi-midan al-tahrir 3–15 li-l-ta'bir 'an rafd al-ta'dilat al-dusturiyya*' (Demonstration in Tahrir Square to express rejection of the constitutional amendments). March 10, 2007. Author's translation. Accessed on February 12, 2009 at http://www.manalaa.net/node/87226.

28. Ikhwanonline. 'Al-Muzhahirat al-rafida li-l-ta'dilat al-dusturiyya tash-mal mu'zham jami'at Misr' (Demonstrations to reject constitutional amendments include most Egyptian universities). March 25, 2007. Accessed on January 17, 2009 at http://www.ikhwanonline.com/Article.asp?ArtID=27259&SecID=304.

29. De Koning, Anouk. 'Café Latte and Caesar Salad: Cosmopolitan Belonging in Cairo's Coffee Shops' in Singerman, Diane and Paul Amar eds., *Cairo Cosmopolitanism: Politics, Culture and Urban Space in the New Globalized Middle East*. Cairo, Egypt: The American University in Cairo Press, 2006, p. 229.

30. Johnson, Steven. *Everything Bad is Good For You: How Today's Popular Culture is Actually Making Us Smarter*. New York, NY: Riverhead Books, 2005.

31. Interview with blogger who wished to remain anonymous, Cairo, Egypt. April 6, 2008.

32. Armbrust, Walter, 'New Media and Old Agendas: The Internet in the Middle East and Middle Eastern Studies.' *International Journal of Middle East Studies* 39 (2007): 531–533 (531).

33. Beinin, Joel. 'Worker's struggles under "socialism" and neoliberalism' in El-Mahdi, Rabab and Philip Marfleet eds., *Egypt: The Moment of Change*. London, UK: Zed Books, Ltd., 2008.

34. McDonough, Ecaterina. 'Is Democracy Promotion Effective in Moldova? The Impact of European Institutions on Development of Civil and Political Rights in Moldova.' *Democratization* 15/1 (2008): 142–161.

35. Slackman, Michael. 'Day of Angry Protest Stuns Egypt.' *The New York Times*, April 6, 2008.

36. Facebook data from http://www.facebook.com/ads/create/ as of July 20, 2008. There were probably considerably fewer members in March 2008.

37. Zuckerman, Ethan. 'The connection between cute cats and web censorship.' ... *My Heart's in Accra*. July 16, 2007. Accessed August 22, 2011 at http://www.ethanzuckerman.com/blog/2007/07/16/the-connection-between-cute-cats-and-web-censorship/.

38. Ibid.

39. Darabnee, Ahmed. 'As-Suhuf-al-qowmiya tashun Hamla Did al-Internet' (The National Media Undertake a Campaign Against the Internet). *Al-Badeel*, April 26, 2008.

40. El-Ghitany, Magda. "Facing Facebook." *Al-Ahram Weekly*, May 1–7, 2008.

41. Howeidi, Fahmy. 'Ghazwat Al-Qursaya.' *Al-Dustur*, December 26, 2007.

42. Interview with the Sandmonkey, Cairo, Egypt. March 23, 2008.

43. Interview with Hossam El-Hamalawy, Cairo, Egypt. May 27, 2009.

44. Matthew, Richard and Shambaugh, George. 'The Limits of Terrorism: A Network Perspective.' *International Studies Review* 2005 (7), 617–627.

45. Hindman, Matthew. *The Myth of Digital Democracy*. Princeton, NJ: Princeton University Press, 2008.

46. Karpf, David. 'Understanding Blogspace.' *Journal of Information Technology & Politics* 5/4 (December 2008): 369–385.

47. Ibid.

48. Facebook.com 'Statistics.' Accessed January 20, 2012 on http://www.facebook.com/press/info.php?statistics.

49. Interview with Hossam El-Hamalawy, Cairo, Egypt. May 27, 2009.

50. Interview with Demagh MAK, Cairo, Egypt. June 18, 2009.

51. Shubaki, Amr. 'Limadha fashala al-idrab al-'am?' (Why did the general strike fail?). *Al-Masry Al-Youm*, April 9, 2009.

52. Interview with Hossam El-Hamalawy, Cairo, Egypt. May 27, 2009.

53. Arab Network For Human Rights Information. 'Istihdaf al-mudawinin al-masriyin: 'ard mustamir' ('Targeting Egyptian Bloggers: An Ongoing Issue'). Accessed on August 7, 2009 at http://www.katib.org/node/7888.

54. Al-Aswany, Alaa. *On the State of Egypt: What Made the Revolution Inevitable*. New York, NY: Random House, 2011.

55. The Sandmonkey. '6th of April…again!' Rantings of a Sandmonkey, April 4, 2009. Accessed on June 24, 2009 at http://www.sandmonkey.org/2009/04/04/6th-of-aprilagain/.

56. El-Hamalawy, Hossam. 'Revolt in Mahalla.' *International Socialist Review* 59 (May-June 2008). Accessed on July 15, 2008 at http://www.isreview.org/issues/59/rep-mahalla.shtml.

57. Posusney, Marsha Pripstein. *Labor and the State in Egypt*. New York, NY: Columbia University Press, 1997.

58. Abdelhamid, Doha. 'Mind the Gap.' *Al-Ahram Weekly*, 14–20 May 2009.

59. Carr, Sarah. 'Doctors' Group Skeptical of Wage Increase Promised By Government.' *Daily News Egypt*, July 16, 2008.

60. Beinin, Joel. *Justice For All: The Struggle For Worker's Rights in Egypt*. The Solidarity Center, 2010.

61. Lesch, Ann M. 'Egypt's Spring: The Causes of Revolution.' *Middle East Policy* Vol. 28, No. 3 (Fall 2011): 35–48.

62. Hindman: *The Myth of Digital Democracy*.

63. 6 April Movement. '6 April 2009, General Strike in Egypt.' Saturday, April 4, 2009. Accessed on June 11, 2009 at http://6aprilmove.blogspot.com/2009/04/6-april-2009-general-strike-in-egypt.html.

64. Interview with Mohamed Adel, Cairo, Egypt. June 10, 2009.

65. Interview with Ahmed Maher, Cairo, Egypt. June 10, 2009.

66. Trager, Eric. 'A Tale of Two Parties.' *Foreign Policy*, November 28, 2010.

67. Interviews with Ahmed Abdel Fattah, Cairo, Egypt, June 14, 2009, and Mohamed El-Gohary, Cairo, Egypt, June 13, 2009.

68. Ben Gharbia, Sami. 'The Internet Freedom Fallacy and Arab Digital Activism.' Nawaat.org, September 17, 2010. Accessed on February 17, 2011 at http://nawaat.org/portail/2010/09/17/the-internet-freedom-fallacy-and-the-arab-digital-activism/.

69. Several mobile phone service centers in Zamalek refused to sell me this device in May and June of 2009 without proof of residency in Egypt and requested my passport and address.

70. Zahur, Sherifa. 'The Lost Calm of Operation Cast Lead.' *Middle East Policy* 16/1: (40–52).

71. 'Demonstration in Solidarity with Gaza at the Faculty of Engineering, Alexandria.' YouTube video. Accessed August 20, 2009 at http://www.youtube.com/watch?v=M5bXQvr8AhI&feature=related.

72. 'Rudud al-fi'l tajtahu shawari' al-'awasim al-arabiyya.' ('Reactions devastate the streets of Arab capitals'). *Al-Ahram*, December 31, 2008.

73. Desvarieux, Jessica. 'Hundreds Protest Closed Egypt-Gaza Border.' *Voice of America News, January 3, 2009. Accessed on July 17, 2009 at* http://www.voanews.com/english/archive/2009–01/2009–01–03voa3.cfm?CFID=26505 3033&CFTOKEN=57849127&jsessionid=8430d305506867ed7e7a1d4e6e77 1932297d.

74. Stern, Johannes. 'Widespread anger in Egypt at Mubarak regime.' World Socialist Web. January 24, 2009. Accessed on June 20, 2009 at http://www.wsws.org/articles/2009/jan2009/egyp-j24.shtml.

75. 'Shurtat Misr tulqi al-qabd 'ala 21 ikhwaniyan bi-sabab muzhaharat Ghazza' (Egyptian police arrest 21 members of the Muslim Brotherhood for Gaza protests.) Masrawy, January 11, 2009. Accessed on January 11, 2009 at http://www.wsws.org/articles/2009/jan2009/egyp-j24.shtml.

76. Interview with Mohamed Khaled, Cairo, Egypt. June 25, 2009.

77. Ibid.

78. Reports available at http://www.anhri.net/en/

79. El-Ghobashy: 'Constitutionalist Contention in Egypt', p. 10.

80. Interview with Nora Younis, Cairo, Egypt. April 2, 2008.

81. See for instance 'Solidarity from Britain', which details a message from the UK Public and Commercial Services Union at http://arabist.net/arabawy/2009/08/11/solidarity-from-britain/

82. El-Hamalawy, Hossam. "In Solidarity With the Egyptian Trade Union Activists." 3arabaway. November 5, 2008. Accessed on November 12, 2009 at http://www.arabawy.org/tag/left-%D9%8A%D8%B3%D8%A7%D8%B1/ page/19/.

83. Hausloner, Abigail. 'As Egypt's Mubarak Comes To Washington, Labor Unrest Surges at Home.' *Time*, August 18, 2009.

Chapter 5 (Amplified) Voices for the Voiceless: Social Media Networks, Minorities, and Virtual Counter-Publics

1. Habermas, Jürgen. *The Structural Transformation of the Public Sphere: An Inquiry Into a Category of Bourgeois Society.* Cambridge, MA: The MIT Press, 1991.
2. Palczewski, C. 'Cyber-movements, new social movements, and counter-publics.' In R. Asen and D. Brouwer (eds.) *Counterpublics and the State* (pp. 161–186). New York: State University of New York, 2001, p. 165.
3. Habermas, *The Structural Transformation of the Public Sphere.*
4. Poor, Nathan. 'Mechanisms of an Online Public Sphere: The Website Slashdot.' *Journal of Computer-Mediated Communications* 10/2 (2005).
5. Ibid., p. 1.
6. Norris, Pippa. *Digital Divide: Civic Engagement, Information Poverty and the Internet World-wide.* Cambridge, MA: Cambridge University Press, 2001.
7. Dahlberg, L. 'Computer-mediated communication and the public sphere: a critical analysis.' *Journal of Computer-Mediated Communication* 7/1 (2001).
8. Hindman, Matthew. *The Myth of Digital Democracy.* Princeton, NJ: Princeton University Press, 2008.
9. Palczewski: 'Cyber-movements, new social movements, and counterpublics', p. 165.
10. Fraser, Nancy. 'Rethinking the Public Sphere: A Contribution to the Critique of Actually Existing Democracies.' in Craig Calhoun, ed. *Habermas and the Public Sphere.* Cambridge, MA: the MIT Press, 1992.
11. Asen, Robert and Brouwer, Daniel C. *Counterpublics and the State.* Albany, New York: State University of New York Press, 2001, p. 7.
12. Edgar, Andrew. *The Philosophy of Habermas.* Montreal: McGill-Queens University Press, 2005, p. 36.
13. Ibid., p. 37.
14. Castells, Manuel et. al. *Mobile Communication and Society: A Global Perspective.* Cambridge, MA: MIT Press, 2007, p. 209.
15. Maratea, Ray. 'The e-Rise and Fall of Social Problems: The Blogosphere as a Public Arena.' *Social Problems* 55/1 (2008): 139–160 (140).
16. Ibid., p. 42.
17. Ibid., p. 147.
18. Bilo, 'Baha'i Faith: Early Days in Egypt.' Baha'i Faith in Egypt, June 6, 2006. Accessed on February 18, 2010 at http://www.bahai-egypt.org/2006/06/bahai-faith-early-days-in-egypt.html.
19. 'State to Appeal Ruling that Favors Egypt's Baha'is.' *Daily News Egypt,* May 5, 2006. Accessed on February 10, 2010 at http://www.dailystaregypt.com/article.aspx?ArticleID=1394.

20. Bayoumi, Amr and Mohamed Azzam. 'Baha'i twins receive first national ID card with a "blank" for religious affiliation. Their father considers it a rescue from "civil death".' *Al-Masry Al-Youm*, August 9, 2009. Accessed on March 2, 2010 at http://www.almasry-alyoum.com/article2.aspx?ArticleID=221981.

21. Interview with Samir Shady, Cairo, Egypt. April 21, 2008.

22. 'On the Baha'is and the Crucifixion of Christ.' Egyptian Baha'i, February 23, 2008. Author's translation. Accessed on 12 July 2010.at http://egyptianbahai.wordpress.com/2008/02/23/christ_crucifixion_and_the_bahai_faith/

23. 'Ya Shaykh?' Egyptian Baha'i, January 29, 2008. Accessed on February 15, 2010 at http://egyptianbahai.wordpress.com/2008/01/29/oh_sheikh/#more-110.

24. 'Introduction.' Wijhat Nazhar Ukhra, August 3, 2006. Accessed on February 22, 2010 at http://fromdifferentangle.blogspot.com/2006_08_01_archive.html.

25. Lovink, Geert. *Zero Comments: Blogging and Critical Internet Culture*. New York, NY: Routledge 2008.

26. 'The Radwan Holiday in Egypt.' Egyptian Baha'i, April 28, 2008. Author's translation. Accessed on January 12, 2010 at http://egyptianbahai.wordpress.com/2008/04/28/ridwan_in_egyp/ .

27. Bilo, 'Egyptian Bah'ais and ID cards.' Baha'i Faith in Egypt, June 2, 2006. Accessed on February 18, 2010 at http://www.bahai-egypt.org/search?updated-max=2006-07-09T19%3A01%3A00-05%3A00&max-results=50.

28. 'Nora Younis khilal takreemha' ('Nora Younis During Her Award Reception'). Egyptian Baha'i. October 30, 2008. Accessed on February 1, 2010 at http://egyptianbahai.wordpress.com/2008/10/30/the_beautifu/2969734075_d676420219/.

29. Interview with Ehab El-Zalaky, Cairo, Egypt. April 11, 2008.

30. Izz Ed-Din, Ahmed. 'Leaders of American Baha'is demand the implementation of administrative court ruling on ID cards…and estimate the number of Baha'is in Egypt at 2000.' *Al-Masry Al-Youm*, August 21, 2008. Author's translation.

31. The Sandmonkey. 'Today's Baha'i Protest.' Rantings of a Sandmonkey, December 17, 2006. Accessed on February 19, 2010 at http://www.sandmonkey.org/2006/12/17/todays-bahai-protest/.

32. Manal and Alaa's Bit-Bucket. 'Waqfa tadamuniyya min al-baha'iyin al-masriyin min ajli haqqihim fi ithbat diyanatihim aw kitaba (ukhra) fi khanat al-diyanah fi-l-awraq al-rasmiyya.' Accessed on January 14, 2010 at http://www.manalaa.net/node/84324.

33. Ibid. 'Ba'd al-hukm 'ala 'Abd al-Karim wa-l-baha'iyin al-kuffar hayniku ukhtak'. Accessed on February 10, 2010 at http://www.manalaa.net/the_heathen_and_your_sister.

34. Ibid. 'Kuntum fein lamma Faransa' (Where were you when France?'). Accessed on July 15, 2009 at http://www.manalaa.net/where_where_you_when_france.

35. Gharbeia, Amr. 'Ni'mil eih fi-l-baha'iyin ba'd ma mana'athum al-mahkama min ithbat dinahum fi al-'awraq al-thubutiyya?' ('What shall we do with the Baha'is now that the courts prohibited them from affirming their religion in evidentiary documents?') Gharbeia.net, December 17, 2006. Accessed on February 18, 2010 at http://gharbeia.net/node/179.
36. 'Court denies Ba'hais legal recognition.' The Arabist, December 17, 2009. Accessed on February 4, 2010 at http://arabist.net/archives/2006/12/16/court-denies-bahais-legal-recognition/.
37. El-Zelaky himself later admitted that there were errors in the coverage of his paper, but argued his reporters were doing their best. Interview with Ehab El-Zelaky, Cairo, Egypt. April 8, 2008.
38. Ibn Abdel Aziz. December 21, 2006. Accessed February 3, 2010 at http://justice4every1.blogspot.com/2006/12/blog-post_116672907886849680.html. Blog open to invited readers only.
39. El-Hamalawy, Hossam. 'Bigotry and sectarianism par excellence.' 3Arabawy, December 16, 2006. Accessed on April 14, 2008 at http://arabist.net/arabawy/2006/12/16/anti-bahaais-bigotry-and-sectarianism/.
40. Whitaker, Brian. 'Egypt's step toward freedom of belief.' The Guardian, March 17, 2009.
41. Stack, Liam. 'Egyptians win right to drop religion from ID cards.' Christian Science Monitor, April 20, 2009, p. 6. It should be noted here that Stack is a personal friend and has extensive social ties in the Egyptian activist community. It is therefore difficult to argue that the power-blogger protest had any effect on his decision to write this article.
42. Slackman, Michael. 'Hints of Pluralism Begin to Appear in Egyptian Religious Debates.' The New York Times, August 31, 2009, p. 6.
43. Photo appears on Hossam El-Hamalawy's December 16, 2010 blog post on 3arabawy, entitled 'Bigotry and sectarianism par excellence.' http://www.arabawy.org/2006/12/16/anti-bahaais-bigotry-and-sectarianism/
44. 'Majma' al-buhuth al-islamiyya: al-baha'iya haraka suhyuniyya tas'a li-nashr al-fasad wa-l-radhila' ('The Islamic Research Center: Baha'ism is a Zionist movement bent on spreading corruption and vice'). Al Masry Al-Youm, May 30, 2009. Accessed on July 15, 2009 at http://www.almasry-alyoum.com/article2.aspx?ArticleID=213030.
45. 'Ahmed 'Abd al-Mu'ti yaktub: mushkilatuna ma'a al-usuliyyin' ('Our problem with the fundamentalists'). Al-Masry Al-Youm, May 7, 2009. Accessed on June 17, 2009 at http://www.almasry-alyoum.com/article2.aspx?ArticleID=210026.
46. Lust-Okar, Ellen. Structuring Conflict in the Arab World: Incumbents, Opponents, and Institutions. Cambridge, England: Cambridge University Press, 2007.

47. Harnisch, Chris and Mecham, Quinn. 'Democratic Ideology in Islamist Opposition? The Muslim Brotherhood's "Civil State".' *Middle Eastern Studies* 45/2 (March 2009): 189–205; Leiken, Robert S. and Brooke, Steven. 'The Moderate Muslim Brotherhood.' *Foreign Affairs*, 86/2 (2007): 107–121; Shehata, Samer, and Stacher, Joshua. 'The Brotherhood Goes to Parliament.' *Middle East Report* 36/3 (Fall 2006): 32–39.

48. Lust-Okar: *Structuring Conflict in the Arab World.*

49. Brownlee, Jason. *Authoritarianism in an Age of Democratization.* New York, NY: Cambridge University Press, 2007.

50. Lynch, Marc. 'Young Brothers in Cyberspace.' *Middle East Report* 245 (Winter 2007). Accessed on January 8, 2008 at http://www.merip.org/mer/mer245/mer245.html.

51. Ibid.

52. Hamzawy, Amr. 'Egypt: Regression in the Muslim Brotherhood's Party Platform?' *Arab Reform Bulletin*, October 2007.

53. Ibid.

54. Lynch: 'Young Brothers in Cyberspace.'

55. Interview with Mohamed Habib, Cairo, Egypt. February 21, 2008.

56. Interview with Ahmed Abdel Fatouh, Cairo, Egypt. February 16, 2008.

57. Interview with Khaled Hamza, Cairo, Egypt. April 27, 2008.

58. 'Khaled Hamza is free.' Ikhwan Web, April 16, 2009. Accessed on March 4, 2010 at http://www.ikhwanweb.com/article.php?ID=16728&SectionID=0.

59. Interview with Abdul-Rahman Monsour, Cairo, Egypt. April 9, 2008.

60. Interview with Abdel Monam Mahmoud, Cairo, Egypt. April 23, 2008. Mahmoud kindly met me for coffee in downtown Cairo and talked at length about what his blog means to him.

61. Interview with Ahmed Abdel Fatteh, Cairo, Egypt. February 16, 2008.

62. Ibid.

63. See for instance, Stack, Liam. 'Egypt targets Muslim Brotherhood moderates.' *Christian Science Monitor*, March 26, 2008, p. 7. Stack, it must be noted, is also a personal friend with extensive ties in the Egyptian activist community.

64. See 'Cairo court jails 25 political opponents.' Reuters, April 16, 2008.

65. 'Egypt police detain Muslim Brotherhood blogger.' Reuters, April 9, 2009. Accessed on July 14, 2009 at http://www.reuters.com/article/internetNews/idUSTRE5342BA20090405.

66. Kassem, Maye. *Egyptian Politics: The Dynamics of Authoritarian Rule.* Boulder, CO: Lynne Rienner Publishers, 2004, p. 38.

67. Stack, Liam. 'Egypt Targets Muslim Brotherhood Moderates.' *Christian Science Monitor.* March 26, 2008. http://www.csmonitor.com/2008/0326/p07s08-wome.html?page=1

68. Kassem: *Egyptian Politics: The Dynamics of Authoritarian Rule*, p. 188.
69. Shehata and Stacher: 'The Brotherhood Goes To Parliament', p. 2006.
70. Ikhwanonline. 'Interview with Mohamed Baligh After Verdict.' June 15, 2008. Accessed on July 17, 2009 at http://www.ikhwanweb.com/article.php?id=17265.
71. See Brownlee: *Authoritarianism in an Age of Democratization*.
72. Interview with Khaled Hamza, Cairo, Egypt. April 27, 2008.
73. Interview with Abdel Rahman Monsour, Cairo, Egypt. April 9, 2008.
74. Interview with Abdullah Al-Shammi, Cairo, Egypt. April 9, 2008.
75. Ibid.
76. Interview with Mohamed Habib, Cairo, Egypt. February 16, 2008
77. http://www.facebook.com/Khairat.Alshater
78. www.ibn-elshater.blogspot.com
79. Photo from www.ibn-shater.blogspot.com.
80. Photo appears on Hossam El-Hamalawy's March 22· 2008 blog entry entitled 'Free Khaled Hamza.' Accessed March 19, 2012 at http://www.arabawy.org/2008/03/02/freekhaledblog/.
81. Snow et. al.
82. El-Hamalawy, Hossam. 'Solidarity from the U.S. for Khaled Hamza.' 3Arabawy, February 24, 2008. Accessed on July 15, 2008 at http://arabist.net/arabawy/2008/02/24/freekhaled_downwithmubarak/.
83. Ibid.
84. 'Egyptian blogs and the Baha'is.' Wijhat Nazhar Ukhra, December 13, 2006. Accessed on February 22, 2010 at http://fromdifferentangle.blogspot.com/2006_12_01_archive.html. Her site does not provide stable URL links to each blog entry.

Chapter 6 We Are All Revolutionaries Now: Social Media Networks and the Egyptian Revolution of 2011

1. Interview with Amr Gharbeia, Cairo, Egypt. July 13, 2011.
2. El-Ghobashy, Mona. 'The Praxis of the Egyptian Revolution.' *Middle East Report* Vol. 41 (Spring 2011).
3. Interview with Ahmed Saleh, Cairo, Egypt. July 6, 2011.
4. Benkler, Yoshai. *The Wealth of Networks: How Social Production Transforms Markets and Freedom*. New Haven, CT: Yale University Press, 2007.
5. Ghonim, Wael. TEDx Talk. Cairo, Egypt. March 4, 2011. Accessed on March 4, 2011 at http://www.youtube.com/watch?v=SWvJxasiSZ8.
6. Khalil, Ashraf. 'Monday's Papers: The Social Insurance Umbrella and the Khaled Saeed Case.' *Al-Masry Al-Youm* English edition. Accessed on April 30, 2011 at http://www.almasryalyoum.com/en/node/48925.

7. Shalaby, Ethar. 'Protesters turn their back to Egyptian police abuse.' Danish Egyptian Dialogue Institute. Accessed on March 11, 2011 at http://dedi.org.eg/index.php/en/hiwar-mag/71-featured/485-protesters-qturn-their-backsq-to-egyptian-police-abuse.

8. 'Al-Amn yuhasir ansar "Khaled Said" fi Iskindariya' (Security forces surround supporters of Khaled Said in Alexandria). Al-Masry Al-Youm, September 25, 2010. Accessed on May 25, 2011 at http://www.almasryalyoum.com/node/167080.

9. Zeinobia. '"Follow-up" Khaled Said Trial "Live" Day One.' Egyptian Chronicles, July 27, 2010. Accessed on May 25, 2011 at http://egyptianchronicles.blogspot.com/2010/07/follow-up-khaled-said-trial-1.html.

10. Shalaby, Ahmed and El Marsfawy, Mostafa. 'Al Masry Al Youm Exclusive: Khaled Saeed Case Investigation.' Al-Masry Al-Youm. December 7, 2010. Accessed May 21, 2011 at http://www.egyptindependent.com/node/55686.

11. Interview with Bassem Fathy, Cairo, Egypt. June 25, 2011.

12. Meier, Patrick. 'Analyzing U-Shahid's Electron Monitoring Results From Egypt.' iRevolution. May 23, 2011.

13. Ibid.

14. El-Ghobashy, Mona. 'The Liquidation of Egypt's Illiberal Experiment.' Middle East Report Online. December 29, 2010. http://www.merip.org/mero/mero122910.

15. Interview with Abdullah Al-Fakharany, Cairo, Egypt. June 26, 2011.

16. Ibid.

17. Hindman, Matthew. The Myth of Digital Democracy. Princeton, NJ: Princeton University Press, 2008.

18. Interview with Amr Gharbeia, Cairo, Egypt. July 13, 2011.

19. Author's translation. Wall post, Kulna Khaled Said, January 14, 2011. Accessed on September 25, 2011 at http://www.facebook.com/ElShaheeed.

20. Author's translation.

21. Interview with Bassem Fathy, Cairo, Egypt. June 25, 2011.

22. Hands, Joss. @ is for Activism. New York, NY: Pluto Press, 2010, p. 124.

23. Madrigal, Alexis. 'Egyptian Activists Action Plan: Translated.' The Atlantic, January 27, 2011. Accessed on March 13, 2011 at http://www.theatlantic.com/international/archive/2011/01/egyptian-activists-action-plan-translated/70388/.

24. Status update, We Are All Khaled Said, 8:55 a.m. CST. Accessed on September 25, 2011 at www.facebook.com/elshaheeed.co.uk.

25. Khalil, 'Monday's Papers.'

26. Status update, We Are All Khaled Said, January 29, 2011, 5:45 p.m. Accessed on September 25, 2011 at www.facebook.com/elshaheeed.co.uk.

27. Status update, We Are All Khaled Said, January 27, 2011, 6:04 p.m. Accessed on September 25, 2011 at www.facebook.com/elshaheeed.co.uk.

28. Status update, We Are All Khaled Said, January 27, 2011, 6:27 p.m. Accessed on September 25, 2011 at www.facebook.com/elshaheeed.co.uk

29. Ibid., status update, January 25, 2011, 11:03 a.m. Accessed on September 25, 2011 at www.facebook.com/elshaheeed.co.uk

30. Author's translation. Status update, *Kulna Khaled Said*, February 3, 2011. Accessed on September 25, 2011 at www.facebook.com/ElShaheeed .

31. Author's translation. Status update, *Kulna Khaled Said*, January 31, 2011. Accessed on September 25, 2011 at www.facebook.com/ElShaheeed .

32. Khamis, Samir and Vaughn, Katherine. 'Cyberactivism in the Egyptian Revolution: How Civic Engagement and Citizen Journalism Tilted the Balance.' *Arab Media and Society 13 (Summer 2011)*.

33. Idle, Nadia and Nunns, Alex. *Tweets From Tahrir*. Doha, Qatar: Bloomsbury Qatar Foundation Publishing, 2011, p. 20.

34. Khamis and Vaughn: 'Cyberactivism in the Egyptian Revolution: How Civic Engagement and Citizen Journalism Tilted the Balance.'

35. Status update, We Are All Khaled Said. February 2, 2011. Accessed September 25, 2011 at www.facebook.com/elshaheeed.co.uk.

36. February 2, 2011.

37. Idle and Nunns: *Tweets From Tahrir*, p. 121.

38. Khamis and Vaughn: 'Cyberactivism in the Egyptian Revolution: How Civic Engagement and Citizen Journalism Tilted the Balance.'

39. Interview with Ahmed Saleh, Cairo, Egypt. July 6, 2011.

40. Ibid.

41. Interview with Amr Gharbeia, Cairo, Egypt. July 5, 2011.

42. Agar, Jon. *Constant Touch: A Global History of the Mobile Phone*. Cambridge, UK: Icon Books, 2003, p. 132.

43. 'Meet Asmaa Mahfouz and the Vlog that Helped Spark the Revolution.' Youtube. February 1, 2011. Accessed February 3, 2011 at http://www.youTube.com/watch?v=SgjIgMdsEuk.

44. Interview with Ahmed Saleh, Cairo, Egypt. July 6, 2011.

45. Sims, David. *Understanding Cairo: The Logic of a City Out of Control*. Cairo, Egypt: American University Press, 2011.

46. Interview with Abdullah Halmy, Cairo, Egypt. June 27, 2011.

47. Ibid.

48. Kaplan, Robert D. 'One Small Revolution.' *New York Times*, January 22, 2011, P. WK11.

49. There was of course, no actual 'kill switch'. Turning off the Internet required the collaboration of Egypt's telecom companies, including Mobinil and Vodaphone.

50. Idle and Nunns: *Tweets from Tahrir.*
51. The full video can be seen at http://www.youtube.com/watch?v= HvRr3xvvXYY.
52. Interview with Amr Gharbeia, Cairo, Egypt. July 5, 2011.
53. Idle and Nunns: *Tweets From Tahrir*, p. 98.
54. 'Timeline: Egypt's Revolution.' Al-Jazeera English, February 14, 2011. Accessed on September 30, 2011 at http://www.aljazeera.com/news/middlee ast/2011/01/201112515334871490.html.
55. El-Hamalawy, Hossam. '#Jan25 Public transportation workers call for over-throwing Mubarak.' 3arabawy, February 9, 2011. Accessed on September 9, 2011 at http://www.arabawy.org/2011/02/09/jan25-public-transportation-workers-call-for-overthrowing-mubarak.
56. El-Hamalawy, Hossam. '#Jan25 Actors for the revolution.' 3arabawy, February 10, 2011. Accessed on September 9, 2011 at http://www.arabawy.org/2011/02/10/cinema-for-the-revolution/.
57. Carr, Sarah. '6 Months Later.' *Inanities.* July 27, 2011. Accessed September 12, 2011 at http://inanities.org/2011/07/6-months-later/.
58. Interview with Bassem Fathy, Cairo, Egypt. June 25, 2011.
59. Conversation with Amr Gharbeia. Cairo, Egypt, July 13, 2011
60. Afify, Heba, and Nadim Audi. 'Egyptian Forces Roust Tahrir Sit-In.' *The New York Times*, August 2, 2011, p. A9.
61. Shirky, Clay. *Here Comes Everybody: The Power of Organizing Without Organizations.* New York, NY: Penguin Press, 2008.
62. Shenker, Jack. 'Egyptian Revolutionary Alaa Abdel Fattah Arrested By Egyptian Junta.' *The Guardian.* October 31, 2011.
63. Lesch, Ann M. 'Egypt's Spring: The Causes of Revolution.' *Middle East Policy* Vol. 28, No. 3 (Fall 2011): 35–48.

Chapter 7 Cascades, Colours, and Contingencies: Social Media Networks and Authoritarianism in Global Perspective

1. http://www.freedomhouse.org.
2. Lust-Okar, Ellen. *Structuring Conflict in the Arab World: Incumbents, Opponents, and Institutions.* Cambridge, England: Cambridge University Press, 2007, p. 172.
3. Brownlee, Jason. *Authoritarianism in an Age of Democratization.* New York, NY: Cambridge University Press, 2007, p. 206.
4. Joyce, Mary (ed.) *Digital Activism Decoded: The New Mechanics of Change.* New York, NY: International Debate Education Association, 2010.

5. Whitten-Woodring, Jennifer. 'Watchdog or Lapdog? Media Freedom, Regime Type, and Government Respect for Human Rights.' *International Studies Quarterly* 53 (2009): 595–625.

6. Milani, Abbas. 'Cracks in the Regime.' *Journal of Democracy* (2009) 16/5: 5–19 (11–15). p. 11.

7. Poulson, Stephen C. 'Nested Institutions, Political Opportunity, and the Decline of the Iranian Reform Movement Post 9/11.' *American Behavioral Scientist* 53/1 (2009): 27–43 (29).

8. Ibid.

9. 'How Iran's opposition inverts old slogans.' BBC News Online, December 7, 2009. Accessed on March 29, 2010 at http://news.bbc.co.uk/2/hi/middle_east/8386335.stm.

10. Ibid.

11. Coughlin, Con. 'Why the Mullahs are Vulnerable.' *The Wall Street Journal*, December 29, 2009. Accessed December 30, 2009 at http://online.wsj.com/article/SB10001424052748703278604574624191585240728.html.

12. Abdel Fatteh, Ahmed. 'Limatha Lem tastati'a Iran qama'a ath-thowra al-khadara'?' (Why couldn't Iran crush the Green Revolution?). Personal correspondence. August 16, 2009.

13. Ibid.

14. Pfeifle, Mark. 'A Nobel Peace Prize for Twitter?' *The Christian Science Monitor*, July 6, 2009.

15. 'Internet Brings Events in Iran to Life.' BBC News Online, June 15, 2009. Accessed December 30, 2009 at http://news.bbc.co.uk/2/hi/middle_east/8099579.stm.

16. 'Surviving The Year of Twitter.' *The Straits* Times, December 27, 2009.

17. Musgrove, Mike. 'Twitter is a Player in Iran's Drama.' *The Washington Post*, June 17, 2009, p. A10.

18. Viner, Katharine. 'Internet has changed foreign policy forever, says Gordon Brown.' *The Guardian*, June 19, 2009.

19. Stone, Brad, and Cohen, Norm. 'Social Networks Spread Iranian Defiance Online.' *The New York Times*, June 16, 2009, p. 11.

20. Ibid.

21. Cohen, Noam. 'Twitter on the Barricades: Six Lessons Learned.' *New York Times*, June 20, 2009. Accessed March 18, 2012 at http://www.nytimes.com/2009/06/21/weekinreview/21cohenweb.html.

22. http://andrewsullivan.thedailybeast.com/

23. Morozov, Eugene. 'Downside to the "Twitter Revolution".' *Dissent* 56/4 (Fall 2009): 10–14.

24. Daragahi, Barzou. 'Exiled, but still insiders; The latest wave in Iran's diaspora is tech-savvy and playing a key role in countering hard-liners at home.' *Los Angeles Times*, December 10, 2009, p.1.
25. Ibid.
26. Mozorov, Eugene. 'From Slacktivism to Activism.' *Foreign Policy. Net.Effect.* September 5, 2009. Accessed on January 14, 2010 at http://neteffect.foreign-policy.com/posts/2009/09/05/from_slacktivism_to_activism.
27. Heaven, Will. 'The fatal folly of the online revolutionaries; Smug Twitter activists are wrong to think they are liberating Iran, says Will Heaven.' *The Daily Telegraph*, December 29, 2009, p. 16.
28. 'Twitter Taken Over By Iranian Cyber Army.' *Brand Republic News Releases*, December 24, 2009.
29. 'Iran.' Freedom of the Press 2009. Freedom House. Accessed March 11, 2010 at http://www.freedomhouse.org/report/freedom-press/2009/iran?page=251&year=2009&country=7627
30. Milani, Abbas. 'Cracks in the Regime.' *Journal of Democracy* (2009) 16/5: 5–19 (11–15).
31. Boromaund, Ladan. 'Civil Society's Choice.' *Journal of Democracy* 20/4 (October 2009): 16–20.
32. Lane, David. 'The Orange Revolution: "People's Revolution" or Revolutionary Coup?' *British Journal of Politics and International Relations* 10/4 (2008): 525–549 (527).
33. 'Freedom in the World 2004 – Ukraine.' Freedom House. Accessed March 22, 2010 at http://expression.freedomhouse.org/reports/freedom_in_the_world/2004/ukraine.
34. Lane: 'The Orange Revolution: "People's Revolution" or Revolutionary Coup?', p. 525.
35. 'Yuschenko and the Poison Theory.' BBC News Online, December 11, 2004. Accessed December 18, 2009 at http://news.bbc.co.uk/2/hi/health/4041321.stm.
36. Lane: 'The Orange Revolution: "People's Revolution" or Revolutionary Coup?', 526
37. Bunce, Valerie and Wolchik, Sharon. 'Getting Real About Real Causes.' *Journal of Democracy* 20/1 (January 2009): 69–73 (70).
38. McFaul, Michael. 'Transitions From Postcommunism.' *Journal of Democracy* 16/3 (2005): 5–19; also quoted in Goldstein, Joshua. 'The Role of Digital Networked Technologies in Ukraine's Orange Revolution.' The Berkman Center for Technology and Society at Harvard. Berkman Center Research Publication 2007–14.
39. Lane: 'The Orange Revolution: "People's Revolution" or Revolutionary Coup?'

40. Ibid., p. 5.
41. McFaul: 'Transitions From Postcommunism.'
42. Ibid., pp. 7–8.
43. http://www.pravda.com.ua/
44. Lane: 'The Orange Revolution: "People's Revolution" or Revolutionary Coup?'
45. Mungiu-Pippidi, Alina and Munteanu, Igor. 'Moldova's Twitter Revolution.' *Journal of Democracy* 20/3 (July 2009): 136–142.
46. McDonagh, Ecaterina. Is Democracy Promotion Effective in Moldova? The Impact of European Institutions on Development of Civil and Political Rights in Moldova'. *Democratization* 15/1 (2008), 142–161. p. 143
47. McDonagh, Ecaterina. Is Democracy Promotion Effective in Moldova? The Impact of European Institutions on Development of Civil and Political Rights in Moldova'. p. 159
48. Mungiu-Pippidi, Alina and Munteanu, Igor. 'Moldova's Twitter Revolution.' p. 142.
49. Stack, Graham. 'Leader of Moldova's "Twitter revolution" goes into hiding: Fugitive surprised by size of protest fears arrest: Organiser says Kremlin behind police targeting.' *The Guardian*, April 16, 2009, p. 19.
50. Mungiu-Pippidi and Munteanu 2009, p. 139
51. Mungiu-Pippidi and Munteanu 2009, p. 140.
52. Ibid.
53. Schell, Jonathan. *The Unconquerable World: Power, Non-Violence and the Will of the People*. New York: Henry Holt and Co., 2004. p. 218.
54. Pippidi and Munteanu 2009, 139.
55. Ibid., p. 141.
56. O'Donnell, Guillermo, Schmitter, Phillippe C., and Whitehead, Laurence, eds. *Transitions From Authoritarian Rule: Comparative Perspectives*. Baltimore, MD: The John's Hopkins University Press, 1986; Przeworski, Adam. *Democracy and the Market: Political and Economic Reforms in Eastern Europe and Latin America*. Cambridge, UK: Cambridge University Press, 1991.
57. Goldstein, Joshua and Rotich, Juliana. 'The Role of Digital Networked Technologies in Kenya's 2007–2008 Post-Election Crisis.' The Berkman Center for Technology and Society at Harvard. Berkman Center Research Publication 2008–9, p. 3.
58. Kiai, Maina. 'The Crisis in Kenya.' *Journal of Democracy* 19/3 (July 2008): 162–168.
59. Ibid., p. 164.
60. Maloney, Brenna. 'A Disputed Election Leads To Violence; Hundreds Killed as Two of the Country's Ethnic Groups Clash.' *Washington Post*, January 7, 2008, p. C12.

61. Gettleman, Jeffrey. 'With Half of Vote Counted, Kenyan Opposition is Poised to Sweep.' *The New York Times*, December 29, 2007, p. 9.

62. Kiai: 'The Crisis In Kenya', p. 165.

63. Maloney, Brenna. 'A Disputed Election Leads to Violence; Hundreds Killed as Two of the Countries Ethnic Groups Clash.'

64. Goldstein and Rotich: 'The Role of Digital Networked Technologies in Kenya's 2007–2008 Post-Election Crisis', p. 5.

65. Gettleman, Jeffrey. 'Kenya's Opposition Switches its Tactics From Street Protests to Business Boycotts.' *The New York Times*, January 19th, 2008. P. 6.

66. Ibid.

67. Kenya Human Rights Commission. "Kenya; Unprecedent State of Violence." *Africa News*. May 21, 2009.

68. Goldstein and Rotich: 'The Role of Digital Networked Technologies in Kenya's 2007–2008 Post-Election Crisis', p. 5.

69. Biz-Community. 'Kenya; Bloggers Keep World Informed.' *Africa News*, January 4, 2008.

70. 'Blogs, SMS, and the Kenyan Election.' Internet & Democracy Blog, January 3, 2008. Accessed December 21, 2009 at http://blogs.law.harvard.edu/idblog/2008/01/03/blogs-sms-and-the-kenyan-election/.

71. *Kenya Pundit*. 'Post-media blackout update, January 1, 4:30 p.m.' Accessed December 21, 2009 at http://www.kenyanpundit.com/2008/01/01/post-media-blackout-update-jan-1–430-pm/.

72. www.kenyanpundit.com

73. The main Tunisian opposition blog, Nawaat, was largely operated from outside of Tunisia.

74. '2008 Freedom of the Press World Ranking.' Freedom House. Accessed March 18, 2010 at http://www.freedomhouse.org/template.cfm?page=442&year=2008.

75. Srinivasan, Ramesh, and Fish, Adam. 'Revolutionary Tactics, Media Ecologies, and Repressive States.' *Public Culture* Vol. 23, No. 3 (2011): 505–510.

BIBLIOGRAPHY

Blogs and Websites

3Arabawy (Hossam El-Hawalamy's blog), http://www.arabawy.org/ (Arabic and English)

Al-Jazeera (Arabic)

Al-Jazeera (English)

Ana Ikhwan (I Am a Muslim Brother), http://ana-ikhwan.blogspot.com (Arabic)

Annals of the Trees (by Amr Gharbeia), http://gharbeia.net (Arabic)

April 6 Youth Movement (Facebook page), https://www.facebook.com/groups/6april2008/ (Arabic)

Baha'i Faith in Egypt, http://www.bahai-egypt.org/ (English)

Baheyya: Egypt Analysis and Whimsy, http://baheyya.blogspot.com/ (English)

Big Pharoah, http://www.bigpharaoh.org/ (English)

Cairo Live, www.cairolive.com (English)

Coalition of Youth Revolution (Facebook page), https://www.facebook.com/Coalition.Of.Youth.Revolution (Arabic)

Daily Dish (Andrew Sullivan's blog), http://andrewsullivan.thedailybeast.com/ (English)

Demagh MAK, http://www.demaghmak.com/ (Arabic)

Egypt Watchman (Mina Zakry's blog), http://www.minazekri.net/ (Arabic)

Egyptian Baha'i, http://egyptianbahai.wordpress.com (Arabic)

Egyptian Chronicles (Zeinobia's blog), http://egyptianchronicles.blogspot.com/ (English)

EgyTimes, http://egytimes.org/ (Arabic)

ElBaradei For President 2011 (Facebook group), https://www.facebook.com/groups/me.elbaradei/ (Arabic)

Ensaa! (Forget!), http://ensaa.blogspot.com (Arabic)

Free Kareem!, http://www.freekareem.org (English)

Global Voices, http://globalvoicesonline.org (English)

Have Your Say (BBC forum), http://www.bbc.co.uk/news/have_your_say/ (English)

Kenya Pundit, www.kenyapundit.com (English)
Kulna Khaled Said (Facebook group),
Living in Egypt Without ID, http://egypt-bahai-id.blogspot.com (English)
Malek X (Malek Mustafa's blog), http://malek-x.net/ (Arabic)
Manal and Alaa's Bit Bucket, http://www.manalaa.net (Arabic and English)
Misr Digital (Wael Abbas's blog), http://misrdigital.blogspirit.com/ (Arabic)
Nawaat (Tunisian group blog)
Nora Younis
Piggipedia, http://www.arabawy.org/tag/piggipedia/ (English)
Pravda (Ukrainian opposition site), http://www.pravda.com.ua/
Rantings of a Sandmonkey, http://www.sandmonkey.org (English)
Save the People of Qursaya Island (Facebook group), http://www.facebook.com/
       wall.php?id=19903372840&page=1&hash=8177ac749eb7a592f4d53da247f
       9c038 (Arabic)
Shabab Baha'i
The Arabist, www.arabist.net (English)
Torture In Egypt, http://tortureinegypt.net/ (Arabic)
U-Shahid (election violation mapping), www.u-shahid.com (Arabic)
We Are All Khaled Said (Facebook group), http://www.facebook.com/elshaheeed.
       co.uk (English)
https://www.facebook.com/ElShaheeed (Arabic)
Wijhat Nazhar Ukhra (Another Viewpoint), http://fromdifferentangle.blogspot.
       com (Arabic)
Wounded Female From Cairo, http://woundedgirlfromcairo.blogspot.com/ (English)

Interviews

Interview with Abdel Monam Mahmoud, Cairo, Egypt. April 23, 2008.
Interview with Abdul-Rahman Monsour, Cairo, Egypt. April 9, 2008.
Interview with Abdullah Al-Fakharany, Cairo, Egypt. June 26, 2011.
Interview with Abdullah Al-Shammi, Cairo, Egypt. April 9, 2008.
Interview with Abdullah Halmy, Cairo, Egypt. June 27, 2011.
Interview with Ahmed Abdel Fattah, Cairo, Egypt. December 10, 2007.
Interview with Ahmed Abdel Fattah, Cairo, Egypt, June 14, 2009.
Interview with Ahmed Maher, Cairo, Egypt. June 10, 2009.
Interview with Ahmed Saleh, Cairo, Egypt. July 6, 2011.
Interview with Amr Gharbeia, Cairo, Egypt. July 13, 2011.
Interview with Amira Howeidy, Cairo, Egypt. April 19, 2008.
Interview with Bassem Fathy, Cairo, Egypt. June 25, 2011
Interview with blogger who wished to remain anonymous, Cairo, Egypt. April 6,
       2008.
Interview with Demagh MAK, Cairo, Egypt. June 18, 2009.
Interview with Ehab El-Zalaky, Cairo, Egypt. April 8, 2008.
Interview with Ehab El-Zalaky, Cairo, Egypt. April 11, 2008.

Interview with Gamal Eid, Director of the Arab Network for Human Rights Information. Cairo, Egypt, February 26, 2008.

Interview with Hossam El-Hamalawy, Cairo, Egypt. May 27, 2009.

Interview with Issandr El-Amrani, Cairo, Egypt. February 16, 2008.

Interview with Khaled Hamza, Cairo,Egypt. April 27, 2008.

Interview with Mohamed Adel, Cairo, Egypt. June 10, 2009.

Interview with Mohamed El-Gohary, Cairo, Egypt, June 13, 2009.

Interview with Mohamed Habib, Cairo, Egypt. February 16, 2008

Interview with Mohamed Habib, Cairo, Egypt. February 21, 2008.

Interview with Mohamed Khaled, Cairo, Egypt. June 25, 2009.

Interview with Mohammed Maree, Cairo, Egypt. July 15, 2011.

Interview with Mina Zakry, Cairo, Egypt. March 24, 2008.

Interview with Mina Zakry, Cairo, Egypt. March 27, 2008.

Interview with Noha Atef, Cairo, Egypt. July 7, 2011.

Interview with Nora Younis, Cairo, Egypt. April 2, 2008.

Interview with Samir Shady, Cairo, Egypt. April 21, 2008.

Interview with The Sandmonkey, Cairo, Egypt. March 23, 2008.

Interview with Tarek Atia, Cairo, Egypt. February 6, 2008.

Interview with Wael Abbas, Cairo, Egypt. April 14, 2008.

References

'2008 Freedom of the Press World Ranking.' Freedom House. Accessed March 18, 2010 at http://www.freedomhouse.org/template.cfm?page=442& year=2008.

6 April Movement. '6 April 2009, General Strike in Egypt.' Saturday, April 4, 2009. Accessed on June 11, 2009 at http://6aprilmove.blogspot.com/ 2009/04/6-april-2009-general-strike-in-egypt.html.

Abbas, Wael. 'Today's Activities in Egypt.' Misr Digital, May 25, 2006. Author's translation. Accessed on May 27, 2009 at http://misrdigital.blogspirit.com/ archive/2006/05/index.html

Abdel Fatteh, Ahmed. 'Limatha Lem tastati'a Iran qama'a ath-thowra al-kha-dara'?' (Why couldn't Iran crush the Green Revolution?). Personal correspondence. August 16, 2009.

Abdel Fattah, Wael. 'Officer from Qism al-Haram torture video arrested.' El-Fagr, November 27, 2006.

Abdel Halim, Khaled Omar. 'Egyptian Human Rights Organization Calls for Amending the Laws to Conform to International Conventions.' Al-Masry Al-Youm, 2 September 2009.

Abdel Qader, Mohamed. 'People's Assembly Human Rights Committee to Visit Police Stations.' Al-Masry Al-Youm, November 30, 2008.

Aclimandos, Tewfik. 'The Muslim Brothers: For a Critique of Wishful Thinking.' Politique Africaine 108 (December 2007): 25–46.

'Ahmed 'Abd al-Mu'ti yaktub: mushkilatuna ma'a al-usuliyyin' ('Our problem with the fundamentalists') *Al-Masry Al-Youm*, May 7, 2009. Accessed on June 17, 2009 at http://www.almasry-alyoum.com/article2.aspx? ArticleID=210026.

Al-A'oumi, Yusef. 'Wazarat al-siyaha: laji'u al-Sudan fi Misr siyah' ('Tourism Ministry: Sudanese refugees in Egypt are tourists'). *Al-Masry Al-Youm*, January 5, 2006.

'Al-Amn yuhasir ansar "Khaled Said" fi Iskindariya' (Security forces surround supporters of Khaled Said in Alexandria). *Al-Masry Al-Youm*, September 25, 2010. Accessed on May 25, 2011 at http://www.almasryalyoum.com/ node/167080.

Al-Saggaf, Yeslam. 'The Online Public Sphere in the Arab World: The War in Iraq on the Al Arabiya Website.' *Journal of Computer-Mediated Communication* 12 (2006): 311–334.

Al-Sayyid, Emad. 'Al-Masry Al-Youm: Alone in publishing the first picture of the officer in Bulaaq accused of torturing Emad Al-Kabir'. *Al-Masry Al-Youm*, December 29, 2006.

Abdel Hamid, Heba and Shaima el-Karnashawi. 'Afrah fil Qursaya b'ad al Hukm bi Tanikinihim min manazilihim' ('Happiness in Qursaya after ruling about expulsion from their homes'). *Al Masry Al-Youm*, November 17, 2008.

Abdelhamid, Doha. 'Mind the Gap.' *Al-Ahram Weekly*, 14–20 May 2009.

Abu Lughod, Lila. 'Islam and Public Culture: the Politics of Egyptian Television Serials.' *Middle East Report*, 180 (Jan/Feb. 1993): 25–30.

Ackerman, Gary, James, Molly, and Casey T. Getz. 'The Application of Social Bookmarking Technology to the National Intelligence Domain.' *International Journal of Intelligence and Counterintelligence* 20/7 (2007): 678–698.

Agar, Jon. *Constant Touch: A Global History of the Mobile Phone*. Cambridge, UK: Icon Books, 2003.

Ajemian, Pete. 'The Islamist opposition online in Egypt and Jordan.' *Arab Media & Society* Issue 7 (January 2008).

Al-Aswany, Alaa. *The Yacoubian Building*. New York, NY: Harper Perennial, 2006

Al-Aswany, Alaa. *On the State of Egypt: What Made the Revolution Inevitable*. New York, NY: Random House, 2011.

Al-Dassouki, Farouk. 'Adawat al-ru'b fi aqsam al-shurta' (Instruments of horror in police stations). *Al-Masry Al-Youm*, August 18, 2007.

Al-Husseini, Amira. 'Arabisc: Sexual Harassment and the Egyptian Blogosphere.' Global Voices, October 30, 2006. Accessed May 27, 2008 at http://www. globalvoicesonline.org/2006/10/30/arabisc-sexual-harrassment-and-the-egyptian-blogosphere/.

Al-Khamissi, Khaled. *Taxi*. Translated by Jonathan Wright. Wiltshire, UK: Aflame Books, 2008.

Al-Malky, Rania. 'Blogging For Reform: The Case of Egypt.' *Arab Media & Society* 1/1 (Spring 2007): 1–9.

Albrecht, Holger. 'How can opposition support authoritarianism? Lessons from Egypt.' *Democratization* 12/3 (June 2005): 378–397.

Anderson, David M. and Michael Cornfield eds., *The Civic Web: Online Politics and Democratic Values*. Oxford, UK: Rowman and Littlefield Publishers, Inc., 2003.

Anderson, Jon W. 'The Internet and Islam's New Interpreters' in Jon W. Anderson and Dale F. Eickelman eds., *New Media in the Muslim World: The Emerging Public Sphere*. Bloomington, IN: Indiana University Press, 2003.

Arab Network For Human Rights Information. 'Istihdaf al-mudawinin al-masriyin: 'ard mustamir' ('Targeting Egyptian Bloggers: An Ongoing Issue'). Accessed on August 7, 2009 at http://www.katib.org/node/7888.

Armbrust, Walter. 'New Media and Old Agendas: The Internet in the Middle East and Middle Eastern Studies.' *International Journal of Middle East Studies* 39 (2007): 531–533.

Asen, Robert, and Brouwer, Daniel C. *Counterpublics and the State*. Albany, New York: State University of New York Press, 2001.

Baaklini, Abdo, Denoeux, Guilain, and Robert Springborg. *Legislative Politics in the Arab World: The Resurgence of Democratic Institutions*. Boulder, CO: Lynne Rienner Publishers, Inc., 1999.

Baheyya. 'Four Myths About Protest.' Baheyya: Egypt Analysis and Whimsy, May 16, 2008. Accessed December 10, 2008 at http://baheyya.blogspot.com/2008/05/four-myths-about-protest.html

Baghdadi, Mohamed. 'Fan ta'dhib al-muwatin' (The art of torturing the citizen). *Al-Masry Al-Youm*, 7 August, 2007.

Barabasi, Albert-Laszlo. *Linked: How Everything is Connected To Everything Else and What It Means For Business, Science, and Everyday Life*. New York, NY: Penguin Books, 2003.

Barlow, John Perry. 'A Declaration of the Independence of Cyberspace.' February 8, 1996. Accessed on May 17, 2009 at https://projects.eff.org/~barlow/Declaration-Final.html.

Bayoumi, Amr and Mohamed Azzam. 'Baha'i twins receive first national ID card with a "blank" for religious affiliation. Their father considers it a rescue from "civil death".' *Al-Masry Al-Youm*, August 9, 2009. Accessed on March 2, 2010 at http://www.almasry-alyoum.com/article2.aspx?ArticleID=221981.

BBC News. 'UN "Shocked" By Violence in Cairo.' December 30, 2005.

BBC World Service. 'An island occupied in Egypt.' Accessed on April 25, 2009 at http://www.bbc.co.uk/worldservice/outlook/2008/01/080121_qursaya_egypt.shtml.

Beinin, Joel. 'Underbelly of Egypt's Neoliberal Agenda.' Middle East Report Online, April 5, 2008. Accessed on June 17, 2008 at http://www.merip.org/mero/mero040508.html

Beinen, Joel. 'Worker's struggles under "socialism" and neoliberalism' in El-Mahdi, Rabab and Philip Marfleet eds., *Egypt: The Moment of Change*. London, UK: Zed Books, Ltd., 2009.

Beinin, Joel. *Justice For All: The Struggle For Worker's Rights in Egypt*. The Solidarity Center, 2010.

Bellin, Eva. 'Coercive Institutions and Coercive Leaders' in Posusney, Marsha Pripstein and Michele Penner Angrist, eds., *Authoritarianism in the Middle East: Regimes and Resistance*. Boulder, CO: Lynne Rienner Publishers, 2005. pp. 21–38.

Ben Gharbia, Sami. 'The Internet Freedom Fallacy and Arab Digital Activism.' Nawaat.org, September 17, 2010. Accessed February 17, 2011 at http://nawaat.org/portail/2010/09/17/the-internet-freedom-fallacy-and-the-arab-digital-activism/.

Benford, Robert D., and Snow, David A. 'Framing Processes and Social Movements: An Overview and Assessment.' *Annual Review of Sociology* 26 (2000): 611–639.

Benkler, Yochai. *The Wealth of Networks: How Social Production Transforms Markets and Freedom*. New Haven, CT: Yale University Press, 2007.

Berk, Richard A. 'A Gaming Approach To Crowd Behavior.' *American Sociological Review* 39 (June 1972): 355–73.

Berman, Jerry, and Deirdre K. Mulligan. 'Digital Grass Roots: Issue Advocacy in the Age of the Internet.' In Anderson, David M. and Michael Cornfield eds., *The Civic Web: Online Politics and Democratic Values*. Oxford, UK: Rowman and Littlefield Publishers, Inc., 2003.

Best, Michael L. and Wade, Keegan W. 'The Internet and Democracy.' *Bulletin of Science, Technology, and Society* 29/4 (August 2009): 255–271.

Bikhchandani, Sushi, Hirshleifer, David, and Ivo Welch. 'A Theory of Fads, Fashion, Custom and Cultural Change as Informational Cascades.' *Journal of Political Economy* 100/5 (1992): 991–1026.

Bilo, 'Baha'i Faith: Early Days in Egypt.' Baha'i Faith in Egypt, June 6, 2006. Accessed on February 18, 2010 at http://www.bahai-egypt.org/2006/06/bahai-faith-early-days-in-egypt.html.

Bilo, 'Egyptian Bah'ais and ID cards.' Baha'i Faith in Egypt, June 2, 2006. Accessed on February 18, 2010 at http://www.bahai-egypt.org/search?updated-max=2006-07-09T19%3A01%3A00-05%3A00&max-results=50.

Bimber, Bruce, Flanagin, Andrew J., and Stohl, Cynthia. 'Reconceptualizing Collecting Action in the Contemporary Media Environment.' *Communication Theory* 15:4 (November 2005): 365–388.

Binder, Leonard. *In a Moment of Enthusiasm: Political Power and the Second Stratum in Egypt*. Chicago, IL: University of Chicago Press, 1978.

Biz-Community. 'Kenya; Bloggers Keep World Informed.' *Africa News*, January 4, 2008.

Black, Jeffrey. 'Egypt's Press: More free, still fettered.' *Arab Media & Society* (January 2008).

'Blogs, SMS, and the Kenyan Election.' Internet & Democracy Blog, January 3, 2008. Accessed December 21, 2009 at http://blogs.law.harvard.edu/idblog/2008/01/03/blogs-sms-and-the-kenyan-election/.

Boas, Taylor. 'Weaving the Authoritarian Web.' *Current History* 103, no. 677 (December 2004): 438–443.

Boroumand, Ladan. 'Civil Society's Choice.' *Journal of Democracy* 20/4 (October 2009): 16–20.

Boyd, Douglas A. *Broadcasting in the Arab World: A Survey of the Electronic Media in the Middle East.* Ames, IA: Iowa State University Press, 1999.

boyd, danah m., and Ellison, Nicole B. 'Social Network Sites: Definition, History, Scholarship.' *Journal of Computer-Mediated Communication* 13(1), article 11.

Bradley, John R. *Inside Egypt: The Land of the Pharoahs on the Brink of a Revolution.* London, UK: Palgrave MacMillan, 2009.

Brinkerhoff, Jennifer. *Digital Diasporas: Identity and Transnational Engagement.* Cambridge, UK: Cambridge University Press, 2009.

Brownlee, Jason. *Authoritarianism in an Age of Democratization.* New York, NY: Cambridge University Press, 2007.

Bucar, Elizabeth M. and Fazaeli, Roja. 'Free Speech in Weblogistan? The Offline Consequences of Online Communication.' *International Journal of Middle East Studies* 40: 403–419.

Bunce, Valerie, and Wolchik Sharon. 'Getting Real About Real Causes.' *Journal of Democracy* 20/1 (January 2009): 69–73.

'Cairo court jails 25 political opponents.' Reuters, April 16, 2008.

'Cairo farmers fight army for land.' *AFP*, November 11, 2007.

Calfano, Brian Robert and Emile Sahlieyeh. 'Transmitting Reform? Assessing New Media Influence on Political Rights in the Middle East.' *Critique: Critical Middle Eastern Studies* 17/1 (Spring 2008): 63–77.

Carapico, Sheila. 'No Easy Answers: The Ethics of Field Research in the Arab World.' *PS: Political Science & Politics* 39/3, July 2006: 429–431.

Carothers, Thomas. 'The End of the Transition Paradigm.' *Journal of Democracy* 13:1 (2002): 5–20

Carr, Sarah. 'Threatened Qorsaya Resident: I was born here and I'll die here.' *Daily News Egypt*, December 20, 2007.

Carr, Sarah. 'Doctors' Group Skeptical of Wage Increase Promised By Government.' *Daily News Egypt,* July 16, 2008.

Carr, Sarah. '6 Months Later.' *Inanities.* July 27, 2011. Accessed September 12, 2011 at http://inanities.org/2011/07/6-months-later/.

Castells, Manuel, et al. *Mobile Communication and Society: A Global Perspective.* Cambridge, MA: MIT Press, 2007.

Castells, Manuel. 'Communication, Power and Counter-Power in the Network Society.' *International Journal of Communication* 1 (2007): 238–266.

Cederman, Lars-Erik. 'Modeling the Size of Wars: From Billiard Balls to Sandpiles.' *The American Political Science Review* 97/1 (Feb. 2003): 135–150.

Clark, Janine. 'Field Research Methods in the Middle East.' *PS: Political Science and Politics* 39/3, July 2006: 417–421.

Cohen, Noam. 'Twitter on the Barricades: Six Lessons Learned.' *New York Times,* June 20, 2009. Accessed March 18, 2012 at http://www.nytimes.com/2009/06/21/weekinreview/21cohenweb.html

Cook, Steven. *Ruling But Not Governing: The Military and Political Development in Egypt, Turkey and Algeria.* Baltimore, MD: The John's Hopkins University Press, 2007

Cook, Steven A. 'Adrift on the Nile.' *Foreign Affairs*, March/April 2009, Accessed on January 18, 2010 at http://www.foreignaffairs.com/articles/64834/steven-a-cook/adrift-on-the-nile

Cook, Steven A. 'Is ElBaradei Egypt's Hero?' Foreign Affairs.com, March 26, 2010. Accessed on May 25, 2010 at http://www.foreignaffairs.com/articles/66178/steven-a-cook/is-el-baradei-egypts-hero?page=show.

Coughlin, Con. 'Why the Mullahs are Vulnerable.' *The Wall Street Journal*, December 29, 2009. Accessed December 30, 2009 at http://online.wsj.com/article/SB10001424052748703278604574624191585240728.html.

'Court denies Ba'hais legal recognition.' The Arabist, December 17, 2009. Accessed on 18 March 2010 at http://arabist.net/archives/2006/12/16/court-denies-bahais-legal-recognition/.

Dahlberg, Lincoln. 'Computer-mediated communication and the public sphere: A critical analysis.' *Journal of Computer-Mediated Communication* 7/1 (October 2001.

D'Anieri, Paul. 'Explaining the success and failure of post-communist revolutions.' *Communist and Post-Communist Studies* 39 (2006): 331–350.

Darabnee, Ahmed. 'As-Suhuf al-qowmiya tashun Hamla Did al-Internet' ('The National Media Undertake a Campaign Against the Internet'). *Al-Badeel*, April 26, 2008.

Daragahi, Barzou. 'Exiled, but still insiders; The latest wave in Iran's diaspora is tech-savvy and playing a key role in countering hard-liners at home.' *Los Angeles Times*, December 10, 2009, p.1.

Dartnell, Michael Y. *Insurgency Online: Web Activism and Global Conflict.* Toronto, Canada: University of Toronto Press, 2006.

Deibert, Ronald. *Parchment, Printing and Hypermedia: Communication in World Order Transformation.* New York, NY: Columbia University Press, 1997.

Deibert, Ronald J., Palfrey, John G. and Rohozinski, Rafal (Editors). *Access Denied: The Practice and Policy of GlobalInternet Filtering.* Cambridge, MA: MIT Press, 2008.

De Koning, Anouk. 'Café Latte and Caesar Salad: Cosmpolitan Belonging in Cairo's Coffee Shops' in Singerman, Diane and Paul Amar eds., *Cairo Cosmpopolitan: Politics, Culture and Urban Space in the New Globalized Middle East.* Cairo, Egypt: The American University in Cairo Presss, 2006.

Delli Carpini, Michael. 'The Internet and an Informed Citizenry,' with Scott Keeter, in David Anderson and Michael Cornfield, eds. *The Civic Web: Online Politics and Democratic Values.* New York, NY: Rowman and Littlefield, 2002.

'Demonstration in Solidarity with Gaza at the Faculty of Engineering, Alexandria.' YouTube video. Accessed August 20, 2009 at http://www.youtube.com/watch?v=M5bXQvr8AhI&feature=related.

Desvarieux, Jessica. 'Hundreds Protest Closed Egypt-Gaza Border.' *Voice of America News*, January 3, 2009. Accessed on July 17, 2009 at http://www.

voanews.com/english/archive/2009–01/2009–01–03-voa3.cfm?CFID=265
053033&CFTOKEN=57849127&jsessionid=8430d305506867ed7e7a1d4e6
e771932297d.

Diamond, Larry. 'Liberation Technology.' *Journal of Democracy* 21/3 (July 2010):
69–83.

Drezner, Daniel and Henry Farrell. 'The Power and Politics of Blogs.' *Public
Choice* 134 (January 2008): 15–30.

Dreyfus, Hubert L. *On the Internet*. London: Routledge, 2001.

Dunne, Michelle. 'Evaluating Egyptian Reform.' *Carnegie Papers* No. 66, January
2006. 1–24.

Edgar, Andrew. *The Philosophy of Habermas*. Montreal: McGill-Queens University
Press, 2005.

'Egypt.' The Open Net Initiative, August 6, 2009. Accessed February 21, 2010
at http://opennet.net/research/profiles/egypt.

'Egypt: Blogger Goes on Trial.' Associated Press, January 19, 2007. Accessed
on April 2, 2009 at http://www.nytimes.com/2007/01/19/world/middleeast/
19briefs-egyptblogger.html

'Egypt editor sentenced to six months, free on bond.' Reuters, March 26, 2008.
Accessed on 8 April 2008 at http://africa.reuters.com/top/news/usn-
BAN635621.html.

'Egypt police detain Muslim Brotherhood blogger.' Reuters, April 9, 2009.
Accessed on July 14, 2009 at http://www.reuters.com/article/internetNews/
idUSTRE5342BA20090405.

'Egyptian army weighs in on disputed Nile island.' Reuters. December 12, 2007.
Accessed on April 20, 2009 at http://www.reuters.com/article/inDepthNews/
idUSL0664802420071212?pageNumber=2&virtualBrandChannel=0.

'Egyptian blogs and the Baha'is.' Wijhat Nazhar Ukhra, December 13, 2006.
Accessed on February 22, 2010 at http://fromdifferentangle.blogspot.
com/2006_12_01_archive.html. Her site does not provide stable URL
links to each blog entry.

Egyptian Center for Human Rights. 'The Collective Harassment During the Eid
El Fitr Holiday and the Absence of a Law.' Press release, October 8, 2008.

Eickelman, Dale F. and Jon W. Anderson. *New Media in the Muslim World: the
Emerging Public Sphere*. Bloomington, IN: Indiana University Press, 2003.

Eid, Gamal. 'The Internet in the Arab World: A New Space of Repression?' The
Arabic Network For Human Rights Information, 2004. Accessed January
21, 2007 at http://www.hrinfo.net/en/reports/net2004/all.shtml#12.

El-Amrani, Issandr. 'Black Referendum Day – demo recap.' The Arabist, May 25,
2006. Accessed on April 21, 2009 at http://arabist.net/archives/2006/05/23/
black-referendum-day-demo-recap/.

El Amrani, Issandr. 'Kifaya and the Politics of the Impossible.' Znet. January 4,
2006. Accessed April 14, 2008 at http://www.zcommunications.org/kifaya-
and-the-politics-of-the-impossible-by-issandr-el-amrani.

El-Dawla, Aida Seif. 'Torture: A state policy' in El-Mahdi, Rabab and Philip Marfleet, eds., *Egypt: The Moment of Change*. London, UK: Zed Books, Ltd., 2009.

Elaasar, Aladdin. 'Is Egypt Stable?' *Middle East Quarterly* 16/3 (Summer 2009): 69–75.

El-Ghobashy, Mona. 'Constitutionalist Contention in Egypt.' *American Behavioral Scientist* 51 (July 2008): 1–21

El-Ghitany, Magda. 'Facing Facebook.' *Al-Ahram Weekly*, May 1–7, 2008.

El-Ghobashy, Mona. 'The Liquidation of Egypt's Illiberal Experiment.' *Middle East Report Online*, December 29, 2010. Accessed on January 22, 2011 at http://www.merip.org/mero/mero122910.

El-Ghobashy, Mona. 'The Praxis of the Egyptian Revolution.' *Middle East Report* Vol. 41 (Spring 2011). Accessed February 18, 2011 at http://www.merip.org/mer/mer258/praxis-egyptian-revolution.

El-Hamalawy, Hossam. 'El-Adly Videogate: Torture Victim Receives 3 Months in Prison for "resisting authorities"!' 3Arabawy, January 9, 2007.

El-Hamalawy, Hossam. 'Resisting Mubarak's Army.' 3arabawy, December 4, 2007.

El-Hamalawy, Hossam. 'Rose Al-Youssef hits new rock bottom', 3arabawy, October 31, 2006. Accessed on March 14, 2009 at http://www.arabawy.org/2006/10/31/rosa-al-youssef-hits-new rock-bottom/.

El-Hamalawy, Hossam. 'Bigotry and sectarianism par excellence.' 3Arabawy, December 16, 2006. Accessed on April 14, 2008 at http://arabist.net/arabawy/2006/12/16/anti-bahaais-bigotry-and-sectarianism/.

El-Hamalawy, Hossam. 'Solidarity from the U.S. for Khaled Hamza.' 3Arabawy, February 24, 2008. Accessed on July 15, 2008 at http://arabist.net/arabawy/2008/02/24/freekhaled_downwithmubarak/.

El-Hamalawy, Hossam. 'Revolt in Mahalla.' *International Socialist Review* 59 (May-June 2008). Accessed on July 15, 2008 at http://www.isreview.org/issues/59/rep-mahalla.shtml.

El-Hamalawy, Hossam. 'In Solidarity With the Egyptian Trade Union Activists.' 3arabaway. November 5, 2008. Accessed on November 12, 2009 at http://www.arabawy.org/tag/left-%D9%8A%D8%B3%D8%A7%D8%B1/page/19/.

El-Hamalawy, Hossam. '#Jan25 Public transportation workers call for overthrowing Mubarak.' 3arabawy, February 9, 2011. Accessed on September 9, 2011 at http://www.arabawy.org/2011/02/09/jan25-public-transportation-workers-call-for-overthrowing-mubarak.

El-Hamalawy, Hossam. '#Jan25 Actors for the revolution.' 3arabawy, February 10, 2011. Accessed on September 9, 2011 at http://www.arabawy.org/2011/02/10/cinema-for-the-revolution/.

Elhafnawy, Nader. 'Societal Complexity and Diminishing Returns in Security.' *International Security* Vol. 29, Issue 1 (Summer 2004): 152–174.

El-Mahdi, Rabab. 'Enough! Egypt's Quest For Democracy.' *Comparative Political Studies* 42 (2009): 1011–1039.

El-Mahdi, Rabab. 'The democracy movement: cycles of protest' in El-Mahdi, Rabab and Philip Marfleet eds., *Egypt: The Moment of Change*. London, UK: Zed Books, Ltd., 2009.

Facebook.com 'Statistics.' Accessed January 20, 2012 at http://www.facebook.com/press/info.php?statistics.

Fandy, Mamoun. 'CyberResistance: Saudi Opposition Between Globalizaton and Localization.' *Comparative Studies in Society and History*, 41/1 (Jan. 1999): 124–147.

Faris, David. 'Revolutions Without Revolutionaries? Network theory, Facebook and the Egyptian blogosphere.' *Arab Media & Society* Issue 6 (Fall 2008).

Faris, David. 'The End of the Beginning: The Failure of April 6th and the Future of Electronic Activism in Egypt.' *Arab Media and Society* Issue. 9 (Fall 2009).

Faris, David. ' (Amplified) Voices for the Voiceless.' *Arab Media and Society* Issue 11 (Summer 2010).

Faris, Robert, and Etling, Bruce. 'Madison and the Smart Mob: The Promise and Limitations of the Internet for Democracy.' *The Fletcher Forum of World Affairs* 32 (2008): 65–85.

Fayza, Hassan. 'The last frontier.' *Al-Ahram Weekly*, 26 July-August 1, 2001.

Fenton, Natalie. 'Mediating hope: New media, politics and resistance.' *International Journal of Cultural Studies* Vol. 11 (2008).

Foot, K.A., and Schneider, S.M. 'Online action in campaign 2000: An exploratory analysis of the U.S. political Web sphere.' *Journal of Broadcasting and Electronic Media* 42/2: 222–244.

Fraser, Nancy. 'Rethinking the Public Sphere: A Contribution to the Critique of Actually Existing Democracies.' in Craig Calhoun, ed. *Habermas and the Public Sphere*. Cambridge, MA: the MIT Press, 1992.

'Freedom in the World 2004 – Ukraine.' Freedom House. Accessed March 22, 2010 at http://expression.freedomhouse.org/reports/freedom_in_the_world/2004/ukraine

Freyberg-Inan, Annette. 'Just how small is this world really?: An application of Network Theory to the Study of Globalization.' *Global Networks*, 6(3) (2006): 221–244.

Gettleman, Jeffrey. 'With Half of Vote Counted, Kenyan Opposition is Poised to Sweep.' *The New York Times*, December 29, 2007, p. 9.

Gettleman, Jeffrey. 'Kenya's Opposition Switches its Tactics From Street Protests to Business Boycotts.' *The New York Times*, January 19, 2008. p. 6.

Gharbeia, Amr. '500 Central Security soldiers around the Judges' Club.' Gharbeia.net, April 26, 2006. Author's translation. Accessed on 22 January 2009 at http://gharbeia.net/node/100 .

Gharbeia, Amr. 'Ni'mil eih fi-l-baha'iyin ba'd ma mana'athum al-mahkama min ithbat dinahum fi al-'awraq al-thubutiyya?' ('What shall we do with the Baha'is now that the courts prohibited them from affirming their religion in evidentiary documents?') Gharbeia.net, December 17, 2006. Accessed on February 18, 2010 at http://gharbeia.net/node/179.

Ghonim, Wael. TEDx Talk. Cairo, Egypt. March 4, 2011. Accessed on April 20, 2011 at http://www.youtube.com/watch?v=SWvJxasiSZ8.

Girl4Cairo. 'LOOK AT ME.' Wounded Girl From Cairo, Thursday, November 9, 2006. Accessed on September 17, 2009 at http://woundedgirlfromcairo. blogspot.com/2006/11/look-at-me.html.

Gladwell, Malcolm. *The Tipping Point: How Little Things Can Make a Big Difference.* New York, NY: Back Bay Books, 2002.

Goldstein, Joshua. 'The Role of Digital Networked Technologies in Ukraine's Orange Revolution.' The Berkman Center for Technology and Society at Harvard. Berkman Center Research Publication 2007–14.

Goldstein, Joshua, and Rotich, Juliana. 'The Role of Digital Networked Technologies in Kenya's 2007–2008 Post-Election Crisis.' The Berkman Center for Technology and Society at Harvard. Berkman Center Research Publication 2008–09.

Garrett, R. Kelly. 'Protest in an Information Society: A Review of Literature on Social Movements and New ICT's.' *Information, Communication, and Society* 9/2: 202–224.

Gould, Roger. 'Collective Action and Network Structure.' *American Sociological Review* 58/2 (Apr. 1993): 182–196.

Granovetter, Mark. 'Threshhold models of collective behavior.' *American Journal of Sociology* 83/6 (May 1978): 1420–1443.

Granovetter, Mark. 'Ignorance, Knowledge, and Outcomes in a Small World.' *Science*, 8/8/2003, 773–774.

Grodsky, Brian. 'Resource Dependency and Political Opportunity: Explaining the Transformation from Excluded Political Opposition Parties to Human Rights Organizations in Post-Communist Uzbekistan.' *Government and Opposition* 42/1 (2007): 96–120.

Gurney, Joan Neff, and Kathleen J. Tierney. 'Relative Deprivation and Social Movements: A Critical Look at Twenty Years of Theory and Research.' *The Sociological Quarterly* 23/1 (Winter 1982): 33–47.

Gurr, Ted Robert. *Why Men Rebel.* Princeton, NJ: Princeton University Press, 1970.

Habermas, Jürgen. *The Structural Transformation of the Public Sphere: An Inquiry Into a Category of Bourgeois Society.* Cambridge, MA: The MIT Press, 1991.

Hamzawy, Amr. 'Egypt: Regression in the Muslim Brotherhood's Party Platform?' *Arab Reform Bulletin*, October 2007.

Hands, Joss. @ *is for Activism.* New York, NY: Pluto Press, 2010.

Hanna, Michael Wahid. 'The Son Also Rises: Egypt's Looming Succession Struggle.' *World Policy Journal*, 2009, vol. 26, issue 3

Harnisch, Chris, and Mecham, Quinn. 'Democratic Ideology in Islamist Opposition? The Muslim Brotherhood's "Civil State".' *Middle Eastern Studies* 45/2 (March 2009): 189–205.

Hausloner, Abigail. 'As Egypt's Mubarak Comes To Washington, Labor Unrest Surges at Home.' *Time*, August 18, 2009.

Heaven, Will. 'The fatal folly of the online revolutionaries; Smug Twitter activists are wrong to think they are liberating Iran, says Will Heaven.' *The Daily Telegraph*, December 29, 2009, p. 16.

Heydemann, Steve. 'Upgrading Authoritarianism in the Arab World.' The Saban Center For Middle East Policy at the Brookings Institution. Analysis Paper Number 13 (October 2007).

Hindman, Matthew. *The Myth of Digital Democracy*. Princeton, NJ: Princeton University Press, 2008.

Hirschkind, Charles. 'The Road to Tahrir'. *The Immanent Frame*. Social Science Research Council. February 9 2011. Accessed March 30, 2011 at http://blogs.ssrc.org/tif/2011/02/09/the-road-to-tahrir/.

Hofheinz, Albrecht. 'The Internet in the Arab World: Playground for Political Liberalization.' *Internationale Politik und Gesselschaft*. (March 2005): 78–96

Howard, Philip N. *The Digital Origins of Dictatorship and Democracy: Information Technology and Political Islam*. Oxford, UK: Oxford University Press, 2010.

Howeidi, Fahmy. 'Ghazwat Al-Qursaya.' *Al-Dustur*, December 26, 2007.

Howeidi, Fahmy. 'Al-Haqa'iq Al-Gha'iba fi milef Al-Qursaya.' *Al-Dustur*. December 20 2007.

Human Rights Watch. 'Egypt: Hold Police Accountable For Torture.' December 12, 2006. Accessed on June 22, 2008 at http://www.hrw.org/en/news/2006/12/22/egypt-hold-police-accountable-torture.

Ibrahim, Saad Eddin. 'Egypt's Democratic Charade.' *Globe & Mail*, January 17, 2006

Idle, Nadia and Nunns, Alex. *Tweets From Tahrir*. Doha, Qatar: Bloomsbury Qatar Foundation Publishing, 2011.

Ikhwanonline. 'Al-Muzhahirat al-rafida li-l-ta'dilat al-dusturiyya tashmal mu'zham jami'at Misr' (Demonstrations to reject constitutional amendments include most Egyptian universities). March 25, 2007. Accessed on January 17, 2009 at http://www.ikhwanonline.com/Article.asp?ArtID=27259&SecID=304.

Ikhwanonline. 'Interview with Mohamed Baligh After Verdict.' June 15, 2008. Accessed on July 17, 2009 at http://www.ikhwanweb.com/article.php?id=17265.

'Internet Brings Events in Iran to Life.' BBC News Online, June 15, 2009. Accessed December 30, 2009 at http://news.bbc.co.uk/2/hi/middle_east/8099579.stm.

'Introduction.' Wijhat Nazhar Ukhra, August 3, 2006. Accessed on January 17, 2010 at http://fromdifferentangle.blogspot.com/2006_08_01_archive.html.

'Iran.' Freedom of the Press 2009. Freedom House. Accessed March 11, 2010 at http://www.freedomhouse.org/report/freedom-press/2009/iran?page=251&year=2009&country=7627

Iskander, Adel. 'Problematizing Arab Media in the Post-Taxonomic Era.' *Arab Media & Society* (May 2007).

Izz Ed-Din, Ahmed. 'Leaders of American Baha'is demand the implementation of administrative court ruling on ID cards...and estimate the number of

Baha'is in Egypt at 2000.' *Al-Masry Al-Youm*, August 21, 2008. Author's translation.

Jankowski, James. *Egypt: A Short History*. Oxford, U.K.: Oneworld Publications, 2000.

Jenkins, J. Craig. 'Resource Mobilization Theory and the Study of Social Movements.' *Annual Review of Sociology*, 9 (1983): 527–53.

Johnson, Steven. *Everything Bad is Good For You: How Today's Popular Culture is Actually Making Us Smarter*. New York, NY: Riverhead Books, 2005.

Joyce, Mary, ed. *Digital Activism Decoded: The New Mechanics of Change*. New York, NY: International Debate Education Association, 2010.

Kalathil, Shanthi, and Taylor C. Boas. *Open Networks, Closed Regimes: The Impact of the Internet on Authoritarian Rule*. Washington, DC: Carnegie Endowment For International Peace, 2003.

Kaplan, Robert D. 'One Small Revolution.' *New York Times*, January 22, 2011, P. WK11.

Karatnycky, Adrian. 'Ukraine's Orange Revolution.' *Foreign Affairs*, March/April 2005.

Karpf, David. 'Understanding Blogspace.' *Journal of Information Technology & Politics* 5/4 (December 2008): 369–385.

Kassem, Maye. *Egyptian Politics: The Dynamics of Authoritarian Rule*. Boulder, CO: Lynne Rienner Publishers, 2004.

Khalil, Ashraf. 'Monday's Papers: The Social Insurance Umbrella and the Khaled Saeed Case.' *Al-Masry Al-Youm* English edition. Accessed on April 30, 2011 at http://www.almasryalyoum.com/en/node/48925.

'Khaled Hamza is free.' Ikhwan Web, April 16, 2009. Accessed on April 15, 2010 at http://www.ikhwanweb.com/article.php?ID=16728&SectionID=0.

Khamis, Sahar, and Vaugh, Katherine. 'Cyberactivism in the Egyptian Revolution: How Civic Engagement and Citizen Journalism Tilted the Balance.' *Arab Media and Society* 13 (Summer 2011).

Kiai, Maina. 'The Crisis in Kenya.' *Journal of Democracy* 19/3 (July 2008): 162–168.

Kramer, Martin. *Ivory Towers on Sand: The Failure of Middle Eastern Studies in America*. Washington, D.C.: Washington Institute For Near East Affairs, 2001.

Kuran, Timur. 'Sparks and Prairie Fires: A Theory of Unanticipated Revolution.' *Public Choice*, Vol. 61, No. 1 (April 1989): 41–74.

Kuran, Timur. 'Now Out of Never: The Element of Surprise in the East European Revolution of 1989.' *World Politics* Vol. 44, No. 1 (October 1991): 7–48.

Kuran, Timur. 'The Inevitability of Future Revolutionary Surprises.' *American Journal of Sociology* 100/6 (May 1995): 1528–51.

Kuran, Timur, and Cass R. Sunstein. 'Availability Cascades and Risk Regulation.' *Stanford Law Review* 54/1 (Apr. 1999): 683–768.

Lane, David. 'The Orange Revolution: "People's Revolution" or Revolutionary Coup?' *British Journal of Politics & International Relations* 10/4 (2008): 525–549.

Leiken, Robert S., and Brooke, Steven. 'The Moderate Muslim Brotherhood.' *Foreign Affairs*. 86/2 (107–121).

Lerner, Daniel. *The Passing of Traditional Society: Modernizing The Middle East*. New York, NY: The Free Press, 1958.

Lesch, Ann M. 'Egypt's Spring: The Causes of Revolution.' *Middle East Policy* Vol. 28, No. 3 (Fall 2011): 35–48.

Lessig, Lawrence. 2008. *Remix: Making Art and Commerce Thrive in the Hybrid Economy*. New York, NY: Penguin Press, 2008.

Levinson, Charles. 'Egypt's Growing Blogger Community Pushes Limits of Dissent.' *Christian Science Monitor*, August 24, 2005. Accessed on September 12, 2006 at http://www.csmonitor.com/2005/0824/p07s01-wome.html.

Lichbach, Mark I. *The Rebel's Dilemma*. Ann Arbour, MI: University of Michigan Press, 1998.

Lohmann, Susanne. 'The Dynamics of Informational Cascades: The Monday Demonstrations in Leipzig, Easter Germany, 1989–91.' *World Politics* 47/1 (Oct. 1994): 42–101.

Lovink, Geert. '*Zero Comments: Blogging and Critical Internet Culture*.' New York, NY: Routledge, 2008.

Lust-Okar, Ellen. *Structuring Conflict in the Arab World: Incumbents, Opponents, and Institutions*. Cambridge, England: Cambridge University Press, 2007.

Lustick, Ian S. and Miodownik Dan. 'Neighborhoods and Tips: Implications of Spatiality for Political Cascades.' Paper presented at the annual meeting of the American Political Science Association, Washington, DC, September 1, 2005

Lynch, Marc. *Voices of the New Arab Public: Iraq, Al-Jazeera and Middle East Politics Today*. New York, NY: Columbia University Press, 2006.

Lynch, Marc. 'Young Brothers in Cyberspace.' Middle East Report 245 (Winter 2007). http://www.merip.org/mer/mer245/mer245.html.

Lynch, Marc. 'After Egypt: The Limits and Promise of Online Challenges to the Authoritarian Arab State.' *Perspectives on Politics*, Vol. 9, Issue 2 (June 2011).

MacKinnon, Rebecca. 'Flatter world and thicker walls? Blogs, censorship and civic discourse in China.' *Public Choice* 134 (2008): 31–46.

Madrigal, Alexis. 'Egyptian Activists Action Plan: Translated.' *The Atlantic*, January 27, 2011. Accessed on March 13, 2011 at http://www.theatlantic.com/international/archive/2011/01/egyptian-activists-action-plan-translated/70388/.

'Majma' al-buhuth al-islamiyya: al-baha'iya haraka suhyuniyya tas'a li-nashr al-fasad wa-l-radhila' ('The Islamic Research Center: Baha'ism is a Zionist movement bent on spreading corruption and vice'). *Al Masry Al-Youm*, May 30, 2009. Accessed on July 15, 2009 at http://www.almasry-alyoum.com/article2.aspx?ArticleID=213030.

Maloney, Brenna. 'A Disputed Election Leads To Violence; Hundreds Killed as Two of the Country's Ethnic Groups Clash.' *Washington Post*, January 7, 2008, p. C12.

Manal and Alaa's Bit-Bucket. 'Waqfa tadamuniyya min al-baha'iyin al-masriyin min ajli haqqihim fi ithbat diyanatihim aw kitaba (ukhra) fi khanat al-diyanah fi-l-awraq al-rasmiyya.' Accessed on January 14, 2010 at http://www.manalaa.net/node/84324.

Manal and Alaa's Bit-Bucket. 'Ba'd al-hukm 'ala 'Abd al-Karim wa-l-baha'iyin al-kuffar hayniku ukhtak'. Accessed on February 10, 2010 at http://www.manalaa.net/the_heathen_and_your_sister.

Manal and Alaa's Bit-Bucket. 'Kuntum fein lamma Faransa.' ('Where were you when France') Accessed on July 15, 2009 at http://www.manalaa.net/where_where_you_when_france.

Mana and Alaa's Bit Bucket. 'Muzhahara bi-midan al-tahrir 3–15 li-l-ta'bir 'an rafd al-ta'dilat al-dusturiyya' ('Demonstration in Tahrir Square to express rejection of the constitutional amendments'). March 10, 2007. Author's translation. Accessed on February 12, 2009 at http://www.manalaa.net/node/87226.

Maratea, Ray. 'The e-Rise and Fall of Social Problems: The Blogosphere as a Public Arena.' *Social Problems* 55/1: 139–160.

Matthew, Richard, and Shambaugh, George. 'The Limits of Terrorism: A Network Perspective.' *International Studies Review* 2005 (7), 617 627. p 618.

McAdam, Douglas, Tarrow, Sidney, and Charles Tilly. *Dynamics of Contention.* Cambridge, UK: Cambridge University Press, 2001.

McDonough, Challiss. 'Muslim Brotherhood to Boycott Local Elections in Egypt After Crackdown.'*Voice of America News.* April 7, 2008.

McDonough, Challis. 'Prison Term for Egyptian Police in Widely-Published Torture Case.' *Voice of America News,* November 6, 2007.

McFaul, Michael. 'Transitions From Post-Communism.' *Journal of Democracy* 16/3 (July 2005): 5–19.

McInerney, Stephen. 'Obama Administration Policy on Democracy in the Arab World.' *Arab Reform Bulletin.* September 2009.

McDonagh, Ecaterina. Is Democracy Promotion Effective in Moldova? The Impact of European Institutions on Development of Civil and Political Rights in Moldova'. *Democratization* 15/1 (2008), 142 — 161.

McFaul, Michael. 'Transitions From Postcommunism.' *Journal of Democracy* 16/3: 5–19.

'Meet Asmaa Mahfouz and the Vlog that Helped Spark the Revolution.' YouTube. February 1, 2011. Accessed February 3, 2011 at http://www.youtube.com/watch?v=SgjIgMdsEuk

Meier, Patrick. 'The Impact of the Information Revolution on Protest Frequency in Repressive Contexts.' Paper presented at the 50th International Studies Association Conference in New York City, February 15–17, 2009.

Meier, Patrick. 'Analyzing U-Shahid's Eleciton Monitoring Results From Egypt.' *iRevolution.* May 23, 2011.

Milani, Abbas. 'Cracks in the Regime.' *Journal of Democracy* 20/4 (October 2009): 11–15.

Milner, Helen. 'The Digital Divide: The Role of Political Institutions in Technology Diffusion.' *Comparative Political Studies*, 39/2 (March 2006): 176–199

Mitchell, Timothy. *Rule of Experts: Egypt, Techno-Politics, Modernity*. Berkeley, CA: University of California Press, 2002.

Moore, Will H. 'Rational Rebels: Overcoming the Free-Rider Problem.' *Political Research Quarterly* 48/2 (June 1995). 417–454.

Morozov, Eugene. 'Downside to the "Twitter Revolution".' *Dissent* 56/4 (Fall 2009): 10–14.

Mozorov, Eugene. 'From Slacktivism to Activism.' *Foreign Policy. Net.Effect.* September 5, 2009. Accessed on January 14, 2010 at http://neteffect.foreignpolicy.com/posts/2009/09/05/from_slacktivism_to_activism.

Morozov, Evgeny. 'The Internet: A Room of Our Own?' *Dissent* 56/3 (Summer 2009): 80–86.

Morozov, Evgeny. *The Net Delusion: The Dark Side of Internet Freedom*. New York, NY: Public Affairs, 2011.

Mosahel, Mohamed Abdel Khaliq. 'Los Angeles Times: Mubarak's Opposition Hums With Disparate Voices'. *Al-Masry Al-Youm*, 29 April 2009.

'Muhafizat al-Giza tatrud sukan jazeerat al-qursaya li hisab al-mustathmareen.' ('The Governate of Giza expels the residents of al-Qursaya island for the sake of investors') *Al-Ahrar*. March 24, 1998.

Monsour, Ibrahim. 'Al-Hukuma ta'tarif bi 'ightiSab jazeerat al-Qursaya' ('Government admits to rape of Al-Qursaya'). *Al-Dustur*, January 4, 2008.

Mukkaled, Diana. 'Egypt's Facebook Girl.' *Asharq Alawsat* (English Edition), April 28, 2008. Accessed on June 11, 2008 at http://www.aawsat.com/english/news.asp?section=2&id=12582.

Mungui-Pippidi, Alina and Munteanu, Igor. 'Moldova's "Twitter Revolution".' *Journal of Democracy* 20/3 (July 2009): 136–142.

Musgrove, Mike. 'Twitter is a Player in Iran's Drama.' *The Washington Post*, June 17, 2009, p. A10.

Nkrumah, Gamal. 'Insecure but incisive.' *Al-Ahram Weekly*. 24–30 November, 2005.

Norton, Richard Augustus. 'New Media, Civic Pluralism, and Political Reform.' in Eickelman and Anderson, eds., *New Media in the Muslim World: The Emerging Public Sphere*. Bloomington, IN: Indiana University Press, 2003.

Norris, Pippa. *Digital Divide: Civic Engagement, Information Poverty and the Internet World-wide*. Cambridge, MA: Cambridge University Press, 2001.

O'Donnell, Guillermo, Schmitter, Phillippe C., and Whitehead, Laurence, eds. *Transitions From Authoritarian Rule: Comparative Perspectives*. Baltimore, MD: The John's Hopkins University Press, 1986

Olson, Mancur. *The Logic of Collective Action: Public Goods and the Theory of Groups*. Cambridge, MA: Harvard University Press, 1965.

'On the Baha'is and the Crucifixion of Christ.' Egyptian Baha'i, February 23, 2008. Author's translation. Accessed on July 12, 2010.at http://egyptianbahai.wordpress.com/2008/02/23/christ_crucifixion_and_the_bahai_faith/

O'Reilly, Tim. 'What is Web 2.0?' September 30, 2005. Accessed on February 12, 2008 at http://www.oreillynet.com/pub/a/oreilly/tim/news/2005/09/30/what-is-web-20.html?page=2

Pajnik, Mojca. 'Citizenship and Mediated Society.' *Citizenship Studies* 9/4 (September 2005): 349–367.

Palczewski, C. 'Cyber-movements, new social movements, and counterpublics.' In R. Asen & D. Brouwer (Eds.), *Counterpublics and the State* (pp. 161–186). New York: State University of New York, 2001.

Pedahzur, Ami, and Perliger, Arie. 'The Changing Nature of Suicide Attacks: A Social Network Perspective.' *Social Forces* 84/4 (June 2006): pp. 1969–1986.

Pfeifle, Mark. 'A Nobel Peace Prize for Twitter?' *The Christian Science Monitor*, July 6, 2009.

Poor, Nathan. 'Mechanisms of an Online Public Sphere: The Website Slashdot.' *Journal of Computer-Mediated Communication* 10/2 (2005).

Postman, Neil. *Amusing Ourselves to Death: Public Discourse in the Age of Showbusiness.* New York, NY: Penguin, 1986.

Posusney, Marsha Pripstein. *Labor and the State in Egypt: Workers, Unions, and Economic Restructuring.* New York, NY: Columbia University Press, 1997.

Poulson, Stephen C. 'Nested Institutions, Political Opportunity, and the Decline of the Iranian Reform Movement Post 9/11.' *American Behavioral Scientist* 53/1 (2009): 27–43.

Przeworski, Adam. *Democracy and the Market: Political and Economic Reforms in Eastern Europe and Latin America.* Cambridge, UK: Cambridge University Press, 1991.

Price, Monroe E. *Media and Sovereignty: The Global Information Revolution and Its Challenge To State Power.* Cambridge, MA: The MIT Press, 2002.

Radsch, Courtney C. 'Core to Commonplace: The evolution of Egypt's blogo-sphere.' *Arab Media & Society* Issue 6 (Fall 2008).

Rafael, Vicente L. 'The Cell Phone and the Crowd: Messianic Politics in the Contemporary Philippines.' *Public Culture* 15/3: 399–425.

Rahimi, Babak. 'Cyberdissent: The Internet in Revolutionary Iran.' *Middle East Review of International Affairs*, 7/3 (September 2003).

Rheingold, Howard. *Smart Mobs: The Next Social Revolution.* New York, NY: Basic Books, 2002.

'Rudud al-fi'l tajtahu shawari' al-'awasim al-arabiyya.' ('Reactions devastate the streets of Arab capitals'). *Al-Ahram*, December 31, 2008.

Rugh, William A. 'Do National Political Systems Still Influence Arab Media?' *Arab Media & Society* (May 2007).

Rutherford, Bruce K. *Egypt After Mubarak: Liberalism, Islam, and Democracy in the Arab World.* Princeton, NJ: Princeton University Press, 2008.

Sakr, Naomi. *Satellite Realms: Transnational Television, Globalization and the Middle East.* London, UK: I.B. Tauris and Co., 2002.

Saleh, Heba. 'Fears for Egypt torture victim.' BBC News, January 16, 2007. Accessed on January 15, 2009 at http://news.bbc.co.uk/1/hi/world/middle_east/6264193.stm.

Saleh, Nivien. *Third World Citizens and the Information Technology Revolution.* Palgrave Macmillan, 2007.

Salih, Khalid. 'Huriyyat al-Sahafa.' Cairo Center for the Study of Human Rights, 2007.

Sandmonkey. 'Al-Qursaya Island.' Rantings of a Sandmonkey, Tuesday, November 13, 2007. Accessed on February 10, 2009 at http://www.sandmonkey.org/2007/11/13/al-qursaya-island/.

Sandmonkey. 'Today's Baha'i Protest.' Rantings of a Sandmonkey, December 17, 2006. Accessed on February 19, 2010 at http://www.sandmonkey.org/2006/12/17/todays-bahai-protest/.

Schell, Jonathan. *The Unconquerable World: Power, Non-Violence and the Will of the People.* New York: Henry Holt and Co., 2004.

Schliefer, S. Abdallah. 'The Impact of Arab Satellite Television on Prospects For Democracy in the Arab World.' *Transnational Broadcasting Studies* 15.

Shalaby, Ahmed. '16 cases of torture inside police stations in July alone.' *Al-Masry Al-Youm,* August 4, 2007.

Shalaby, Ahmed and El Marsfawy, Mostafa. 'Al Masry Al Youm Exclusive: Khaled Saeed Case Investigation.' *Al-Masry Al-Youm.* December 7, 2010. Accessed May 21, 2011 at http://www.egyptindependent.com/node/55686.

Shalaby, Ethar. 'Protesters turn their back to Egyptian police abuse.' Danish Egyptian Dialogue Institute. Accessed on 11 March 2011 at http://dedi.org.eg/index.php/en/hiwar-mag/71-featured/485-protesters-qturn-their-backsq-to-egyptian-police-abuse.

Shapiro, Samantha. 'Revolution, Facebook-Style.' *New York Times Magazine,* January 22, 2009.

Shehata, Samer, and Stacher, Joshua. 'The Brotherhood Goes to Parliament.' *Middle East Report* 36/3 (Fall 2006): 32–39.

Shenker, Jack. 'Egyptian Revolutionary Alaa Abdel Fattah Arrested By Egyptian Junta.' *The Guardian.* October 31, 2011.

Shirky, Clay. 'Social Software and the Politics of Groups.' Originally published on the 'Networks, Economics, and Culture' mailing list, March 9, 2003. Available at http://shirky.com/writings/group_politics.html

Shirky, Clay. *Here Comes Everybody: The Power of Organizing Without Organizations.* New York, NY: Penguin Press, 2008.

Shorbagy, Manar. 'The Egyptian Movement For Change – Kefaya: Redefining Politics in Egypt.' *Public Culture* 19/1 (2007): 175–196.

Shubaki, Amr. 'Limadha fashala al-idrab al-'am?' (Why did the general strike fail?). *Al-Masry Al-Youm,* April 9, 2009.

Shumate, Michelle and Justin Lipp. 'Connective collective action online: An examination of the hyperlink network structure of an NGO issue network.' *Journal of Computer-Mediated Communication* 14 (2008): 178–201.

'Shurtat Misr tulqi al-qabd 'ala 21 ikhwaniyan bi-sabab muzhaharat Ghazza' (Egyptian police arrest 21 members of the Muslim Brotherhood for Gaza protests.) Masrawy, January 11, 2009. Accessed on February 20, 2010 at http://www.wsws.org/articles/2009/jan2009/egyp-j24.shtml.

Sifry, David. 'State of the Blogosphere, April 2006 Part 1: On Blogosphere Growth.' Accessed at http://www.sifry.com/alerts/archives/000432.html on September 11, 2006.

Sims, David. *Understanding Cairo: The Logic of a City Out of Control.* Cairo, Egypt: American University Press, 2011.

Singer, Michaela. 'Angry Qursaya Residents Complain at State Council.' *Daily News Egypt*, November 29, 2007.

Slackman, Michael. 'Egypt Says It Won't Deport Any of the Jailed Sudanese.' *New York Times*, January 18, 2006.

Slackman, Michael. 'Day of Angry Protest Stuns Egypt.' *The New York Times*, April 6, 2008.

Slackman, Michael. 'Hints of Pluralism Begin to Appear in Egyptian Religious Debates.' *The New York Times*, August 31, 2009

Slaughter, Anne-Marie. 'America's Edge: Power in the Networked Century.' *Foreign Affairs* 88/1 (Jan/Feb 2009).

Snider, Erin A. and Faris, David M. 'The Arab Spring: U.S. Democracy Promotion in Egypt.' *Middle East Policy* Vol. 28, No. 3 (Fall 2011): 49–61.

Somer, Murat. 'Cascades of Ethnic Polarization: Lessons from Yugoslavia.' *Annals of the American Academy of Political and Social Science*, Vol. 573 (January 2001): 127–151.

Somer, Murat. 'Resurgence and Remaking of Identity: Civil Beliefs, Domestic and External Dynamics, and the Turkish Mainstream Discourse on Kurds.' *Comparative Politics* 38/6 (August 2005): 591–622.

Sreberny, Annabelle. 'Mediated Culture in the Middle East: Diffusion, Democracy, Difficulties.' *Gazette*, 63/2–3: 101–119, 2001.

Srinivasan, Ramesh, and Fish, Adam. 'Revolutionary Tactics, Media Ecologies, and Repressive States.' *Public Culture* Vol. 23, No. 3 (2011): 505–510.

Stack, Graham. 'Leader of Moldova's "Twitter revolution" goes into hiding: Fugitive surprised by size of protest fears arrest: Organiser says Kremlin behind police targeting.' *The Guardian*, April 16, 2009, pg. 19.

Stack, Liam. 'Egypt targets Muslim Brotherhood moderates.' *Christian Science Monitor*, March 26, 2008.

Stack, Liam. 'Egyptians win right to drop religion from ID cards.' *Christian Science Monitor*, April 20, 2009

Starkey, Paul. 'Modern Egyptian culture in the Arab world.' In Daly, M.W., ed., *The Cambridge History of Egypt, Volume 2: Modern Egypt, from 1517 to the end of the twentieth century.* Cambridge, U.K.: Cambridge University Press, 1998.

'State to Appeal Ruling that Favors Egypt's Baha'is.' *Daily News Egypt*, May 5, 2006. Accessed on February 10, 2010 at http://www.dailystaregypt.com/article.aspx?ArticleID=1394.

Stern, Johannes. 'Widespread anger in Egypt at Mubarak regime.' World Socialist
    Web. January 24, 2009. Accessed on 20 June 2009 at http://www.wsws.org/
    articles/2009/jan2009/egyp-j24.shtml.

Sunstein, Cass. *Republic.com*. Princeton, NJ: Princeton University Press, 2001.

Sunstein, Cass. *Infotopia: How Many Minds Produce Knowledge*. New York, NY.
    Oxford University Press, 2006.

Surowiecki, James. *The Wisdom of Crowds: Why the Many Are Smarter Than the Few
    and How Collective Wisdom Shapes Business, Economies, Societies and Nations*.
    New York, NY: Doubleday, 2004.

'Surviving The Year of Twitter.' *The Straits Times*, December 27, 2009.

Tarrow, Sydney. *Power in Movement: Social Movements and Contentious Politics*.
    Cambridge, UK: Cambridge University Press, 1998.

Teitelbaum, Joshua. 'Dueling for *Da'wa*: State vs. Society on the Saudi Internet.'
    Middle East Journal 56/2 (Spring 2002): 222–239.

'The Radwan Holiday in Egypt.' Egyptian Baha'i, April 28, 2008. Author's
    translation. Accessed on 12 January 2010 at http://egyptianbahai.wordpress.
    com/2008/04/28/ridwan_in_egyp/ .

The Sandmonkey. '6th of April…again!' Rantings of a Sandmonkey, April 4, 2009.
    Accessed at 24 June 2009 on http://www.sandmonkey.org/2009/04/04/6th-
    of-aprilagain/.

Tilly, Charles. *Social Movements, 1768–2004*. Boulder, CO: Paradigm Publishers,
    2004.

'Timeline: Egypt's Revolution.' Al-Jazeera English, February 14, 2011. Accessed
    on September 30, 2011 at http://www.aljazeera.com/news/middleeast/2011/
    01/201112515334871490.html.

Trager, Eric. 'A Tale of Two Parties.' *Foreign Policy*, November 28, 2010.

'Twitter Taken Over By Iranian Cyber Army.' *Brand Republic News Releases*,
    December 24, 2009.

Viner, Katharine. 'Internet has changed foreign policy forever, says Gordon
    Brown.' *The Guardian*, June 19, 2009.

Vitalis, Robert. 'American Ambassador in Technicolor and Cinemascope:
    Hollywood and Revolution on the Nile' in *Mass Mediations: New Approaches
    to Popular Culture in the Middle East and Beyond*. Berkeley: University of
    California Press, 2000.

Watts, Duncan. *Small Worlds: The Dynamics of Networks between Order and
    Randomness*. Princeton, NJ: Princeton University Press, 1999.

Watts, Duncan. *Six Degrees: The Science of a Connected Age*. New York, NY: W.W.
    Norton and Co., 2003.

Wheeler, Deborah L. 'Empowering Publics: Information Technology and
    Democratization in the Arab World: Lessons From Internet Cafes and
    Beyond.' *Oxford Internet Institute, Research Report* No. 11, July 2006: 2–18.

Wheeler, Deborah L. 'Egypt: Building an Information Society for International
    Development.' *Review of African Political Economy*, No. 98 (2003): 627–642.

Wheeler, Deborah L. *The Internet in the Middle East: Global Exectations and Local Imaginations in Kuwait.* Albany, NY: State University Press of New York, 2006.

Whitaker, Brian. 'Egypt's step toward freedom of belief.' *The Guardian*, March 17, 2009.

Whitten-Woodring, Jenifer. 'Watchdog or Lapdog? Media Freedom, Regime Type, and Government Respect for Human Rights.' *International Studies Quarterly* 53 (2009): 595–625.

Wickham, Carrie. *Mobilizing Islam: Religion, Activism, and Political Change in Egypt.* New York, NY: Columbia University Press, 2002.

Winston 2003

Wolff, Sarah. 'Constraints on the promotion of the rule of law in Egypt: insights from the 2005 judges' revolt.' *Democratization* 16/1 (2009): 100–118.

Woodly, Deva. 'New competencies in democratic communication? Blogs, agenda setting and political participation.' *Public Choice* 134 (January 2008): 109–123.

Wright, 'Activists Demand Probe in Cairo Killings'. Reuters, January 1, 2006

'Ya Shaykh?' Egyptian Baha'i, January 29, 2008. Accessed on February 15, 2010 at http://egyptianbahai.wordpress.com/2008/01/29/oh sheikh/#more-110.

Yzer, Marco C. and Brian G. Southwell. 'New Communication Technologies, Old Questions.' *American Behavioral Scientist* 52/1 (September 2008): 8–20.

Zahur, Sherifa. 'The Lost Calm of Operation Cast Lead.' *Middle East Policy* 16/1: (40-52).

Zeinobia. '"Follow-up" Khaled Said Trial "Live" Day One.' Egyptian Chronicles, 21 March 2011. Accessed on May 25, 2011 at http://egyptianchronicles. blogspot.com/2010/07/follow-up-khaled-said-trial-1.html.

Zetter, Kim. 'TED Interview: Tribes Author Says People, Not Ads, Build Social Networks.' *Wired*. 2/4/09.

Zherebkin, Maksym. 'In search of a theoretical approach to the analysis of the 'Colour Revolutions.': Transition studies and discourse theory.' *Communist and Post-Communist Studies* 42 (2009): 199–216.

Zittrain, Jonathan. *The Future of the Internet—And How to Stop It.* New Haven, CT: Yale University Press, 2008.

Zuckerman, Ethan. 'The connection between cute cats and web censorship.' ... *My Heart's in Accra.* July 16, 2007. Accessed August 22, 2011 at http://www.ethanzuckerman.com/blog/2007/07/16/the-connection-between-cute-cats-and-web-censorship/

Zuckerman, Ethan. 'Success. Success? Success.'... *My Heart's in Accra.* January 24, 2008. Accessed March 21, 2010 at http://www.ethanzuckerman.com/blog/2008/01/24/success-success-success/

INDEX